FRENCH INTERVENTIONISM

To Mum and Dad

French Interventionism

Europe's last global player?

ADRIAN TREACHER
Sussex European Institute,
University of Sussex, UK

ASHGATE

Published by
Ashgate Publishing Limited
Gower House
Croft Road
Aldershot
Hampshire GU11 3HR
England

Ashgate Publishing Company
Suite 420
101 Cherry Street
Burlington, VT 05401-4405
USA

Ashgate website: http://www.ashgate.com

British Library Cataloguing in Publication Data
Treacher, Adrian
French interventionism : Europe's last global player?
1. France - Foreign relations - 1995- 2. France - Politics
and govenment - 1995-
I. Title
327.4'4'009045

Library of Congress Cataloging-in-Publication Data
Treacher, Adrian.
French interventionism : Europe's last global player? / Adrian Treacher.
p. cm.
Includes bibliographical references and index.
ISBN 0-7546-3179-6 (alk. paper)
1. France--Military policy. 2. National security--France 3. Security,
International. I. Title.

UA700 .T68 2002
355'.033544--dc21

2002074727

ISBN 0 7546 3179 6

Printed and bound in Great Britain by Antony Rowe Ltd, Chippenham, Wiltshire

Contents

Acknowledgements

I guess that my francophilia began as a boy with family camping trips to Burgundy, Beaujolais and Normandy. This condition then developed with language training at school and probably then became permanent at Bradford University where I took European Studies, specialising in French and politics.

This particular volume is the ultimate expression of a project that began back in 1994 when I launched, or stumbled, in to doctoral study. This was in the Department of Political Science and International Studies at the University of Birmingham, and the original source of inspiration for the PhD was my now valued friend Stuart Croft. Several articles on French security policy followed, and now this volume. The key primary research was undertaken during a series of visits to the *Institut Français des Relations Internationales* (IFRI) in Paris, for which I'm particularly indebted to Frédéric Bozo. My gratitude also extends to Dominique David and especially the staff at the Documentation Centre. Another invaluable piece of field-work was undertaken at the Western European Union's Institute for Security Studies, again in Paris. Here again, I acknowledge the assistance of all the staff. A fair number of people, during these trips, accepted to suffer a Treacher research interview and they are too numerous to mention individually here. My thanks go to them all.

Certain individuals do, however, merit a particular mention. Stuart has been a constant source of support throughout this period, and he also gets the credit for this volume's title. Maintaining the Birmingham link, I also need to acknowledge Jolyon Howorth, Lucy James, John Redmond, Wolf-Diether Roepke, Terry Terriff and all the support staff. Jim Rollo and Helen Wallace and the rest of my colleagues at the Sussex European Institute likewise deserve some of the spotlight. And I could not leave out Robert Elgie whose undying support for this volume over the last two years still humbles me. Finally, I wish to extend my appreciation to all those at Ashgate with whom I have worked.

As always, any errors and omissions are my responsibility alone.

List of Abbreviations

BAe	-	British Aerospace
BIAS	-	Bataillon Interarmé de Somalie
CDU	-	(German) Christian Democratic Union
CFA	-	Communauté Financière Africaine
CFSP	-	Common Foreign and Security Policy
CJTF	-	Combined Joint Task Forces
CSCE	-	Conference on Security and Cooperation in Europe
DASA	-	DaimlerChrysler Aerospace
DOM-TOM	-	Département d'Outre-Mer-Territoire d'Outre-Mer
EADS	-	European Aeronautic, Defence and Space Company
EC	-	European Community
ECOMOG	-	ECOWAS (Economic Community of West African States) peacekeeping mission for Liberia
EEC	-	European Economic Community
EMU	-	Economic and Monetary Union
ESDI	-	European Security and Defence Identity
ESDP	-	European Security and Defence Policy
EU	-	European Union
FAR	-	Force d'Action Rapide
FN	-	Front National
G8	-	Group of the world's eight leading industrialised countries
GATT	-	General Agreement on Tariffs and Trade
GDP	-	Gross Domestic Product
IFRI	-	Institut Français des Relations Internationales
IGC	-	InterGovernmental Conference
IRIS	-	Institut des Relations Internationales et Stratégiques
MINURCA	-	United Nations force the Central African Republic
MISAB	-	Inter-African force for the Central African Republic
NAC	-	North Atlantic Council
NACC	-	North Atlantic Cooperation Council
NATO	-	North Atlantic Treaty Organisation
OAU	-	Organisation for African Unity
ONU	-	Organisation des Nations Unies
OSCE	-	Organisation for Security and Cooperation in Europe
OTAN	-	Organisation du Traité de l'Atlantique du Nord

PCF	-	Partie Communiste Française
RECAMP	-	Reinforcement of African Peacekeeping Capabilities Programme
RPF	-	Rwandan Patriotic Front
RPR	-	Rassemblement Pour la République
RRF	-	Rapid Reaction Force
SDECE	-	Service de Documentation Extérieure et de Contre-Espionage
SDI	-	Strategic Defence Initiative
SFOR	-	Stabilisation Force (Bosnia)
SHAPE	-	Supreme Headquarters Allied Powers Europe
SPD	-	(German) Social Democratic Party
UDF	-	Union Démocratique Française
UK	-	United Kingdom
UN	-	United Nations
UNAMIR	-	United Nations Assistance Mission to Rwanda
UNAVEM	-	United Nations Mission for Angola
UNIFIL	-	United Nations Interim Force in Lebanon
UNITAF	-	Unified Task Force (Somalia)
UNOSOM	-	United Nations Operation in Somalia
UNPROFOR	-	United Nations Protection Force (in the former-Yugoslavia)
UNSC	-	United Nations Security Council
US	-	United States
USSR	-	Union of Soviet Socialist Republics
WEU	-	Western European Union

Chapter 1

Introduction – The Origins of Contemporary French Security Policy

France has traditionally been classed as one of the most enigmatic and vociferous state actors in international relations. It has been accepted as a power on the world stage to an extent which nations of roughly comparable size and equivalent richness in historical tradition have not.[1] Doelnitz called it *'un monstre. Petite par la taille, énorme par l'esprit'*.[a] [2] A superpower in the seventeenth century, a great power by the time of the First World War, this mature west European country, although now only a 'medium power', manages to sustain into the twenty-first century an almost unparalleled level of European and global economic and strategic influence given the extent of its demographic and geographic resources. Acknowledging this, General de Gaulle readily admitted that, at times, France had gone to the international bargaining table with no material of military substance and no assets in the accepted currency of international relations.[3]

The country stands, in the first years of the new century, as a permanent member of the United Nations Security Council (UNSC), as a major component of the European Union (EU), as an automatic member of the now G8 international negotiation forum, as the world's fourth-largest exporter,[4] as a member of around 100 international organisations (reputedly more than any other country);[5] as part of the restricted club of states with nuclear weapons capability, as one of the few countries in the world capable of projecting military force outside of its immediate geostrategic region, as directly responsible for around one and a half million dependants around the globe in *Départements et Territoires d'Outre-Mer (Dom-Toms)*;[b] and it sits, as a former imperial power, at the head of a large francophone commonwealth stretching from Vietnam to Burkina Faso to Haiti (in 1999, 52 countries assembled in Moncton (New Brunswick, Canada) for the eighth francophone summit). Moreover, while, having considered themselves to have been at the cultural centre of the known universe in the nineteenth

---

[a]   'a monster. Small in size, enormous in spirit'. Note that all translations are the author's own.

[b]   'Overseas Departments and Territories'. Martinique and Guadeloupe in the Caribbean, Guyane on the South American mainland and Réunion in the Indian Ocean constitute the overseas departments, and these are run directly from Paris. The overseas territories, meanwhile, have diverse degrees of autonomy but retain economic dependence on the Hexagon (a common term used to describe metropolitan France) – these comprise French Polynesia, New Caledonia, the Wallis and Futuna Islands and the New Hebrides.

century, France's diplomats and military continue to be overtly active all over the world.

This volume claims a vibrant coherency for French security policy and its use of military intervention, namely the perpetual promotion of national *grandeur* and the relentless pursuit of an elevated global standing that was once automatic. These ultimate objectives have remained unaltered since at least the end of the Second World War, it is just the tactics have been changing and will continue to do so. To this end, one recurring theme of the volume will be the role of the French 'exception'. Hence, there has been a continued willingness, an almost instinctive desire, to actively engage in world affairs, and there remains an absolute readiness to 'intervene', whether this is by diplomatic or military means. The outside world, ever since the country's momentous 1789 revolution, has become accustomed to seeing French forces being stationed, and often becoming actively engaged, around the globe. To this end, the global deployment of French military forces with a predisposed readiness to intervene when necessary has been one of the key policy instruments employed by the country's political leaders to promote national claims to *grandeur* and an elevated international rank. However, the nature of this intervention has changed quite significantly over the last 10-15 years. There has been a shift away from solo operations towards participation in multinational humanitarian and peacekeeping operations on behalf of the world community. Seen from this perspective, French policy assumes a certain consistency and a certain predictability. It is hence the purpose of this volume to chart how the justifications for this global vocation have been adapted and how the necessary instruments to maintain this approach have been introduced. In addition, the whole 'process' of European security is currently in a state of flux, particularly regarding the future of the European Union as a military actor. Hence, a detailed understanding of the French position may provide for greater clarity in the wider picture.

On a more theoretical level, France represents an interesting subject of analysis in terms of the structure-agency debate within the discipline of international relations. Much of this volume is dedicated to national politicians attempting to portray France as an autonomous security actor, largely unconstrained by the bipolar, Cold War, international system, or at least as able to behave independently. This suggests, in this instance, the predominance of agency over structure. Such a view goes against Waltz and the neo-realists who tell us that it is systemic pressures which produce a 'rough behavioural uniformity' among states. Although neo-realists accept that all states are self-interested, they claim that their actions are shaped by the structural constraints.[6] By evaluating the performance of France, with its claim to autonomy from the confines of global structures, this book makes a further contribution to the question as to whether the international system conditions the foreign (here read security) policy of given states. For Hollis and Smith, the collapse of the Cold War system has meant 'questions concerning the nature of agency and the meaning of structure and the relationship between them are now more relevant than ever in international relations theory'.[7]

And France proffers another twist to this in view of its relative concentration, when compared to other Western liberal democracies, of security decision-making authority in the hands of one person – the President. This, including the limitations of this authority, is expanded upon later in this Introduction. Hence, at a lower level, the emphasis is still on the primacy of agency, the Presidency, over structure, the French political system. France thus gives us two dimensions of agency. It is a principle argument here that with the end of bipolarity, and the re-emergence of multipolarity, in the international system, France's political leaders have been forced to significantly de-emphasise the country's singularity as an agent in return for continued influence within the international system via various 'alliances' with other states. It is, however, harder to discern whether the French Presidency, as an agent, has likewise lost much of its dominance over structure. This appears to be largely dependent on whether the corresponding French Government belongs to the same political bloc.

This book thus elaborates on the evolution of French foreign policy, and principally its interventionist tendencies, through the Fifth Republic, arguing that the one constant has been an almost automatic claim to greatness (*grandeur*) and the corresponding elevated global status (*rang*). What have changed have been the various tactics adopted by France's national leaders towards achieving these twin and closely interrelated ends according to the international geostrategic environment in which they had to operate and the domestic resources available to them. Hence, broadly speaking, policy during much of the Cold War was one of asserting French independence and autonomy of action, of promoting the French 'exception' (*spécificité*). This was deemed by President de Gaulle and his successors to be the most appropriate course of action given the circumstances of the time: nuclear parity between the two superpowers, a Europe divided into two fixed strategic blocs, and a booming, initially at least, domestic economy. Then, with the new security order emerging out of the end of the Cold War, Paris (namely, France's political leadership) eventually concluded that fresh tactics were required. The approach adopted since 1958, and which had built up something of its own momentum, no longer delivered sufficient benefits given the new multipolarity of the international system and the evolving economic situation. Indeed, it was proving detrimental to the pursuit of *grandeur* and *rang*. Systemic and economic pressures were such that much of the emphasis on national independence had to be sacrificed in exchange for greater cooperation and, in some instances, integration, with the country's principal partners. At the national level, the agent was less able to manipulate the structure, indeed, it was having to be more responsive to it. A graphic illustration of this was French diplomacy remodelling itself as a supporter and instrument of international peacekeeping on behalf of the United Nations (UN).

The practical results of this tactical shift could be seen in the much greater emphasis placed on Europe as a singular security actor. Put simply, policy-makers in Paris concluded that France no longer had the resources to, nor, to some extent, the opportunity, to persist with its often solo path through international relations. It was no longer profitable to act as the lone agent within the global structure; the utility of the French exception as a policy tool came to be seriously questionable. If it were to maintain and augment national *grandeur* and *rang*, and the possibility of not doing so was never really publicly debated, then France would henceforth require assistance. (Western) Europe had to perform the functions and attain the goals that French political culture could no longer achieve by itself. The national leadership thus strove to forge some autonomous European security and defence identity, obviously to be guided from Paris, that would be in a position to promote and defend Europe's (read French) interests. In this respect, to point to the end of the Cold War as a finite and decisive watershed for French security policy is to be overly simplistic. Even during the 1980s, before the momentous transformation of the international system, France, in the guise of President François Mitterrand, had attempted to push forward (west) European integration within the context of the EU, although he did seek to retain the maximum autonomous room for manoeuvre on the international stage. This somewhat contradictory approach proved increasingly difficult to sustain. At the same time, economic imperatives had been exponentially gaining in prominence well before the collapse of the Berlin Wall.

This introductory chapter addresses the more analytical questions associated with this topic in terms of defining the principal concepts involved. First, what notion of security policy best helps us to understand the French experience? Second, what do scholars mean when they refer to France as a security actor? How can a country with all its diverse components be described as a unitary actor? Key to this is an understanding of the significance of the State in France. France's cultural and historical heritage is then outlined, this being a fundamental factor determining the way France behaves as it does. Finally, this chapter explores certain domestic elements of the contemporary Fifth Republic that impact on France as a global security actor: the malleable Constitution and an apparent popular consensus on foreign policy.

The rest of the volume then makes something of a chronological journey through the life of the Fifth Republic. Chapter Two analyses de Gaulle's perceptions of France and of what was the most effective national strategy to adopt in the quest for the *grandes lignes* of sustained *grandeur* and elevated global *rang*. In applying his tactics in practice, de Gaulle, as key architect and first President of the Fifth Republic, attempted to foster and expand French *singularité* and sought to maximise France's scope for manoeuvre and independent action on the international stage. This is best demonstrated by his manipulation of the rigidity of the bipolar system and the withdrawal of France from the integrated military command structure of NATO (the North Atlantic Treaty Organisation).

Chapter Three examines a certain tactical reappraisal undertaken by de Gaulle's presidential successors, notably Mitterrand with his double *septennat*, in response to an evolving set of domestic and international circumstances. Some of the key tenets of the Gaullist approach to France's position in the world began to be brought in to question. While not being prepared to rein in the ultimate strategic security policy objectives, French leaders had to acknowledge their country's limitations regarding their attainment. But instead of a commensurate scaling down of French global ambitions, they were almost instinctively transferred to the (west) European level. The European Union would become the surrogate for the perpetuation of French strategic goals. France's relations with NATO and the European security architecture at this time are also discussed. Thus, from having dedicated itself, in the 1960s, to breaking down the inflexibility of Cold War bipolarity, French leaders began to perceive the latter as being extremely well suited to French interests.

French security policy is then brought up to date, with an evaluation of the post-Cold War years up to the start of the new century. Structural changes in the international system were to serve as something of a catalyst for the tactical realignment of policy instruments. As a result, these years have been marked by an accelerated process of downplaying the hitherto flaunted French exceptionalism combined with the promotion of multinational initiatives. At the same time, strategic doctrine has been reassessed as, almost for the first time, the debate on French security policy went public. German reunification, in particular, was the source of much soul-searching among French political elites. The 1993 legislative victory of the centre-right and the departure of Mitterrand from Presidential office two years later then served to accentuate these adjustments. The tactical response of France's leaders was primarily to push for even deeper European integration. Meanwhile and as described in Chapter Four, French security policy-makers were able to quite successfully reinvent the country's global mission. They achieved this by dedicating the armed forces to multinational peacekeeping and humanitarian operations on behalf of the international community as encapsulated by the UN; the latter having become a principal instrument of French security policy. The Gulf War and Bosnia are given particular prominence here.

Chapter Five analyses the French re-evaluation of Europe's security architecture through the 1990s. In the face of their key European partners' reluctance to be seen to be encouraging an American withdrawal from the continent, the policy-makers in Paris had, for the time being at least, to abandon attempts at forging an autonomous and fully functioning multilateral European military and defence organisation. Instead, they began to focus their efforts on forging a European Security and Defence Identity (ESDI) *within* the Atlantic Alliance. This represented an acknowledgement that for at least the short to medium-term the latter was really 'the only show in town' for the realisation of French strategic ambitions. But then, and somewhat to the surprise of many of the relevant actors in French administration, the policy was able to almost come full circle. Largely as a result of a dramatic change in British policy in 1998, the European Union is now well on its way to absorbing the Western European Union and becoming a military actor able to operate outside of the NATO framework and unshackled by American hegemonic diplomacy. Meanwhile, the downplaying of the French exception and the implicit emphasis placed on the normalisation of French security policy has been further illustrated by increased military cooperation with France's European partners, the denationalisation of national defence industries and the symbolic and emotive professionalisation of the French armed forces. These practical adjustments are dealt with in Chapter Six and represented tactical changes to reflect economic constraints, shifting domestic politics and a transformed global geopolitical picture.

French security policy towards the wider world is covered in Chapter Seven. This points to a key component of the tactical emphasis on French *spécificité*, essentially the privileged status and influence France enjoyed among its former colonial possessions, principally in sub-Saharan Africa. Here, the global vocation of France's political elites is especially highlighted. At first, the transformation of the international system with the end of the Cold War and domestic economic constraints were not sufficient to prevent the perpetuation of solo military initiatives in sub-Saharan Africa. This became almost the only region in the world where France could perpetuate the myth of its status as a great power. Nevertheless, here too France's mission has undergone a major tactical revision. The contrast in the responses to the successive crises in Rwanda and Zaire could not have been starker. As in other areas of French security policy, there has been a transferral of French ambitions to multinational solutions, both Western and local. Perhaps the trigger-happy *gendarme* is being replaced by a more considered approach.

The Conclusion states that throughout the life of the Fifth Republic, the national leaderships have been driven by their quest for continued *grandeur* and *rang*. This has been illustrated by a series of significant tactical shifts in order to preserve these widely held, at least among most French political elites, military leaders and intellectuals, strategic imperatives. But the Conclusion goes on to speculate about the state of French national identity and characterises an international actor that has largely been driven by a sense of vulnerability and insecurity and that which may now be becoming more at ease with its medium power status.

But before this volume can proceed, there is one crucial concept that requires elaboration: what here is understood by 'security policy'? While acknowledging the myriad interpretations of security and the merits of taking security as being something much more than inter-state military relations, this volume adopts a narrow theoretical approach. Firstly, it deals with the French State operating in an international system dominated by states as the principal object of analysis. Sub and non-state actors evidently play a role, and this is acknowledged in the study; but it is the behaviour of France as a collective unit that is our main concern here. Hence, the book examines the range of French agency, alluded to earlier, within the international structure of states. Secondly, it is France's behaviour in implementing what is commonly termed security *policy* that is the crux of the analysis. Whereas the term security can today have multiple connotations, security policy is held by all to have at its core defence and military matters. For our purposes here, the broader notions of security are dealt with by other elements of foreign policy. Hence, security policy is but one element of a state's all-encompassing foreign policy, reflecting the creation and projection of military power within the state system. But privileging military matters does not preclude the incorporation of political, societal and economic elements in accounting for France's security policy.

France as a Security Actor and the Emergence of the Global Vocation

What actually is inferred in international relations when reference is made to 'France'? Empirically, it can be described as a sovereign state in the sense that it possesses territory, a population and government. But as Fowler and Bunck observe, this comprises but one element of a definition for sovereign statehood.[8] Total sovereignty for a state would also imply internal supremacy, whereby the government is clearly the dominant authority over all other power centres within that territory and population, and external independence, namely autonomy from the authority of other states. In contemporary western Europe however, these qualifications have to be moderated in view of the degree of interpenetration and interdependence among the region's states and in view of the increasingly pluralistic nature of Western society as a whole. And a modern state bases much of its authority on, and justifies its existence in terms of, a national constitution as recognised by international law. States thus remain the framework of order and represent the highest form of political authority that humanity has, to date, been able to develop and sustain.[9]

However, it is hard to specify what is meant by the state and to pinpoint it as a behavioural unit; interpretations vary, it is a contested concept. Certainly, there is a distinction to be made between state machinery and a population's *perception* of the state. One can point to the various institutions such as the government and the judiciary as the focus of state identity, but the experience of France would appear to indicate that here at least the State is something more than the sum of its institutions, and that there is something more to it than simply a physical base comprising a territory and a population. The French popular conception of the State bestows it with something of its own persona; it is an idea in people's minds, even if this idea takes manifold forms. It has been strong enough, for example, to withstand periods of significant institutional weakness. Clearly then, the notion of the State is fundamental to any true understanding of what is meant by 'France'.

To this end, it is not so much the geographic entity that is of concern in this work, rather the decision-makers which act on behalf of the French people and the forces and elements which impact upon the decision-making process. In reality, sovereign states are not unitary actors – government policy is the combined output of several key elements, of a conglomeration of large organisations and political actors. Equally, the French populace cannot be regarded as simply sharing one single current of political thought. It embraces multiple interpretations of the past, and the future. For Jean Blondel, 'French political history can be seen as a maze of threads beginning in various places, frequently crossing and tangling with one another, with new strands entering from time to time'.[10] Political traditions came in all shapes and sizes in France, including: clerical, monarchist, pacifist, liberal, nationalist, communist and republican. As Hazareesingh noted, '[t]he centrality of the notion of rupture in French political discourse attests to the turbulent and centrifugal character of public life since 1789'.[11] However, generally speaking, most analysts and observers tend to perceive security policy as the more or less purposeful acts of unified national governments.[12] In Graham T. Allison's view, '[t]reating national governments as if they were centrally coordinated, purposive individuals provides a useful shorthand for understanding problems of policy'.[13] But unity does not imply uniformity, the lack of disagreement does not translate as a harmony of political beliefs. And this makes for a certain ambiguity. But generally speaking, the state is held to be more than a collection of individual decision-makers, and as constituting more than the sum of its parts. Throughout this volume, references will be made to 'Paris', 'French security policy-makers', 'French political elites', 'France's leaders', and so on. These are all taken as references to France as an international actor, and infer a certain compliance among the general population to the lead taken by the national leadership.

From a historical perspective, contemporary France had clearly been established as a geographical and political entity by the end of the Middle Ages, and it has enjoyed fairly constant frontiers, with the exception of Alsace Lorraine in the east, since the early nineteenth century. But by any standards, this was a dramatic and somewhat perilous journey. What had emerged in 842 as the kingdom of Western Francia, on the division of the Holy Roman Empire, had evolved into a 'Great Power' by the middle of the seventeenth century. It had been particularly well constructed in order to assume such a role and to meet the demands of protracted international competition: effective armed forces, an able bureaucracy and, according to Craig and Alexander, a 'theory of state that restrained dynastic exuberance and defined political interest in practical terms'.[14] Added to this were a self-sufficiency in agriculture and a relatively large population. France was then to constitute the foremost military power in the European arena for generations to come, seeking, in its time, continental hegemony under Louis XIV and then Napoleon Bonaparte. However, unlike, successively, Spain, Britain and the United States (US), it was never able to become the dominant world power, and it largely ceased to have expansionist ambitions within Europe after 1815.

It has been observed that, in France, the state and the territorial configuration preceded the nation.[15] This was an interesting development if one accepts, as does Jean-Paul Briseul, that the state is the judicial expression of the nation.[16] Voltaire described France as having been the creation of its kings, who had 'made' France by placing under royal sovereignty people who had been divided by their feudal lords and religious leaders and who, on universally enjoying the Kings' peace, became a 'people'.[17] And the principle instrument for this development was the pre-eminence of the Monarchy's military power. Louis XIV was famously to remark, for example, that '*l'Etat, c'est moi*'. Equally, Burghardt credits the French monarchs with establishing national unity.[18] Cecile Labourde referred to the state, out of necessity, having been forcibly constructed against what was then civil society.[19] To a large extent, regional specificities were destroyed for the sake of the stronger whole. There was a sense of fusion and homogenisation.[20] The various ancient nationalisms found common ground in the nation-State. The latter gave meaning to the diverse and dispersed interests that prevailed at the time. According to Doelnitz, '*[b]atailles, mariages, alliances, ruses, trahisons, tout fut bon pour assembler petit à petit les pièces de ce qui allait devenir ce fameux "Hexagone"*'.[c] He went on to point out that Louis XIV and his successor Louis XV were careful not to over-extend France beyond what they deemed were its natural frontiers; those that are, for the most part, in place today.[21] Certainly, the geographic expansion was relatively slow, taking place over centuries. And perhaps this gave greater provision for the growing centralism of the French system to be assimilated by the population.

During the reign of Louis XIV, in the seventeenth century, the notion of the activist state was to emerge out of the actions of his chief minister, Jean-Baptiste Colbert. Cardinal Richelieu built on these foundations, extolling the administrative and theoretical skills that would exemplify the very ideal of modern French statehood.

---

^c   'Battles, marriages, alliances, trickery, betrayal, all worked to assemble little by little the pieces which would become this famous *Hexagon*'.

Then, under Napoleon Bonaparte, the apparatus of the State was expanded, becoming an arbitrary instrument with a force of its own. Interestingly, it was Bonaparte who introduced the usage of plebiscites, or referenda, to appeal directly to his political constituency. This tactic would become a common feature of the Fifth Republic that is the focus of this volume. Progress and modernisation were hence controlled by a centralised bureaucracy in the interests of the State. If the monarchy, and later the Empire, had not provided a strong and coherent administrative apparatus, the country, in all likelihood, would not have survived.[22] A nation-state forged together by force and marriage and lacking any sense of distinct ethnicity or geography would most likely have succumbed to its inherent centrifugal forces but for the guiding hand of the leadership in Paris.

Present day France was thus constructed over centuries from the centre. The nation has been modelled on the State. Hence, *l'Etat* means so much more in France than in most countries. It conveys the notion of a coherent and self-confident institution charged with promoting the proper ordering of society, and with countering the inherent centrifugal tendencies referred to earlier. It has traditionally been expected of the State that it direct all the country's *grands projets*. As recently as 1995 for example, it was credited with spending some 55 per cent of French GDP (a higher proportion than in any other major industrial country).[23] De Gaulle was to claim 'that the nation and those who direct its affairs define political reality, which determines economic and cultural values; material factors are fundamentally subordinate to the acts of political will that impose themselves on the behaviour of men'.[24] In Gaullist mythology, of which much will be discussed later, there is a hierarchy headed by *la France* as a mystical, although historically grounded, apolitical ideal. Then, there is *l'Etat* 'which is called into being by the nation and thereafter becomes the custodian of national self-expression'.[25] Thirdly, there is *la République* that represents the constitutional arrangements that the people and their representatives have accepted as being the best adapted to France's historical tradition.[26]

However, the relative position of France in Europe was to go into something of a decline following the heights of the first Napoleonic era. It would take some considerable time for French political elites to recover their self-esteem and global status following, from 1870, three successive invasions by the German neighbour which culminated, in 1940, in military defeat inside three weeks, the humiliation of occupation and the establishment of the collaboratist Vichy government. The Fourth Republic guided the French somewhat haphazardly through the difficult post-Second World War years. This was a period characterised by domestic political inertia and debilitating military excursions in Indo-China and Algeria. The Fifth Republic, inaugurated in 1958, was largely the creation of General Charles de Gaulle. He forcibly crafted a workable and efficient political apparatus and eased the French people's adjustment to their country's reduced international standing. France was now, for all intents and purposes, only a medium-sized power. Nevertheless, it remained at the centre of international institutions like the UN and the then EEC (European Economic Community). Equally significant was the *rapprochement* with West Germany. The end of the Cold War was to come at a time when France was enjoying significant benefits from its somewhat maverick role within the bipolar international system.

The highly centralised nature of French society was maintained throughout this time. Under the Fifth Republic, the French have retained, for example, their aversion to pressure groups; a sentiment dating back to Jacobin times.[27] For Jean Blondel, the 1789 revolution had been fought, in part, against groups which were 'held to have been previously instruments of "selfish" sectionalism against the general will; individualism prevailed as an ideology'.[28] And the whole episode of the subsequent "Terror" was attributed to the inadequacies of popular sovereignty.[29] It had been Rousseau who had introduced this notion of the 'General Will', claiming that modern society could only properly function if its members renounced selfish individualism in favour of a unity of purpose centred on shared citizenship.

Even in the Fifth Republic, there has been a strong conception of politics that rejected the group as a legitimate actor. French society, in Blondel's view, is not yet fully pluralistic since groups are viewed as inevitable evils rather than natural instruments for the transmission of demands.[30] This universalist approach aids explanations pertaining to the suspicion in French society with regard to political parties and pressure groups, these being enemies of the aforementioned General Will. This gives understanding, in part at least, to the absence over the years of any strong equivalent to Britain's Campaign for Nuclear Disarmament. In the analysis of Jean-Marie Domenach, democracy has never been popular in France. What has been important has been equality, to the extent that the elites are simultaneously deferred to, imitated, envied and disparaged.[31] And the dominance of the centre extends to the industrial sector. The corporate structure comprises a tight network of cross-shareholdings and directorships linking banks, insurers and industrial groups. Controlling all this is an elite of leaders with *a grande-écoles* [d] education and a strong strand of government intervention. To this author at least, the apparent interpenetration of the State and private industry is striking. As alluded earlier, the state-owned sector remains significant to this day, although it is diminishing.

Hence, what has emerged as 'France' within the contemporary international system rests on the dominant role of the State first developed by the monarchy, with a strong emphasis on citizenship. It has been built from the centre. And being French rests on being a citizen of this State, as opposed to any purely ethnic qualification. This is not to deny the existence of a multicultural society in terms of, for example, ethnic origin or religion, but it stresses a diversity which is bound together by adherence to the French State. According to Dabezies, the French are not a race, a view hotly contested by supporters of Jean-Marie Le Pen's *Front National*, they comprise a nation-state with fixed frontiers.[32] To attack the State would be to attack France. Buzan's description of the State as more of a metaphysical entity, as an idea held in common by a group of people,[33] fits well when talking about France. In Serge Berstein's interpretation, 'France was a reality that could not be subsumed into any

---

[d]   A group of elite colleges, principally the *Ecole Polytechnique* and the *Ecole Nationale d'Administration*, which have a virtual monopoly of the supply of graduates for the highest posts in public service and industry.

other entity. It was imperative that in all circumstances her interests should prevail, her voice should be heard and respected – in other words that her destiny should be guaranteed. Her destiny was more important than that of any individual group, since each group was only a part of the whole'.[34] And what binds all this together is the common cultural heritage discussed below. Although it should be acknowledged that, evidently, this has lost some of its cohesiveness with the immigration of new citizens, principally from former-French colonies.

The Cultural and Historical Legacy

A nation's past impacts on its present, and this holds particularly true for French history with its strong mythological dimension. Even in its earlier guises, French political culture had a vision of the country as being something exceptional, as having a special mission in the world. French monarchs, as far back as the twelfth century, idealised their heritage. They perceived themselves not just as the heirs of the Gauls, with a recurring obsession to reconstruct the holy kingdom of Charlemagne,[35] but also of ancient civilisation, including both pagan and Christian elements. One could point, even then, to an aspiring national mentality. In the thirteenth and fourteenth centuries, French bishops, having studied Roman law, recognised only the spiritual authority of the bishops of Rome and proclaimed the kings of France emperor in their own kingdom, thereby resurrecting the Roman concept of the *imperium*, which had no earthly superiors.[36] French political culture thus had developed an essentially Roman sense of *grandeur*. A return to this golden age became the primary purpose of political action. This claimed heritage, which reached its height under Louis XIV, when Paris was the undoubted capital of Europe, supposedly bequeathed the French with special privileges as the defenders of European civilisation itself, not simply of France and its interests.[37] The legacy of Louis XIV, in particular, and the concept of *grandeur* have thus been fundamental to a specific interpretation of the ideal structures of French foreign policy for four centuries.

With the momentous fall of the monarchy, in the fallout of the 1789 revolution, glory was transformed to reflect upon the nation as a whole rather than on the king. *Citoyen* and *citoyenne* became common forms of address, thereby replacing the notion of people being subjects.[38] And in 1790 the French declared themselves *la grande nation*. The revolution served as a powerful nationalist motor. The nation became the transcendent bond, uniting all citizens in patriotic fervour. The latter consumed Paris, and parts of the provinces, as the fledgling revolutionary state fought to stay alive in the face of successive foreign threats. The whole population was thus implicated in the defence of *la patrie*. The nation and its army had been forged together as one. Conscription was introduced in 1798, the Jacobin nation in arms became the Napoleonic conscript army.[39] For Hague, Harrop and Breslin, '[a] duty of military service to the fatherland went hand in hand with the hard-won rights and privileges of citizenship; the French revolutionary armies thus foreshadowed the vast conscript armies of the twentieth century'.[40] Conscription also served to bind the people together by negating regional or social disparities. The military and the use of force thus lie at the heart of French national identity.

The qualification for being French is not ethnic per se, it is political. One is French if one is a citizen of the French State. The individual has a stake in the national community. In this way, the French do not consider people from francophone Switzerland or Belgium as French because they are not part of the French State. Napoleon Bonaparte was to expand upon and promote the idea that each individual French citizen should give their supreme loyalty to their country and devote themselves to the pursuit of national greatness. *La patrie* had been created as an alternative focus of identification for the new society, to replace the monarchy, the church and the nobility which had all, in theory, been zealously swept away.[41]

It was during these first republican, and then imperial, years that the idea of France's universal mission emerged. Immanuel Wallerstein observed, '[w]hen French troops crossed European frontiers (under the Convention, the Directory and the Empire) they came, at least at first, as triumphant harbingers of a universalizing ideal'.[42] Having already claimed for itself the mantle of defender of European civilisation, France, in its 1792 Edict of Fraternity, offered help to peoples abroad wishing to gain freedom by overthrowing their kings. Bonaparte himself was motivated, at least in part, by the desire to construct, by force if need be, a pacific European confederation which dissolved national differences with him as its *protecteur*.[43] However, it is also evident that he was driven by a thirst for *gloire*.[44] The French Revolution, with its rallying cry of '*liberté, égalité, fraternité*', had been about much more than the removal of the monarchy, as for many it had involved a qualitative change in which revolutionary ideals of justice flourished. A new political culture, the Universal Republic, was supposed to emerge.

The fallout from the Revolution was to emphasise the universality of the principles and values created by the new political order. Governments' legitimacy, their claim to authority, henceforth derived from the consent of the Nation. The Declaration of the Rights of Man was adopted by the first National Assembly in August 1789 and stated that men are born free and equal, and that law is the expression of the sovereign will of the people. Many republicans believed that the emancipation of their society from the bonds of servitude was simply the prelude to a general transformation of the entire globe.[45] Thus, despite the First Republic being a disastrous social and political experiment, the Revolution was to survive as an almost purely golden legend. Robespierre was to write:

> [a]insi a commencé la plus belle révolution qui ait honoré l'humanité; disons mieux, la seule qui ait eu un objet digne de l'homme, celui de fonder enfin les sociétés politiques sur les principes immortels de l'égalité de la justice et de la vertu.[e] [46]

Hence, French political culture's special concern with human rights began to take hold.

---

[e]   'Thus began the finest revolution to grace humanity; or rather, the only one with a worthy objective for mankind, that is to finally base political societies on the immortal principles of equality, justice and virtue'.

Although France had been a major player in the opening-up of the New World since the seventeenth century, these ideas would not find full expression until the reign of Napoleon III onwards (mid-nineteenth century), as France competed with its European rivals for fresh colonial conquests. Hoffman claimed that France acquired colonies solely for the purpose of boosting its global *rang* and for spreading its universal values.[47] That the whole process was underpinned by a belief in cultural superiority perhaps overstates things somewhat. But what certainly made the French different to the other imperial powers, was that the belief in the universalism of their values rested at the very heart of the national psyche;[48] and this notion was particularly lauded by politicians, intellectuals and journalists. But there would inevitably have been some degree of crude economic motives hidden behind these 'higher' justifications which dominated the imperialist debate. Nevertheless, Boissy d'Anglas wrote in 1794 that the 1789 Revolution had not just been for Europe but for the universe. And that the French had devised the one right way for administering, therefore why should the colonies be deprived of it? [49] There was, hence, an extremely powerful cultural, ideological and psychological strain running through France's colonial operations. The French political elites, not uniquely, believed in their intellectual and moral duty to expand French territory and influence. The policy was one of assimilation, whereby native peoples would be converted to French citizens and their countries made part of France, or be closely attached. The principal instrument of this declared civilising mission was naturally the French language. It was assumed that the natives would naturally desire this, believing that nothing better could happen to them. Promises of equality through integration were, however, never fulfilled.

Thus, what had emerged in France by the twentieth century was a political culture with a strong motivation to pass on its special message to the rest of the world, and a belief in the prerogative of the French nation to speak on behalf of humanity. This was an almost mythical and ostentatious interpretation of a nation's history. There was still a sense of pride that it had been Frenchmen who had crafted the values of the eighteenth century Enlightenment as enshrined by the American Declaration of Independence in 1776 and by the 1789 Declaration on the Rights of Man and the Citizen. Frenchmen were to be equally instrumental in ensuring the adoption in 1948 by the UN General Assembly of the Universal Declaration of Human Rights. President Giscard d'Estaing, for example, was to refer, in the 1970s, to France's superiority of spirit as 'that of a country which understands best the problems of its times and which brings to them the most imaginative, the most open, the most generous solutions'.[50] French political leaders traditionally had little difficulty in equating the universal cause of freedom and justice with the independence and greatness of their own country.[51] This provided, for example, the explanation and basis for a post-Second World War claim, along with the US, to global leadership. Both countries shared a similar historical experience and set of values, and a belief that their experiences could help the rest of the world. French political culture was later to perceive part of its global role as being the cultural counterbalance to the US in the Western hemisphere.[52] But claims to cultural pre-eminence, at least, had become ever harder to justify following the 'heights' of the nineteenth century. The notion of a civilising mission, based around the French language, was proving increasingly anachronistic.

Perhaps in an effort to overcome an inherent national anxiety, French political elites have demonstrated a remarkable capacity to retain a claim to greatness for their country even in the face of apparently total defeat. Part of the healing process, following the traumas of the Second World War for example, involved the revival of patterns of nationalistic thought and attitudes which were based on the traditional assumption of the inherent superiority of French culture and manners over those of the Germanic world.[53] Solace for successive military defeats came from invoking France's inherent *grandeur*. This was something eternal, not transitory, which would far out-last the recent disasters. Moreover, Kolodziej describes how de Gaulle was able to put forward the following rationale with regard to the *débâcle* of 1940. Pétain's Vichy government had forfeited any right to be the legal representative of France when it prematurely capitulated to Germany, when there were still individuals and groups with the resources to assume the nation's defence. Thus, in the General's eyes, France's sovereignty had been temporally transported, in the form of his own person, to London until Vichy was overturned.[54]

De Montbrial was unquestionably correct when he stated that the French have retained 'a lofty conception of their history, and of the wealth of their literary, philosophical, artistic or scientific culture'.[55] Hence, according to Michel Winock, France cannot be defined simply by its geography, it is above all else an idea.[56] And for Dominique Moïsi, 'France's fascination with her own past pushes her to give a high priority to the historical dimension of political phenomena'.[57] For example, Alfred Grosser described Gaullism, one of the dominant, if vague, forces running through the Fifth Republic, as being the double heritage of the nation born out of royal direction and the nation forged by the Jacobins in the name of the people.[58] Doelnitz, meanwhile, has noted the high frequency with which the word 'France' is used in French writings in comparison to, say, Germany, Italy and Spain. Equally, he points to the number of literary references to *la patrie* and *l'identité nationale*.[59]

Domestic Provisions of the Fifth Republic

Having attempted to establish whence came contemporary France's global vocation, the final purpose of this introductory chapter is to outline certain aspects of the Fifth Republic that facilitated the continuing endurance of the Gaullist approach to security policy that is discussed in the next chapter. The 1958 French Constitution was largely inspired by the vision of de Gaulle, and he was to use its often ambiguous provisions to extend Presidential authority to almost unprecedented levels. As intended, the result has been that security policy has largely become the sole preserve of the Presidency. Within the whole security policy decision-making framework, the President was to be the dominant agent and was to be possessed of every available means with which to operate free from the systemic pressures of the bipolar world. The experiences of the Fourth Republic had demonstrated that a political system that placed primary authority with the National Assembly had weakened France's ability to be a powerful and decisive actor on the global stage. By focusing the main responsibility for security policy on the Presidency, a certain amount of coherence and effectiveness would be restored. Meanwhile, the lack of scope for public input into the policy debate has helped to foster something of a popular consensus, or perhaps apathy, with regard to France's international actions. This consensus, although more mythical than real, has facilitated France's successive leaderships' consistent pursuit of the strategic objectives.

A Malleable Constitution

As argued above, France had already emerged as a relatively unitary, highly centralised, actor by the time the somewhat ambiguous 1958 Constitution inaugurated the Fifth Republic. The new institutional structure was largely based on the experiences and conclusions of de Gaulle and was designed to maximise French influence in the world and to support France's claims to Great Power status. *Rang* and *grandeur* were the strategic objectives. And the principal innovation was the engineering of an emphatic reorientation, as compared to the Third and Fourth Republics, away from political parties, the standing of which was already inherently weak given the traditional popular aversion to political groups, and towards the Presidency. De Gaulle, in his famous press conference of 31 January 1964, encapsulated his vision, stating that there can be no duality of authority at the summit of the State. It is the President, the argument went, who is *l'homme de la Nation*, who is the source and holder of national power.[60] He was convinced that only some form of presidential government, with a democratic base, could be equal to his, and what he perceived to be popular, ambitions for France. Hence, the 1958 Constitution provided the potential for the Presidency to assume a significant and unprecedented extension of prerogatives, thereby making it the key institutional actor at the expense of the National Assembly and other political actors, notably in security matters. Henceforth, for example, the President could now only be forced to resign in the event of high treason (article 68). For Edward Kolodziej, '[s]ucceeding a confusing parade of prime ministers, cabinet heads, and legislators under the Fourth and Third Republics, de Gaulle as President of the Republic spoke for France'.[61]

This potential for Presidential pre-eminence in security policy-making, or of the agent dominating the structure at the domestic level, was brought about by the manipulative efforts of de Gaulle himself. He and his successors at the Elysée accorded themselves considerably more power than the Constitution appeared to give. The General, in setting this precedent, was able to discernibly demonstrate that 'a constitution is both a text and something that is applied'.[62] On paper, the Constitution provided for a balanced division of power between Executive and Government. In practice it has clearly been seen to favour the Executive. Hence, somewhat ambiguous constitutional provisions were augmented by the General's introduction, in 1965, of Presidential election by universal suffrage, thereby forging a direct link with the people and providing the incumbent with power and legitimacy of unrivalled quality within the Hexagon. Other key constitutional amendments which worked towards the same ends were de Gaulle's 14 January 1964 decree bestowing the President with sole authority on the use of nuclear force, and President Pompidou's subsequent decree of 10 December 1971 placing the Joint Chief of Staff under the authority of the President.

Security Policy-Making in the Fifth Republic

These measures were all to mean that, in theory at least, the exercise of Presidential power regarding security policy had the potential to be virtually unrestrained. Political practice would henceforth prove that the key decisions in defence and security policy would largely be the sole responsibility of the President. For Marr, 'France enjoys the symbolism and language of republicanism, but the reality is that it is ruled by a monarch, with powers which seem absolutist ...; it's just that the monarch is elected'.[63] In this vein, there has never been any doubt since 1958, with the exception of Michel Debré's ministerial term during which he attempted to assert some autonomy and possibly during periods of *cohabitation* (see below), that the President is the real Defence Minister. The Defence Ministry as a whole has had little significant input in the formulation of national strategic and security policy, or in the decision-making process. The Foreign Ministry has been equally subservient. Mitterrand, when President, was to define the latter's role as not to define policy but to act as 'a powerful and efficient instrument' implementing policy designed at the Elysée.[64]

The unprecedented popular support given to the Fifth Republic would appear to endorse the predominant position accorded to the Presidency. There have, for example, been no serious calls for a new Constitution that would take power away from the executive. Furthermore, successive Presidents have been able to accentuate this apparent dominance by operating almost exclusively through a network drawn from graduates of the *grandes écoles*. This network has been described by Massie as 'a self-perpetuating and small elite, who move between politics, the civil service, the management of the public sector and top jobs in those private-sector businesses that depend on the public sector for support'.[65] The top echelon of France's administration has thus traditionally been a relatively closed shop. In addition, the Presidents have taken to developing their own diplomatic machinery parallel to those of the Quai d'Orsay (the location of the Foreign Ministry). These have been comprised of personal emissaries in whom they have held the highest confidence. Mitterrand, for example, was accused of personalising French foreign policy during his two terms in office, sending his own advisors or friends on secret diplomatic missions while the relevant diplomats were themselves left in the dark.[66] References were made to him running something akin to a royal court.[67]

But it would be a gross oversimplification to claim that the grip of the Presidency on security policy has been absolute under the Fifth Republic. For one thing, it is not a given that the President and the Government should come from the same political coalition, although this was the case until 1986. During this time, it was generally in the Prime Minister's interests, for reasons of political survival, to consent to the President's initiatives regardless of his or her own inclinations. The period was distinctive for the lack of open challenges to the dominant power of the Executive emanating from the Government. On the surface at least, the Presidency was the dominant agent within the French political system. Then, with the 1986 legislative elections producing a Government of the right in opposition to the incumbent Socialist President, the ambiguities of the Constitution were highlighted. This has equally been the case with the two subsequent periods of *cohabitation*, 1993-5 and 1997-2002.

These have demonstrated, if indeed this was needed, that Presidential power can be seriously constrained by political circumstance.

During this first *cohabitation*, differences of interpretation concerning the Constitution were highlighted, and became the subject of intense public debate. Whereas the President can, in certain circumstances, assume emergency powers (article 16), can (only once every 12 months) dissolve the National Assembly (article 12), appoints the military Chief of Staff, negotiates treaties (article 52) and is 'the guarantor of national independence, and of the integrity of the territory' (article 5), the National Assembly retains the right to authorise any declaration of war (article 36) and to ratify and ensure respect of treaties (articles 5, 52 and 53). Moreover, while the President is supreme head of the armed forces and chairs all defence committees (article 15), it is the Prime Minister who has responsibility for national defence (article 21).[68] And the Prime Minister traditionally stands at the head of a parliamentary majority, certainly not a negligible mandate. The post does bring with it a certain diplomatic responsibility, not least by accompanying the President to international conferences and bilateral summits. Indeed, certain Prime Ministers have been able to leave their indelible mark on certain foreign policy dossiers: Mauroy and the 1981 Polish crisis; Fabius with human rights and South Africa's apartheid policy; Rocard in the south Pacific; Cresson and the Maastricht Treaty; and Bérégovoy with the GATT negotiations.[69] Evidently, Prime Ministers faced with *cohabitation* have been especially keen to exert their international influence; Balladur and his Stability Pact to name but one instance. But equally there have been rebuttals. Mitterrand, for example, vetoed Chirac's original nominees for foreign and defence minister, Jean Lecanuet and François Léotard. Both men were considerable political figures in their own right and would have been in a position to strengthen the government challenge to the *domaine réservé*.

This being the case, the President's power-base is further weakened by the fact that he (the Presidency remains a male bastion) does not control the administrative apparatus responsible for the discharge of policy. Many agents act on behalf of the French State, and inevitably they have their own impact on policy implementation. Civil servants at the Hôtel de Brienne, the Ministry of Defence, as in other Ministries, attempt to ensure that their Minister, traditionally the puppet of the President, follows an agenda that they themselves set.[70] This practice would appear to be a common feature of parliamentary democracies. The Armed Forces likewise have their own agenda and try to influence particular debates in their favour, not least, those concerning the defence budget. The Counter-Espionage Service (SDECE – *Service de Documentation Extérieure et de Contre-Espionnage*) also has carved out something of its own freedom of manoeuvre. Officially, it is controlled by the Defence Ministry, but it evolved into a semi-autonomous unit with allegiance to nobody. It was able to shed direct command links to the Presidency, and the Prime Minister and Interior Minister were equally sidelined. It appears, for instance, that, in the early years of Mitterrand's Presidency, the SDECE was manipulating evidence in order that the President be persuaded to sanction a major intervention in Chad.[71]

In addition to the Elysée, the Matignon, the Quai d'Orsay, the Armed Forces and the various State agencies, another significant power centre in the determination of

French security policy is the Ministry of Finance. From the late 1980s, with economic pressures mounting, the latter has assumed increased prominence in security policy decision-making. And the role played by public and private big business should not be underestimated, notably those operating in strategic areas like military equipment. They have proved highly persuasive in promoting and protecting their interests. The activities of French multinationals in the more remote parts of Africa, in the exploitation of energy and mineral resources, have often represented the, sometimes uncontrolled, front-line of French foreign policy.

It should likewise be noted that the President does not step into a policy vacuum on entering the Elysée. France's world interests are deeply rooted in history, and there is the legacy of Presidential predecessors to contend with. The new incumbent cannot simply start with a clean slate. The state of public opinion, often fuelled by the media, can also act as a constraint on Presidential power, be this via mass demonstrations in the streets, local elections or opinion polls. In 1994, for example, there was widespread popular mobilisation in response to events in Bosnia-Herzegovina. Nevertheless, given the aforementioned extensive powers in the field of security, there is considerable scope for the individual personality of each President to leave an indelible impression on policy decisions. And his or her view of the world, temperament and working methods will already have been massively shaped by their own long experience.[72] Indeed, the history of the Fifth Republic is broken down according to the respective President; namely the *gaullienne*, *pompidolienne*, *giscardienne* and *mitterrandienne* periods (presumably, Chirac will also be so honoured). Hence, the actions, and indeed non-actions, of France's Heads of State have impacted significantly, and frequently indelibly, on the output of French foreign and defence policy. As Blondel observed, the Presidential office 'gives independence to the holder; the holder needs to give meaning to the position'.[73] In addition, the President has the advantage of a seven-year popularly-elected mandate, or *septennat*, in which to enact his/her policies (in October 2000, a national referendum voted for a five-year presidential term to replace the *septennat*). Governments are only elected for a five-year term, but few have survived that long. Moreover, the French electorate has shown itself reluctant to elect governments for consecutive terms. In the 13 years prior to 1997, four different governments sought re-election and they were all denied. Equally, the Elysée's power position has been enhanced by the relatively high turnover of Prime Ministers, nine in the same 13-year period.

In practice it has been the President who has authorised the deployment of French troops around the globe. In addition, and crucially, he has, since the 1964 Presidential decree, had sole responsibility for the launch of nuclear weapons with all the stature that that implies. Maire even referred to France as a nuclear monarchy.[74] The Presidents have traditionally enjoyed a *domaine réservé* (Michel Chamard credits the late political doyen Jacques Chaban-Delmas for having come up with the term in the 1960s),[75] not actually set out explicitly in the Constitution but widely acknowledged in practice, in which power can be exercised to its fullest extent, most especially in security matters. It has been the President who has generally set the policy guidelines and taken the decisions of any real international significance for French security policy. Equally, the Presidency has become the international face of France.

To this end, Parliamentary supervision is minimal, particularly in comparison to the American Congress system. The National Assembly has 'the power of knowledge', to know what is going on, but it lacks 'the power of influence'.[76] A senior French government official declared 'the strength of French diplomacy is that it is isolated from political parties and the political system'.[77] The Constitution's article 53, for example, states that all treaties agreed by the Government must be subject to parliamentary scrutiny. That this was not taking place in practice was clearly illustrated by Brouillet's 1978 study that found that most of France's bilateral military agreements had never been submitted to the National Assembly.[78] Moreover, those Parliamentary and Senate Select Committees responsible for foreign and defence matters can only question the relevant civil servants and military staff with the permission of the Minister of Defence. Jean-Louis Arnaud observed that Mitterrand, as President during the 1980s, exonerated the government of all responsibility in the area of foreign policy.[79] It is the President who determines just what constitutes France's vital and strategic interests, these are then pursued and defended by the armed forces; he does not have to wait for some form of consensus to emerge within some council. Hence, for instance, Mitterrand's 1983 decision to send French troops to Chad to counter Libyan territorial advances was only put in front of the Prime Minister's Cabinet two weeks after the launch of the operation, and most Ministers learnt of the decision via the media.[80] Parliamentary supervision of Presidential authority would be further weakened in 1995 when President Chirac broadened the scope for national referenda, effectively extending the scope for bypassing the National Assembly.

A Compliant National Consensus

The traditional, and almost infamous, absence of anything resembling a popularly supported security policy alternative to the *grandes lignes* outlined above, as well as the notion of a universal mission, or indeed to the tactics adopted to obtain them, has given the Presidents of the Fifth Republic an even freer rein in this field than they might otherwise have expected. Questions, for example, as to why France sought to be a world power have been largely ignored, they were not deemed relevant because France, as far as the ruling elites have been concerned, was a global actor and, what is more, it could afford to be.[81] Balaj notes that French policy-makers refer to a 'broad public consensus' on foreign affairs and consider themselves removed from public opinion and interest group pressures. They deem themselves to be the arbiters of the national interest.[82] Presumably, there is a sense here of benevolent leadership, of knowing what is best for France and its people. However, this apparent consensus did not emerge in the National Assembly until the mutations of the Left with regard to security policy, encouraged and cajoled by Mitterrand and his supporters, towards the political centre-ground during the Giscard *septennat*. But, in a sense, the very vagueness of de Gaulle's policies, summarised by Pierre Hassner as 'strategic simplicity, diplomatic flexibility and political ambiguity',[83] facilitated the emergence of a broad agreement regarding France's position in the world.

Furthermore, certain institutional factors contributed to the blocking of challenges to the *grandes lignes* of *rang* and *grandeur*. Firstly, as alluded to above, French security policy has not, for the most part, been the result of compromises between competing bureaucratic agencies. Respective Presidents have set a clear path and have, effectively, arbitrated among the various options presented to them. Hence, policy largely reflected individual Presidential preferences within the *grandes lignes* and has been little affected by domestic political considerations. Secondly, France had retained the highly centralised, elitist and technocratic decision-making process fashioned by generations of autocratic rulers. Constitutional dispersal of power is less apparent in France than elsewhere. According to John Mason, 'the influence of party leaders over the national political agenda and later the pressures of parliamentary discipline once in power, ensured that grass-roots movements were denied institutional support from unions, churches, and the leftist press'.[84] No grass-roots, social, movement has been able to overcome the huge systemic obstacles and emerge with sufficient influence to challenge the monopoly of security policy specialists over decisions concerning vital strategic questions and to foster political change. Even the National Assembly, due to its relative impotence as a formal check on executive authority, is not perceived as a conduit for the views of constituents. At the same time, less than ten per cent of the workforce belong to trade unions.

A third institutional explanation is the fact that any peace movement to emerge in France during the Fifth Republic, which perhaps elsewhere would have challenged the country's highly militarised international stance, would have automatically been associated in the popular mind-set with the Communist Party. The electoral decline of the latter, from one of three dominant political parties immediately after the Second World War to one touching less than ten per cent of the popular vote led to the marginalisation of these movements. Fourthly, the Catholic Church, historically opposed to republicanism, came to support the Fifth Republic and the positions adopted by France's leaders. It even subsequently acknowledged the moral right of a state to pursue a policy of nuclear deterrence.[85] Fifthly, the absence of a truly investigative journalistic tradition in France reinforced the view that the 'consensus' was not to be questioned,[86] and that the need to preserve it was paramount. It became an end in itself. Sixthly, the retention of National Service translated itself into greater military awareness throughout the population and among the political elites than was found in countries like Britain that did not have conscription. This common experience, it is argued, meant that there was a relatively high level of general understanding of the needs for a strong and independent military operating within France's traditional foreign policy objectives.[87] In a sense, conscription, in addition to its military function, served as a form of soft indoctrination. As François Léotard was to note, 'Defence is the sum of financial, industrial and human effort. It also represents what the country is prepared to devote its armed forces which are an essential element of its global presence, of the defence of its national territory, of the assertion of its values'.[88] Finally, some observers like Menon have pointed to a certain degree of collusion between French scholars and policy-making elites, thereby implying a certain absence of academic criticism of prevailing policies.[89]

This relative passivity, where public opinion on security policy has tended to follow the lead of the political elites, was carried over into the nuclear age as something of a natural progression. This was perhaps surprising given that France was largely similar socially and politically to neighbouring countries where a widespread pacifist and anti-nuclear sentiment did take hold, particularly during the 1980s: it was equipped with advanced social organisations, and it was urbanised, secularised and industrialised. In addition, pacifist-orientated policy-making had been popular during the inter-war years, especially among French intellectuals and veterans of the 1914-18 conflict, and in the early days of the Cold War when the *Mouvement de la Paix* political party was at the height of its popularity. Nevertheless, a truly unified anti-nuclear movement failed to materialise, due not least to the wide diversity of pacifist discourse, ranging from fundamentalist expressions of an absolute aversion to the use of force to the calculated pseudo-pacifism of the Communist Party.[90] At the same time, a general reflection on the humiliation of 1940 and the subsequent occupation concluded that pacifism and anti-militarism were associated with defeatism. A new consensus on defence was to emerge, based on the will to guarantee France's security by all available military means.

In many countries, any debate over the development of a national nuclear capacity, and the permanent global projection of military power, would have required a clear statement of national interest, whereas in France it appeared to be enough for the President to simply call on the nation to rally around the flag, or to justify France's actions as 'doing good for others'.[91] Since 1958, French society had been, to some extent, shielded, both physically and conceptually, from the battlefield and was thus immune to much of the general west European debate concerning defence. An editorial in 1992 pondered, 'whether the French have really understood the purpose of nuclear weapons. They have been told so much that these were non-usable weapons that they have finally come to believe that they were indeed destined never to be used. The French consensus is based perhaps on a misunderstanding'.[92] For Stanley Hoffman, the French have been proud of their independence and nuclear capability, they did not therefore require a strong peace movement to protest against American hegemony over decisions of life and death.[93]

Conclusion

Having, at the outset, set out the parameters of this volume, this introductory chapter has examined the emergence of 'France' as a political and security actor. Each country evolves out of a particular set of circumstances; those for France help to explain the emergence and retention of the vibrant and forthright global vocation that concerns us here. This almost existential external focus is crucial to any understanding of France. It forms the basis upon which the fundamental goals of French security policy rest. And these have necessitated that the policy-makers in Paris, rather than being constrained by the parameters of the international system, attempt to manipulate it for the purposes of national gain. In addition, this chapter has charted some key domestic aspects of the Fifth Republic that have either facilitated or were crucial to the security policy designed by de Gaulle as President and that remains the reference point for France's political elites today. It is the formation of this Gaullist legacy, with its key distinction between the *tactical* and the *strategic*, that occupies Chapter Two.

Notes

1   Blondel, Jean (1974), *The Government France*, Methuen, London, pp.231-2.
2   Doelnitz, Tristan (1993), *La France Hantée par sa Puissance*, Belfond, Paris, p.207.
3   Blondel, Jean, *op cit*, p.231.
4   Cohen, Roger, 'Form and substance: France's dual model', *International Herald Tribune*, 25 August 1997.
5   Lewin, André (1995), 'La France et la coopération multilatérale', in André Lewin (ed), *La France et l'ONU (1945-1995)*, Collection Panoramiques, Condé-sur-Noireau, p.31.
6   Wendt, Alexander, 'Levels of analysis vs. agents and structures: part III', *Review of International Studies*, vol.18, no.2, April 1992, pp.181-2.
7   Hollis, Martin and Smith, Steve, 'Two stories about structure and agency', *Review of International Studies*, vol.20, no.3, July 1994, p.241.
8   Fowler, Michael Ross and Bunck, Julie Marie, 'What constitutes the sovereign state?', *Review of International Studies*, vol.22, no.4, October 1996, p.383.
9   Buzan, Barry (1983), *People, States and Fear*, The University of North Carolina Press, Chapel Hill, p.1.
10 Blondel, Jean, *op cit*, p.6.
11 Hazareesingh, Sudhir, *Political Traditions in Modern France*, Oxford University Press, Oxford, 1994, p.29.
12 Allison, Graham T. (1971), *Essence of Decision: Explaining the Cuban Missile Crisis*, Little Brown and Co., Boston, p.4.
13 *Ibid*, p.3.
14 Craig, Gordon A. and George, Alexander L. (1990), *Force and Statecraft: Diplomatic Problems of our Time*, Oxford University Press, Oxford, p.5.
15 Jenkins, Brian (1987), 'Nation, nationalism and national identity in France since 1789: some theoretical reflections', in Jeff Bridgford (ed), *France: Image and Identity*, Newcastle Upon Tyne Polytechnic Products, Newcastle.
16 Briseul, Jean-Paul, 'Structures territoriales françaises et construction de l'Europe', *Défense Nationale*, vol.49, January 1993, p.17.
17 Cranston, Maurice (1988), 'The sovereignty of the nation', in Colin Lucas (ed), *The Political Culture of the French Revolution*, Pergamon Press, Oxford, p.101.
18 Burghardt, A.F., 'The bases of geographical review', *Geographical Review*, vol.63, 1973, p.255.
19 Labourde, Cecile, seminar at the University of Birmingham, 22 October 1997.
20 David, Dominique, Chargé de Mission auprès du Directeur, Institut Français des Relations Internationales (IFRI), in interviews with the author, Paris, June/July 1996.
21 Doelnitz, Tristan, *op cit*, p. 215.
22 Blondel, Jean, *op cit*, p.29.
23 Grimond, John, 'First nation singular', *The Economist*, 25 November 1995.
24 Kolodziej, Edward A. (1974), *French International Policy under De Gaulle and Pompidou: The Politics of Grandeur*, Cornell University Press, Ithaca, p.23.

25 Gaffney, John (1991), 'Language and politics: the case of neo-Gaullism', in John Gaffney and Eva Kolinsky (eds), *Political Culture in France and Germany*, Routledge, London, p.94.
26 *Idem.*
27 Mény, Yves (1989), 'Interest groups and politics in the Fifth Republic', in Paul Godt (ed), *Policy-Making in France*, Pinter Publishers, p.91.
28 Blondel, Jean, *op cit*, p.37.
29 Labourde, Cecile, *op cit.*
30 Blondel, Jean, *op cit*, p.38.
31 Domenach, Jean-Marie, quoted in Walden, George, 'France says no', *The Observer* (Prospect section), 19 October 1997.
32 Dabezies, Pierre, Professeur at Paris I University and former advisor to Jacques Chirac, in an interview with the author, Paris, June 1996.
33 Buzan, Barry, *op cit*, p.38.
34 Berstein, Serge (1989), *The Republic of De Gaulle: 1958-1969*, Cambridge University Press/Editions de la Maison des Sciences de l'Homme, Paris, p.244.
35 Price, Roger (1993), *A Concise History of France*, Cambridge University Press, Cambridge, p.26.
36 Goubert, Pierre (1991), *The Course of French History*, Routledge, London, p.91.
37 Morse, Edward L. (1973), *Foreign Policy and Interdependence in Gaullist France*, Princeton University Press, Princeton, p.132.
38 Sewell (jr), William H., 'Activity, passivity, and the revolutionary concept of citizenship', in *The Political Culture of the French Revolution, op cit*, p.113.
39 Blondel, Jean, *op cit*, p.8.
40 Hague, Rod, Harrop, Martin and Breslin, Shaun (1992), *Comparative Government and Politics: An Introduction*, MacMillan, London, p.76.
41 Hazareesingh, Sudhir, *op cit*, p.73.
42 Wallerstein, Immanuel (1992), *Geopolitics and Geoculture*, Cambridge University Press, Cambridge, pp.4-5.
43 Bourgeois, Bernard, 'L'apport de la pensée française à une organisation collective du monde', in *La France et l'ONU (1945-1995), op cit*, p.49.
44 McLynn, Frank, 'Napoleon', as reviewed in *The Times*, 20 November 1997.
45 Hazareesingh, Sudhir, *op cit*, p.72.
46 Hampson, Norman, 'La Patrie', in *The Political Culture of the French Revolution, op cit*, p.132.
47 Hoffman, Stanley, quoted in Frears J.B. (1981), *France in the Giscard Presidency*, Allen and Unwin, London, p.109.
48 David, Dominique, 'The search for a new security strategy in a shifting international arena', in Tony Chafer and Brian Jenkins (eds), *France: From the Cold War to the New World Order*, MacMillan, Basingstoke, p.66.
49 Quoted in Hayward, Jack (1973), *The One and Indivisible French Republic*, Weidenfeld and Nicolson, London, p.248.
50 Giscard d'Estaing, Valéry, quoted in Frears, J.B., *op cit*, p.127.
51 McMillan, James F. (1992), *Twentieth Century France: Politics and Society 1898-1991*, Edward Arnold, London, p.65.
52 Chevènement, Jean-Pierre (1985), *Le Pari sur l'Intelligence; Entretiens avec Hervé Hamon et Patrick Rotman*, Flammarion, Paris, pp. 177, 206-7 and 210.

53 Schubert, Klaus (1991), 'France', in Regina Cowen Karp (ed), *Security with Nuclear Weapons?: Different Perspectives on National Security*, Oxford University Press, Oxford, p.164.

54 Kolodziej, Edward A., *op cit*, p.25.

55 De Montbrial, Thierry, 'French "exception", yes, and it isn't likely to fade away soon', *International Herald Tribune*, 14 September 1995.

56 Winock, Michel, quoted in Jeambar, Denis, 'La France et les Frances', *Le Point*, 28 January 1995.

57 Moïsi, Dominique, 'Franco-Soviet relations and French foreign policy: between adjustment and ambition', in *Policy-Making in France*, *op cit*, p.217.

58 Grosser, Alfred (1984), *Affaires Extérieures: La Politique de la France 1944-1984*, Flammarion, Paris, p.159.

59 Doelnitz, Tristan, *op cit*, p.195.

60 De Gaulle, Charles, quoted in Duhamel, Alain, 'Le monarque républicain', *Le Point*, 22 April 1995.

61 Kolodziej, Edward A., *op cit*, p.19.

62 Grosser, Alfred, *op cit*, p.151.

63 Marr, Andrew, 'Vive la république! Et vive le roi!', *The Independent*, 8 August 1995.

64 Mitterrand, François in a speech to the National Assembly, 3 December 1981.

65 Massie, Allan, 'Arrogance meets its match at the barricades', *The Observer*, 10 December 1995.

66 Accusation made, for example, during a televised interview accorded by François Mitterrand on 16 December 1984 to Anne Sinclair, Dominique Bromberger, Michel Colomès, Paul-Marie de la Gorce, André Mazières and Michel Tatu; quoted in *Le Monde*, 18 December 1984.

67 Védrine, Hubert (1996), *Les Mondes de François Mitterrand: A l'Elysée 1981-1995*, Fayard, Paris, p.66.

68 Howorth, Jolyon (1990), 'Foreign and defence policy: from independence to interdependence', in Jack Hayward, Peter A. Hall and Howard Machin (eds), *Developments in French Politics*, MacMillan, London, p.201; and Cohen, Samy (1986), *La Monarchie Nucléaire: Les Coulisses de la Politique Etrangère sous la Cinquième République*, Hachette, Paris, p.21.

69 Védrine, Hubert, *op cit*, pp.51-2.

70 *Ibid*, p.50.

71 Howorth, Jolyon (1993), 'The President's special role in foreign and defence policy', in Jack Hayward (ed), *De Gaulle to Mitterrand: Presidential Power in France*, Hurst and Co., London, p.181.

72 *Ibid*, p.150.

73 Blondel, Jean, *op cit*, p.255.

74 Maire, Edmond, writing in *Le Monde*, 20 November 1980.

75 Chamard, Michel, 'Les fissures du "domaine réservé"', *Le Figaro*, 27 August 1991.

76 Balaj, Barbara S., 'France and the Gulf War', *Mediterranean Quarterly*, vol.4, no.3, Summer 1993, p.99.

77 Quoted in *Ibid*, p.110.

78 Brouillet, Alain, 'Le Parlement français et la politique étrangère', *Le Monde Diplomatique*, May 1979.

79 Arnaud, Jean-Louis, 'L'interprétation Mitterrandienne du "domaine réservé"', *Le Matin*, 18 December 1984.

80 Cohen, Samy, *La Monarchie Nucléaire: Les Coulisses de la Politique Etrangère sous la Cinquième République*, op cit, p.19.
81 Bozo, Frédéric, Chargé de Récherches, Institut Français des Relations Internationales (IFRI), in an interview with the author, Paris, April 1995.
82 Balaj, Barbara S., *op cit*, p.110.
83 Hassner, Pierre, quoted in Menon, Anand, 'Continuing politics by other means: defence policy under the French Fifth Republic', *West European Politics*, vol.17, no.4, October 1994, p.77.
84 Mason, John G. (1989), 'Mitterrand, the Socialists and French nuclear policy', in *French Security Policy in a Disarming World: Domestic Challenges and International Constraints*, Lynne Reinner, London, p.59.
85 Foley, James B. (1985), 'Pacifism and anti-nuclearism in France: perceptions of the crisis of deterrence and détente', in James E. Dougherty and Robert L. Pfaltzgraff (eds), *Shattering Europe's Defence Consensus: The Antinuclear Movement and the Future of NATO*, Pergamon/Brasseys, Oxford, p.176.
86 Menon, Anand, 'Continuing politics by other means: defence policy under the French Fifth Republic', *op cit*, p.80.
87 Roper, John, then Director of the Western European Union's Security Studies Research Institute, in an interview with the author, Paris, April 1995.
88 Léotard, François (1993), Preface to Pierre Pascallon (ed), *Quelle Défense pour la France?*, Institut des Relations Internationales et Stratégiques/Dunod, Paris, p.9.
89 Menon, Anand, speech at the University of Birmingham, May 1996. This view was supported by Jean-Yves Haine, Maître de Conférences, Centre D'Etudes Des Conflits, Paris Institut D'Etudes Politiques, in an interview with the author, Paris, July 1996.
90 Hazareesingh, Sudhir, *op cit*, p.203.
91 Smith, Tony, 'In defense of intervention', *Foreign Affairs*, vol.73, no.6, November/December 1994, p.44.
92 Les débats, *Défense Nationale*, Décembre 1982, p.92.
93 Hoffman, Stanley, 'La politique internationale de Mitterrand, ou le gaullisme sous un autre nom', in Stanley Hoffman and Sylvia Malzacher (eds), *L'Expérience Mitterrand: Continuité et Changement dans la France Contemporaine*, Presses Universitaires de France/Basil Blackwell, Cambridge, p.384.

Chapter 2

Gaullist Security Policy: Forging the Legacy

This chapter considers General Charles de Gaulle as the driving force behind the creation and ultimate success, in terms of stability and durability at least, of the Fifth Republic. His appreciation of what was good for France and what France stood for, particularly his popularisation of the notion of *rang* as a strategic objective, retains a fundamental significance, and has never seriously been publicly challenged. In addition, he placed great emphasis on the policy of non-dependence as a tactical response to what he perceived as structural pressures inherent in the bipolar international system with which he was faced. In practice, this primarily involved his guidance of France to an international position that was apparently, if not in reality, distinct from the two superpower blocs. In public at least, the General was not prepared to accept the constraints of the Cold War system. This approach would be characterised by the withdrawal of France from NATO's integrated military command and by the deepening *rapprochement* with West Germany (evidently, the development of the autonomous nuclear weapons capability was likewise a tactical choice, and this is discussed in Chapter Six).

The General and *La France*

Some 30 years or so after his death, the spectre of de Gaulle still looms large over French security policy-making structures. It is thus crucial that this chapter additionally sets out just how the General interpreted and adapted the cultural and historical legacy described in the preceding chapter. It was, for example, de Gaulle who catapulted the concepts of *rang* and *grandeur* to the forefront of security policy strategic thinking. To this end, this chapter will now demonstrate his obsession with *rang* and how, having evaluated the lessons of history and having applied his own experiences, he concluded, over time, that a tactical course of non-dependence was the best way to guarantee for France elevated global status. It was clear that de Gaulle would not allow France, as an agent, to be cowed by the Cold War structure.

Throughout his political life, de Gaulle practised his own analysis of French history. But to a large extent, his conclusions only followed a long and illustrious line of French leaders in believing that France had a special right and duty to play the role of world power just because it was France.[1] Even the leaders of the relatively weak and divisive Fourth Republic, with their greater tolerance for subordination to American foreign policy, never forgot France's grand past and its claimed world role.[2] France was special, it was a *puissance spécifique*, it had something high and unique to offer. And this was something eternal, far greater than how it may seem at one moment in time. To this end, according to Cerny, the idea of *grandeur* had been adopted to 'create a new and deeper sense of national unity that would enable the traditional cleavages in French political life to be overcome by reinforcing the consensus around a strengthened and dynamic state that incarnated the general interest within a stable political system'.[3] And, like others before him, de Gaulle was able to exploit the traditional French affinity for heroic leadership. Grand gestures were used to disguise relative national decline. The French people came to believe that because de Gaulle, as their leader, was supposedly a great man then they too could be great.

The General had a simple vision of the international system and the place France should occupy within it. This was a system that was inevitably hostile and competitive, and one that was based on transient balances of power between states permanently acting according to their own interests. The latter were, in his view, the fundamental reality and 'the only entities with the right to issue orders, and the power to be obeyed'.[4] Hence, the nation-state represented the ultimate focus of people's loyalty. But the General went further: all states were equal, but France was more equal than all the others. This helps to explain France's rejection of the supranational and federalist models for the then still emerging EEC. This rejection was graphically confirmed by the French counter-proposal for an alternative method of European political cooperation – the Fouchet Plan (this is discussed further later in this chapter). De Gaulle placed the national idea at the top of the scale of political values. To this end, according to Grosser, the prosperity and wellbeing of the French people were not ends in themselves, but 'a means to improve the destiny of France'.[5] And de Gaulle always looked for a sense of continuity and tradition in countries, speaking of nations and peoples rather than of transitory regimes. He was consistently referring, for instance, to the Soviet Union as Russia. In addition, traditional references to *la France* as a woman were commonplace. The French have frequently adopted female figures as symbols of their country. 'Unlike the other nations of post-war western Europe', states Steven Philip Kramer, 'France continued to conceive of itself almost entirely in traditional nation-state terms'.[6] This vision, as described by Hazareesingh, held that 'all states were primarily motivated by interests, and that grand ideologies such as communism or capitalism simply provided the language in which these conflicting interests were articulated. These interests were relatively constant, and were determined by national identity and character, geography, cultural attributes, and the legacy of past political experiences'.[7]

It is, however, sometimes forgotten that de Gaulle, with all his strength of character and independence of thought, respected all the fundamental security decisions made by the Fourth Republic: the *force de frappe*, NATO (he never withdrew France from the organisation as a whole), Franco-German *rapprochement*, decolonisation and the development of the EEC. What changed was the tone and the style. The fundamental choices open to France had not changed, de Gaulle just modified the way of dealing with them. Hence, his major contribution to French security policy was to translate the aspirations that had been prevalent prior to 1958 into an overall coherent, almost aggressive, policy, backed by sufficient means and will. He built a new declaratory diplomatic discourse promoting France's return as a world power of stature and importance. For Gordon, '[t]he Gaullist years represent a crystallization of traditional French attitudes towards national security into a coherent, well-articulated and largely implemented doctrine'.[8] In addition, *grandeur* was adapted to France's new medium-power status. The General taught the French that they were no longer a Great Power in material terms, although the sense of moral predominance was instinctively retained. Membership of the EEC was hence deemed essential to French national interests, although not to the extent of sacrificing any major tenets of independence and freedom of action. At the same time, he was striving to prioritise national over sectional interests, believing that much of the former had been hijacked by the latter.

Roger Price asserted that the General's 'frequent references to the eternal values of France thus concealed a determination to adapt to the realities of a rapidly changing world'.[9] But adapting did not mean simply conducting a reactive relationship with the pressures of the international system; de Gaulle's France would be proactive, manipulating the system to its own advantage. As James F. McMillan noted, '[i]t was never de Gaulle's ambition to pursue power and glory in the manner of Louis XIV, but rather, by developing a renewed sense of national pride, to legitimise the Fifth Republic and to enhance the authority of the French state'.[10] He was convinced that only with the restoration of patriotism and national pride could the state overcome the divisions deriving from its wrecked polity and economy. The forging of the social cultural and political unity of the French nation was a categorical imperative to restore France's international stature. Internal policies were hence only mechanisms for the pursuit of foreign policy. Economic, technical, scientific and even social progress was prioritised *behind* international progress. What had traditionally been the primary objective of France's leaders became, for the General, an internal means to an external end. De Gaulle was to refer to 'a certain idea of France' which fused foreign and domestic policy into a supposed coherent whole.

Rank

De Gaulle was to reveal an obsession with France's relative standing within the international system. And this obsession remains the pre-eminent and unswerving guiding principle in French security policy strategic planning today, this is the ultimate objective. Like many national leaders before him, de Gaulle believed that national legitimacy was born in history, it came from the respect and support of the citizens for their *patrie* and the affinity they felt for their compatriots.[11] He played on the belief in France's historic mission, that French genius would further the interests of mankind as a whole, that the world had been conditioned to look to France for inspiration. A doctrine so flattering to national sensibilities, one that readily proclaimed national importance, was bound to appeal, especially in a country with a belief system given toward national exceptionalism. As Gordon noted, the French have traditionally been more than ready to accept a role that distinguished them from others and assumed a universal interest in their own culture and ideas.[12] To this end, there has consistently been a willingness to give a high priority to the international projection of French culture.

Although it clearly was not a superpower in this new bipolar age, France had to be restored to its position as a great world power. As de Gaulle put it, 'France is not really herself unless she is first rank'.[13] Everything had to be subordinated to this end. De Gaulle himself would direct this quest and become the very embodiment of the country's international status. The overriding imperative was that France once again be recognised by the international community as a significant power, as a country that mattered. As will be discussed in Chapter Three, France's leaders would have, in later years, to change tack by seeking to preserve the country's global rank by downgrading independence and embracing integration with the country's European partners. But in the meantime, in Klaus Schubert's analysis, 'the "grandeur" of the nation is the most important national concern ... National independence and maximum world status have been characteristic imperatives of French policy. Any asset or resource which promises to strengthen the nation, which seems suitable for improving the global status and glory of France, becomes a worthwhile policy device'.[14]

This almost unrivalled obsession with *rang* has dominated France's security policy since the Second World War. An intrinsic element of 'Frenchness' remains this overtly external outlook. That is essentially, an inherent preoccupation with international standing and status and paranoia of what any loss of these would bring. General Michel Cot referred to a secular global evangelism.[15] Mitterrand, as President, even suggested that France's position in the world was better appreciated outside France than within.[16] In his 1981 inaugural address, he emphasised that a great nation should entertain only noble projects and that France should 'enlighten humanity's progress'.[17] Grosser referred to a French volition to provide aid to developing countries as 'the logical outcome of a national ambition to play a part wherever the future of the world is being decided'.[18] The image of France as the spokesperson for the disadvantaged around the world still holds some credence. 'Her ambitions of grandeur', according to Marie-Claude Smouts, 'still feed on the dreams of distant horizons. She cannot imagine herself powerful without a presence beyond her borders and an influence overseas'.[19] France cannot be without *grandeur*. Equally, Grosser points to international prestige as not being a policy instrument, but an end in itself.[20] Or as the then President of Chad, Hissène Habré, put it, 'France is France, thanks to the role she plays in the world'.[21] For his part, Moïsi stated that France stands among a select group of countries, which also includes China, Russia and the United States, 'which believes, rightly or wrongly, not only that the world matters to them but that they matter to the world. For these nations, international identity is an essential part of national identity; they can and must make a difference on the international scene'.[22] This assertive, interventionist, foreign policy outlook is, thus, rare. Dominique David, meanwhile, stresses geography as part explanation for France's external vocation. Its multiple frontiers, facing different directions, and its location at the end of the historic migratory route across Europe from east to west, and as the crossroads of Latin, Germanic and Anglo-Saxon cultures, made it the repository for numerous peoples and produced an inherent international perspective.[23]

De Gaulle, himself, was worried about the consequences for his country should it not pursue this inherent external and universal vocation, expressing the opinion that '[u]nless France and its people are devoted to great enterprise abroad, they find themselves ... always in "mortal danger", susceptible to internal collapse or foreign domination'.[24] In a similar vein, Bozo, writing in 1995, was to attribute French diplomacy with being embedded in 'a global conceptual framework that generated a sense of general coherence and direction'. And he claimed that the ability to deliver a strong international message was a significant element in the nation's approval of an active foreign policy.[25] To this end, France's diplomatic network remains among the most extensive and dense. And this national self-perception naturally raised the profile of the military as a foreign policy tool. Hence, military prowess was deemed by de Gaulle's security policy-makers to be just as important as economic might as they dedicated themselves to the aforementioned *grandes lignes* and as they sought to demonstrate national sovereignty and autonomy. To this day, France, rarely among the Western world, continues to hold a major military display on its national day. Equally, the General encouraged strong resistance to any constraints on the country's global status that might be derived from multilateral alliances.

Non-dependence

If the pursuit of *rang* and *grandeur* was the strategy, then non-dependence would become the tactic. In 1945, a resurrected but shattered France had only nominally been among the elite club of states which, at the end of the Second World War, negotiated the new world order centred, on paper at least, on the UN. With its great power status all but disappeared, Paris had reluctantly been forced to accept an international framework that lowered its standing and imposed strict rules of solidarity with allies. French leaderships were subsequently driven by the desire to restore traditional prestige and, at the time, this implied reasserting national independence. This was as much the case for the Fourth Republic as for the Fifth. Initially, the overwhelming priority was to avert further conflict at all costs, to guarantee the protection of the national territory from invasion and occupation, and to police the colonies. To this end, France signed up to a series of defensive alliances, firstly to counter the threat of German aggression (with Britain in 1947, with Britain and the Benelux countries in 1948) and subsequently against the Soviet Union (the 1949 Atlantic Alliance). The French, in the early 1950s, were also to be both the architects and eventual wreckers of the abortive European Defence Community. But by the early years of the Fifth Republic, war had ceased to be a daily preoccupation, there was deepening *rapprochement* with West Germany, and, for the French planners at least, the Soviet Union did not appear to pose a direct military threat. Hence, with the integrity of the Hexagon seemingly re-established, the tactical focus shifted away from the need to provide a large conventional force capable of fighting in the European arena. De Gaulle's Administration could concentrate on reasserting France's global rank via independence.

The General accepted that no sovereign state could act without constraints, he simply strove to augment French autonomy of decision-making in a restrictive geopolitical environment. The security framework that had emerged by 1958 was not one that corresponded to de Gaulle's preferences. To him this implied that he must strive to break down the bipolar system inaugurated at the Second World War Yalta and Potsdam conferences (to which France had not been invited) and in its place build a new European construction that was halfway between East and West. Hence, the objective was to overcome the logic of the two blocs. This would allow France the maximum possible room for manoeuvre as it pursued the *grandes lignes* of its security policy and for the execution of what de Gaulle felt were France's international responsibilities.

Unlike their west European allies at this time, French policy-makers did not perceive defence as something that could be afforded to France by another power as a guarantee. Instead, they claimed that defence was something for which each state should be directly and solely responsible.[26] To preserve its international position, France had to have independence of military strategy from both ally and enemy alike. Failure to recognise this in the past had produced cataclysmic consequences. In Wendl's view, '[n]either the alliance system before World War I nor the attempt to construct a system of collective security between the wars, saved France from great suffering and a feeling that she had been used as an advance pawn and as a source of manpower in terms of the peripheral strategy of the Anglo-American powers'.[27] From Paris, it seemed as though the Americans had waited three years to see how the first global conflict developed before getting involved on the side of the French. Equally, in the face of the challenges posed by the axis powers in the 1930s, the attempts of France's leaders at security system-building, once again reliant on alliances (including recent ones concluded with Belgium, Czechoslovakia, Poland, Romania and Yugoslavia) had crumbled, and France's sovereignty had been compromised. It had been forced to stand helpless as the very country it had used diplomatic means to contain rebuilt its force capacity and subjugated the French nation-state. There then followed the humiliation of having the British, supposed allies, sinking the French fleet at Mers-el-Kébir. And once again Paris had an agonising wait, this time for two years, before the Americans would intervene. Moreover, there was speculation that World War Two may have been avoided had the United States committed itself to the League of Nations.

The lesson here was that a militarily weak France, reliant on others for its security was an enslaved and vulnerable France. The perceived failure of the Americans to back-up French forces in Vietnam in 1954 gave further credence to the calls for non-dependence. The US was defined as a capable ally, but one whose provision of security should not be taken for granted. This view was then compounded in 1956 when the Franco-British and Israeli intervention in the Suez crisis with its swift veto by the two superpowers. Paris' international humiliation reinforced its determination to possess the necessary means to enhance France's status and to bolster its functional independence free of the superpowers (Britain was to draw contrasting conclusions and was to move, metaphorically, much closer to Washington). Hence, France would become among the first of the Western states to exploit the dilemmas of the balance of terror that restrained both superpowers from resorting to nuclear war to resolve their differences. France could act with relative autonomy at a minimal cost and with low risk. And no distinction was made between French and European interests. As described by Cole, 'Europe was to be led to independence from American hegemony under France's enlightened military and political leadership. Only France, the lone continental European nuclear power, was strong enough to provide an alternative to American leadership'.[28]

De Gaulle's attempts to preserve and promote France's *grandeur* and *rang* would thus focus on pushing French 'exceptionalism', and fostering the notion of France as a country apart. Pierre Lellouche espoused this outlook, '*[c]'est parce que la France est ainsi faite, avec son histoire, avec sa mémoire, avec sa culture, qu'elle ne saurait renoncer aux fondements de l'indépendance nationale'.*[a][29] In this way, de Gaulle, once free from the constraints of the Algerian conflict, set about, from 1964 to 1967, demonstrating France's autonomous foreign policy line: active engagement with Mexico and Latin America, attacks on the dollar-dominated international financial system, a visit to the Soviet Union, condemnation of the American war in Vietnam, continued rejection of the British application for EEC membership and the withdrawal from NATO's integrated military structures. He was determined that France was not going to be the vassal of, or display deference to, the US, as the acknowledged leader of the Western world. Rather, the two countries would be partners. On each occasion that Paris perceived the Americans to be attempting to augment their influence on western Europe's security mechanisms, it responded with measures to revive the notion of a solely European security identity.

But the emphasis on independence should be understood more in terms of non-dependence, or of minimising dependence within interdependence. As de Gaulle himself put it, '[w]hat is independence? – certainly not isolationism or narrow nationalism. A country can be a member of an alliance, such as the Atlantic Alliance, and remain independent ... To be independent means that one is not at the mercy (*à la discrétion*) of any foreign power'.[30] Hence for Menon, de Gaulle's 'defence policy was not ideologically driven. Rather, it was based on a Machiavellian view of the nature of international politics and the duties of the state within an anarchic international system ... Hence the philosophical underpinning of the need for national independence was simply the belief that reliance on another for security was inconceivable'.[31] Furthermore, as pronounced by Edouard Balladur, as Prime Minister in the 1990s: '[a] country's international influence is measured by its ability to carry its partners with it on the international stage. But its power to do this is very weak if it does not have the means and political will to act by itself'.[32] Goldstein's reasoning was that French political elites had by now completely lost confidence both in alliance-based security as the ultimate guarantee, and the notion of 'free riding' on the security patronage of a superpower.[33] They would increasingly turn to the notion of self-reliance.

---

[a]   'Because France is as it is, with its history, with its memory, with its culture, it would not know how to renounce the foundations of national independence'.

De Gaulle and the Cold War Game

To this end, the 1961 Fouchet Plan[34] was, to a large extent, an answer to US President Kennedy's 'grand design' for Europe. The latter aimed to avert the re-emergence of destructive nationalism across the European continent, and implied the obsolescence of the nation-state in Europe with the possible emergence of a United States of Europe under American tutelage. With this system, it was argued, traditional rivalries for European hegemony would disappear. In contrast, de Gaulle's vision of Europe was based on the continued pre-eminence of the nation-state. As a result, he vigorously sought to counter integrationist and federalist schemes that threatened to dilute its authority. The Fouchet Plan sought to pre-empt any assumption of a political identity by the EEC by establishing an alternative mechanism for political cooperation between the EEC Six (EC6). For Howorth, de Gaulle's principal motivation was to increase the pressure on the US to revise NATO's structure in order to give the Europeans a more balanced representation and influence; the General was even referring to a 'European defence'.[35] Indeed, a system of regular intergovernmental meetings to discuss defence matters *outside* of NATO could only be interpreted as a challenge to that Organisation. And as always, de Gaulle was driven by the perceived need to contain and perpetuate the subordination of West Germany and by the determination to counter possible 'Anglo-Saxon' domination.

The collapse of the negotiations due to the reticence of France's EEC partners, despite certain concessions by the French, was a severe blow to de Gaulle. One of his arguments had been that the main instrument by which greater European independence was to be achieved was France's nuclear force (discussed below). However, this was discredited as soon as it became clear that France's aims for integration under Fouchet did not extend to integrated control of these nuclear forces. Without the Plan, the General concluded there was no hope of maintaining French continental supremacy. As a result, de Gaulle had to reject Britain's application for EEC membership. It had not been part of his vision for France, based on *rang* and *grandeur*, that it share western continental hegemony with another power. Furthermore, with the EC6 having failed to adopt a common political agenda, any EEC with Britain as a member would inevitably be inclined to lean towards the US on key political and economic matters. De Gaulle's successors would subsequently launch their own initiatives that could have been interpreted as countering other American projects for Europe. US Secretary of State Kissinger's 'year of Europe' (1973) was met with French calls for a revival of the Western European Union (WEU). President Mitterrand's similar stance in the 1980s could also be interpreted as a way to enable France to reassert its presence *vis à vis* the US in dealing with Europe's security issues. Some observers, whether rightly or wrongly, thus created the image of France as the wrecker of all international moves which it believed it would not be in a position to control.[36]

Diplomatic and military independence were deemed fundamental. To this end, French representatives insisted upon, and perhaps even exaggerated, the doctrinal differences separating their military strategy from that supported by their allies. The French leaders, in the view of François de la Rose, were '*si profondément attachés á la notion, sinon á la réalité de leur indépendance, qu'ils refusent toute intégration dans un ensemble dominé par une superpuissance même alliée'.*[b] [37] But the anti-American stance was not based so much on ideology but on a rational decision to allow France the maximum room for manoeuvre in its international role, thereby boosting its international rank. Thus, the development of an effective national military capacity was to be used as a tool for diplomatic leverage, and as a means to maintain the country's *rang* and central international role transcending its regional limitations. Simultaneously, the links with Moscow, a traditional ally, would be reaffirmed. At the time of the French Third Republic, spanning the decades either side of the dawn of the twentieth century, these two great powers, France and Russia, had had common cause, situated as they were at the western and eastern extremities of the continent, to stand together in the face of the potential threats emanating from an Austro-Hungarian and Germanic central Europe. The subsequent emergence of a distinct Soviet ideology was not allowed to interfere with historical links or with the immediate, *détente*-orientated, political concerns.

However, as Paul Kennedy points out, it should be acknowledged that, to a certain degree, '[a]ll of France's posturings of independence have taken place behind the American shield and guarantee to western Europe, both conventional and nuclear'.[38] And this was a guarantee obtained remarkably cheaply by the French. For Lellouche, France at this time 'benefited from a divided Germany and a strong Western alliance without incurring the full costs of Western discipline'.[39] This afforded France remarkable latitude within which to demonstrate autonomy. Nevertheless, the moment there was an international crisis of significant magnitude, as with the crises in Cuba and Berlin in the early 1960s, France stood immediately, without hesitation, behind, or next to, the US.

Thus, independence and freedom to act would be the means by which France would gain a greater standing in the international community. This approach would permit the country's political leaders to carve out a 'third way', enabling France to act as a kind of bastion against the superpower division of the world. 'By defining its own unique status within the Atlantic construction, while at the same time offering an alternative design for transatlantic relations', wrote Bozo, 'France managed to maximise her political influence in the West and beyond'.[40] Jean-Pierre Chevènement, meanwhile claimed that the non-alignment subsequently made France more capable than other countries to reflect more effectively on the post-Cold War European order.[41] France's diplomatic profile was thus raised to unprecedented levels. Moreover, the declaratory opposition to the bipolar order served to augment French international prestige, and to enhance the national leadership's perceived role for France as the principle link between the West and the Third World, between North and South. For Daniel Vernet, French diplomacy could be seen representing the country 'in the guise of defender of the weak and oppressed, acting as the goad constantly spurring the big powers to action but bearing no responsibility for the consequences of the positions it adopted'.[42]

---

[b]   'so deeply attached to the notion, if not the reality of their independence, that they refuse any integration in a group dominated by a superpower, even an ally'.

Economic reconstruction was to complement this political regeneration by forming the springboard for de Gaulle's ambitious foreign policy. From the end of the Second World War, the French economy enjoyed some three decades of rapid and dynamic growth, *les trente glorieuses*. This undoubtedly made it easier for de Gaulle to pursue ambitious diplomatic schemes abroad. But he nevertheless had to acknowledge economic imperatives and sacrifice expenditure on conventional armed forces in favour of the nuclear programme. The negative impact of subsequent conventional force deficiencies was to come fully to the fore with the end of the Cold War. At the same time, de Gaulle was using armaments exports as a key tool of foreign policy. There was some expectation that increasing sales abroad would enlarge French political influence in recipient states. For instance, they were key to his efforts at challenging the US' influence in Latin America. The questionable comportment of these regimes, mostly dictatorships, was hence not a major consideration. Mirage fighter planes were, for example, sold to Peru in 1968 and a whole programme of industrial cooperation with Brazil, including the purchase of Brazilian aircraft, was launched. As noted by Grosser, concerns for the balance of payments and for the maintenance of production lines useful to the French armed forces were deemed to outweigh notions of distinguishing between those states who were and who were not suitable clients for France to be selling arms to.[43]

Thus, while not accepting the validity of the bloc system, de Gaulle learnt to play the Cold War game to full advantage. For Davidson, 'France was able to take advantage of the lethal menace of the Soviet Union, on the one side, and the solidity of all the other members of the Atlantic Alliance, on the other, to claim for herself a unique status of moral independence, as a gratuitous defiance of the domination of the two superpowers'.[44] Moïsi summarised France's Cold War tactics at this time as 'firmness toward the Soviet Union, generosity towards the Third World, ambiguity toward the United States'.[45] However, any relaxation in superpower tensions served to fuel fears in Paris of a bipolar condominium, while periods of raised superpower tension and confrontation reduced France's room to manoeuvre within its own, Western, camp. So in actual fact, for Menon, 'the Cold War and the accompanying bipolar international order, although vilified in French rhetoric, provided the ideal setting for the exercise of national independence'.[46] Touraine saw in this approach a remarkable capacity to employ the maximum possible margin for manoeuvre in an international system that was frozen.[47] At the same time, the fact that, since 1962, France had not been embroiled in a major military conflict allowed a certain latitude of action. Moreover, the lack of direct challenges to France's global rank permitted its leaders to believe they were steering a great power.

But from an objective perspective, outside of diplomatic language, de Gaulle failed to develop any viable, practical, alternative to the bipolar division of Europe. The tactical approach based on the French exception and non-dependence could only be taken so far in practice. France under de Gaulle just came to occupy an anomalous position, never fully leaving the Western bloc but often making sorties towards the Eastern bloc. The General additionally failed to promote much enthusiasm, in the early 1960s, for his attempts to establish a third international bloc, based on the states that stood along the Rhine, the Alps and the Pyrenees, that, if need be, could act as arbiter between the Americans and the Soviets.[48] Equally, his vision of a united Europe 'from the Atlantic to the Urals', as elaborated in a February 1965 press conference, came to nothing in his lifetime. France's only success in this area was in Africa, where a bloc of newly independent states, out of economic necessity and cultural affinity, grouped themselves around Paris. Flynn referred to the General's time in office as the period of 'high gaullism' where image and reality stayed some distance apart.[49] The bloc system that the General's rhetoric had consistently railed against remained intact. In time, he came to see the system as ultimately being beneficial to French interests.

When the Cold War was to finally come to an end, France, lacking sufficient resources, was not, in any sense, a country in a position to assume a dominant role in the new international politic in which states would form and dissolve fluid coalitions. Europe, as Kolodziej observed, was supposed to 'move under the spur provided by France's *détente* policy from a bloc system to an interpenetrated security and economic system'.[50] But the notion was full of contradictions. France, naturally, was to be at the centre of this new Europe, but de Gaulle never seriously tackled the inconsistencies between French national interests and those of France's neighbours. Equally, self-determination in the Third World was championed at the same time as he was proposing big-power rule by France and the four other nuclear powers as the best way to ensure global order.

In economic terms, the attempt to forge a third way would finally peter out with the collapse in 1983 of the two-year Socialist, Keynesian, experiment after successive devaluations of the French franc. From the 1960s, according to Jenkins and Chafer, France's leaders had been unable to resist the powerful 'economic and political logic of the global confrontation between capitalism and Communism'.[51] De Gaulle's talk of an alternative to these two approaches based on the market and the plan respectively, a kind of social capitalism, remained largely empty rhetoric. This may have been more symbolic gesturing than a *bona fide* vision, he lacked any real innovative economic strategy, the economy largely ran itself. Nevertheless, the French economy would try to remain largely *dirigiste*, with the State, as opposed to the financial markets, dictating policy. As Ross observed, 'France has had statist, centralizing perspectives on economic life since Louis XIV mobilised luxury goods producers to compete with English capitalism'.[52]

'Withdrawal' from NATO

France's membership of, and role in, NATO had been negotiated during de Gaulle's absence from office. As early as November 1959, he began berating moves within the Alliance towards integration and was promoting the notion of an almost solely national defence.[53] To this end, he withdrew France's Mediterranean fleet from its NATO command (the Atlantic fleet would follow suit in 1964) and then, in 1963, he refused to allow the First Army Corps, formed from units kept intact from the Algerian war, to be subordinated to NATO. The General garnered a deep resentment towards Washington following President Eisenhower's rejection, backed by British Prime Minister MacMillan, of his 1958 memorandum proposing a reshaping of the Alliance via a Franco-British-American triumvirate. This was to have determined the *grandes lignes* of global policy and give direction to the Atlantic Alliance, giving it worldwide responsibilities. De Gaulle had envisaged that this inner core would acquire something of a superior equality. The triumvirate powers would be equal with each other but more equal than the other Alliance members. The view in the Elysée was also that ever since the Soviet Union had gained the means to destroy at least part of the US there had been no assurance that the Soviets were certain that the Americans would actually risk suicide by defending western Europe. If the US nuclear guarantee could no longer be relied upon then, so the reasoning went, the Atlantic Organisation had become obsolete. This was because it simply was not credible that the US would risk mass destruction on its own soil in order to protect and defend western Europe from Soviet attack. No country would now be willing to take a nuclear risk for another one, for its own very survival would be at stake.

As a result of all these considerations, membership of NATO's integrated military command ceased to serve any purpose and was, moreover, becoming detrimental to what de Gaulle perceived as French interests. He even believed that continued integration for France with NATO was weakening the national strength of both the government and the people.[54] The nuclear balance between the two superpowers ruled out any possibility that either would launch a direct strike against the other since this would only lead to mutual destruction. A conflict waged on the territory of western Europe, on the other hand, would present greatly reduced risks. Thus, for France's leaders at this time, NATO membership deprived *la patrie* not only of autonomy, in the face of growing American hegemony, but also of any real protection. The idea that the Americans would provide automatic security to western Europe no longer had credence. At the same time, the instinct of the French leadership was to feel constrained by a system of strict solidarity with France's NATO partners. De Gaulle was searching for ways for France to express an independent vocation. As Bozo points out, 'by defining its own unique status within the Atlantic construction, while at the same time offering an alternative design for transatlantic relations, France managed to maximise her political influence in the West and beyond'.[55] The final, formal, break came in 1966 when France left NATO's integrated military command structure.

There were further incentives behind the withdrawal: the desire to avoid becoming embroiled in conflicts in which France had no direct interest and the belief that the Soviet Union did not pose a direct threat to western Europe. In public at least, de Gaulle was no longer concerned about war in Europe. Henceforth, participation in any joint military effort would be conditional. De Gaulle was to consistently refuse to give any formal guarantee of France's commitment to the defence of its Western partners. The knowledge that its allies were under attack would not be sufficient, France would demand to know who had started the conflict. Furthermore, NATO represented a hindrance to de Gaulle's bid to lead a west European power bloc to rival, and balance, the two superpowers. Not least because the integrated military command structure, and the implied reliance on the US, was having a debilitating effect on the commitment of the European members to their own defences. Finally, Gordon points to another reason, the psychological needs of the French army. For the General, army and nation were linked organically and therefore there should be no attempts to separate them. The army was weighed down with what it perceived to be the double betrayal of

IndoChina and Algeria. In both cases there was a prevailing sense of having fought and died for nothing. It was now critical that the army be reintegrated into the nation, to re-establish the link. This implied that the army should now primarily serve within the Hexagon. It would not again be assigned objectives that were not French objectives, and it would not be asked to risk wars that were not France's wars.[56]

Four factors combined to make withdrawal from the integrated military structures a relatively risk-free manoeuvre. First, the credibility of NATO's extended deterrence and the protracted presence in western Europe of significant American nuclear and conventional forces, indeed, the latter formed a reassuring buffer between France and the Soviet army. Second, the commitment of the major Western powers to a collective, forward defence, thereby bestowing France with a physical security buffer. Third, the fixed binding of the German Federal Republic into the Western fold. And fourth, the special Franco-German political, economic and military partnership (for example, Germany consistently worked to prevent French isolation from NATO). Moreover, this action never represented anything like a shift to neutrality. De Gaulle's France remained fully committed to Article V of the North Atlantic Treaty even though the General's rhetoric often indicated otherwise and it refused to allow any foreign military presence on its soil, save for joint exercises. Contingency procedures were quickly established to compensate for any potential deterioration in western Europe's security and defence. A series of extensive agreements were immediately signed with the Alliance, beginning with the Ailleret-Lemnitzer Accord, concerning the nature of any French participation alongside its allies in a European conflict. Franco-NATO cooperation was to actually increase following the French withdrawal. And it is almost certain that plans were drawn up to allow for France's allies, should the need arise, to store fuel in France in hardened bunkers and to have access to French airfields and ports. And, from the mid-1970s, French armed forces were acting as an uncommitted reserve for NATO.[57]

The German Question

The determination to either contain or balance German power, had been a major feature of French foreign and defence policy since the mid-nineteenth century rise of Bismarck's Prussia. Anti-German sentiment had been based on territorial proximity, military conflict, cultural and religious opposition, economic rivalry and ideological cleavages. It became a French political maxim that the hegemony, prosperity and unity of France depended on Germany not being politically united; the historical lesson being that when politically united, Germany invaded France. In this sense, German reunification post-Second World War was not perceived to be in French interests. For Lacouture, '[w]hat made the German question so important to de Gaulle was that the answers to it conditioned the three debates that formed the basis of any French diplomacy worthy of the name: national independence, the construction of Europe, peaceful East-West relations'.[58]

Bonn's ambitions had to be tamed and French interests protected. As Gregory put it:

[a]fter the failure to provide a long-term resolution of the German question in history through collective security, neutralisation, or disarmament, France in the second half of the twentieth century has embraced Germany through a variety of bilateral and multilateral arrangements intended to constrain Germany and to provide a means by which France can influence developments in Germany.[59]

There were also attempts to compensate for France's relative economic weakness by pursuing something of a political guardianship of, and a psychological edge over, the 'German minor'. By exercising some control over Germany, French leaders were seeking to calm national historical fears. The principal instruments for the first notion were the *force de frappe* and France's status as one of the four occupying powers in Berlin. The second stemmed from the fact that Germany had produced a Hitler whereas France had not. What emerged, at least from the French point of view, was an implicit French assent for West German economic leadership in Europe, in return for support from Bonn on issues of *grande politique*. Thus, much of France's international manoeuvrability at this time was due to the implicit constraints governing its German neighbour, a potential rival for influence. Germany was enlisted by de Gaulle as an instrument to steer France away from potential superpower domination by enabling it to remain independent. For Patrick McCarthy, this was not, initially at least, an alliance of two friendly powers against outside forces, it was more the means for one power to control the other and for the other to control itself as it had not done in the first half of the century.[60] From the French perspective, Germany was being offered legitimacy but not equality. Hence, no contradiction was perceived in Paris between economic cooperation and a national *force de frappe*.

For Friend, '[g]aullist foreign policy since the mid-1960s had operated on the unspoken premise that since West Germany was utterly loyal to the United States, France could afford to dance out of line, remaining loyal to the Atlantic Alliance but in its own independent and idiosyncratic way'.[61] But this approach was largely dependent on the fluctuating state of East-West relations. At times of raised tension the Federal Republic proved highly attractive to the US, and France thus lost influence. When tensions relaxed, the Federal Republic, according to Grosser, 'relapsed into the role of a pawn on the international chessboard while France again became one of the Big Four discussing the German problem'.[62] Additionally, at times of Cold War crisis, the French were swift to promote NATO and to ensure (West) German and American commitment to it.

Then, as the West German economy surged ahead in the 1960s, the ominous prospect of a newly dominant Germany looked increasingly likely. France simply did not have the capacity alone to successfully maintain the policy of containment. French disillusionment with the plan for a privileged Franco-German relationship as a possible alternative to NATO was accentuated in 1964 by the German Bundestag's amendment of the previous year's Elysée Treaty which undermined its very meaning by making it clear that Bonn remained firmly committed to the Atlantic Alliance. The Treaty, a bilateral version of the failed Fouchet Plan, had provided for a merging of military doctrines, three-monthly meetings of the respective Defence Ministers (two-monthly meetings for the Chiefs of Staff), exchanges of military personnel and cooperation on armaments and civil defence. With the Treaty compromised, de Gaulle's

Administration searched for help to counterbalance the potentially dominant unified Germany within Europe. With Russia no longer capable of being this counterweight, French security policy-makers looked to European integration to restrain any German tendencies for going it alone. De Gaulle, having fought to hold back the forces of European integration, was now convinced that the only solution to the German question was a European one. Thus he pursued a policy aimed at consolidation of the West around Germany. The priority was to ensure that Germany retained its Western orientation and that it was not in a position to completely dominate the continent. As Howorth has noted, 'the posing of the "German problem" in a wider European framework, has been a central element of France's security policy ever since'.[63] The obvious dilemma of such a policy was that it ran counter to the General's requirement for French independence.

Conclusion

This chapter has emphasised the formative nature of French security policy during de Gaulle's presidential term and the first 11 years of the Fifth Republic (he retired from public service in 1969). To a large extent, it was a question of continuity. Traditional ideas of *grandeur* and *rang* were adopted as were the key security policy decisions made by the leaders of the Fourth Republic. As established in Chapter One, the new Constitution was purposely crafted, and thereafter methodically manipulated, in order that France, in the guise of the President, was able to reassert itself on the international stage. Security policy would not henceforth be driven by the incoherent parliamentary in-fighting characteristic of the Fourth Republic. France would have an international voice that befitted her raised stature. For at least as long as the Cold War lasted, policy-makers were to endeavour that France was not dictated to by the confines of the international system. However, policy actions did not always live up to the flamboyant rhetoric. The country fell far short, during this period, of forging a third way in international relations between the two ideologically opposed superpower blocs. Nevertheless, the continued development of the independent nuclear weapons capacity (see Chapter Six) and the policy towards NATO were principal indicators of the French exception. But more than this, they represented a national resolve to attain and preserve *rang* and *grandeur*.

Many of the foundations for de Gaulle's security policy had been laid years, decades and, in some cases, centuries before his accession to presidential office. He brought these together into a coherent whole and gave them his own personal spin. France's world *rang* and its inherent *grandeur* were the driving forces behind his actions in this field, as they would be for his successors. And these actions, in responding to the particular set of circumstances at the time, would be characterised by the expression of France's non-dependence on other countries and by the promotion of the apparent French exception. Hence, it is to overstate matters to claim that de Gaulle was the creator of the French exception and that he was the architect of French security policy. His principle contribution was to crystalise and give popular expression to policy approaches that had evolved over two centuries or more and which were being formalised during the Fourth Republic. He would then subsequently become the symbol and very epitome of French *rang* and *grandeur*. Furthermore, it was down to the General's personal beliefs that the Presidency would subsequently have the capacity to be the dominant agent in the French political structure. And this 'exception' was itself simply one of many tools that French policy-makers used to attain the strategic objectives. As will be shown in this volume, it, like other tactics, was transitory; it would be employed so long as it produced positive results in the bigger picture.

Nevertheless, de Gaulle was to 'bequeath' to France's future policy-makers a foreign policy apparatus that was entirely geared to maximising the country's global presence. The subsequent life of the Fifth Republic would be one that fully embraced this legacy. Chapter Three examines how this external and interventionist vocation was retained despite shifting geopolitical and economic circumstances. Instead of adjusting their country's strategic objectives to reflect these new national shortcomings, France's political leaderships simply strove to engage the country's west European partners. The latter were to enable France to attain the strategic goals it could no longer achieve by itself.

Notes

1   Gordon, Philip H. (1993), *A Certain Idea of France: French Security Policy and the Gaullist Legacy*, Princeton University Press, Princeton, p.15.
2   *Ibid*, p.5.
3   Cerny, P.G. (1980), *The Politics of Grandeur*, Cambridge University Press, Cambridge, p.18.
4   De Gaulle, Charles, quoted in Nayeri, Farah, 'Chirac takes his cue from de Gaulle', *Wall Street Journal Europe*, 11 August 1995.
5   Grosser, Alfred, 'General de Gaulle and the foreign policy of the Fifth Republic', *International Affairs*, vol.41, no.2, April 1963, p.201.
6   Kramer, Steven Philip (1994), *Does France Still Count?: The French Role in the New Europe*, Center for Strategic and International Studies/Praegar, Washington DC, p.26.
7   Hazareesingh, Sudhir (1994), *Political Decisions in Modern France*, Oxford University Press, Oxford, p.276.
8   Gordon, Philip H., *A Certain Idea of France: French Security Policy and the Gaullist Legacy*, op cit, p.6.
9   Price, Roger (1993), *A Concise History of France*, Cambridge University Press, Cambridge, p.319.
10   McMillan, James F., *Twentieth Century France: Politics and Society 1898-1991*, Edward Arnold, London, 1992, p.167.
11   Gordon, Philip H, *A Certain Idea of France: French Security Policy and the Gaullist Legacy*, op cit, p.10.
12   *Ibid*, p.164.
13   De Gaulle, Charles (1954), *Mémoires de Guerre*, Plon/Livres De Poche, Paris, p.5.
14   Schubert, Klaus (1991), 'France', in Regina Cowen Karp (ed), *Security with Nuclear Weapons?: Different Perspectives on National Security*, Oxford University Press, Oxford, pp.162-3.

15 Cot, Michel, Président de Groupe de Réflexion, Fondation pour les Etudes de Défense, in an interview with the author, Paris, July 1996.

16 Mitterrand, François (1986), *Réflexions sur la Politique Extérieure*, Fayard, Paris, reproduced in 'M. François Mitterrand et la politique extérieure', *Le Monde*, 31 January 1986.

17 Mitterrand, François, quoted in Moïsi, Dominique, 'Mitterrand's foreign policy: the limits of continuity', *Foreign Affairs*, Winter 1981-2, p.347.

18 Grosser, Alfred, 'General de Gaulle and the foreign policy of the Fifth Republic', *op cit*, p.201.

19 Smouts, Marie-Claude (1989), 'The Fifth Republic and the Third World', in Paul Godt (ed), *Policy-Making in France*, Pinter Publishers, London, p.235.

20 Grosser, Alfred (1995), 'Le rôle et le rang', in André Lewin (ed), *La France et l'ONU (1945-1995)*, Collection Panoramiques, Condé-sur-Noireau, p.64.

21 Habré, Hissène, quoted in Randal, Jonathan C., 'Outlook for France in Chad: at best, a standoff', *International Herald Tribune*, 14 March 1986.

22 Moïsi, Dominique, 'The urge to be different', *The Financial Times*, 25 July 1995.

23 David, Dominique, Chargé de mission auprès du Directeur, IFRI, in interviews with the author, Paris, June-July 1996. See also for example, David's chapter 'France: l'illusion de la puissance', in *Les Fractures de l'Occident: Eliments de Géopolitique*, La Découverte, Paris, 1994, p.74.

24 Kolodziej, Edward A. (1974), *French International Policy Under De Gaulle and Pompidou*, Cornell University Press, Ithaca, p.35.

25 Bozo, Frédéric (1995), 'France and security in the new Europe: between the Gaullist legacy and the search for a new model', in Gregory Flynn (ed), *Remaking the Hexagone: The New France in the New Europe*, Westview Press, Boulder, p.221.

26 Lellouche, Pierre (1988), 'Guidelines for a European defence concept', in Jonathan Alford and Kenneth Hunt (eds), *Europe in the Western Alliance*, Macmillan/IISS, London.

27 Mendl, Wolf (1970), *Deterrence and Persuasion: French Nuclear Armament in the Context of National Policy 1945-69*, Faber and Faber, London, p.70.

28 Cole, Alistair (1998), *French Politics and Society*, Prentice Hall, Hemel Hempstead, p.239.

29 Léotard, François, 'Défense européenne: le temps de la volonté', *Le Figaro*, 3 January 1995.

30 De Gaulle, Charles, quoted in Howorth, Jolyon (1996), 'France and European security 1944-94: re-reading the Gaullist "consensus"', in Tony Chafer and Brian Jenkins (eds), *France: From the Cold War to the New World Order*, Macmillan, London, p.22.

31 Menon, Anand, 'From independence to cooperation: France, NATO and European security', *International Affairs*, vol.71, no.1, 1995, p.20.

32 Balladur, Edouard, in a speech given to the Institute of Higher National Defence Studies, Paris, 8 September 1994.

33 Goldstein, Avery, 'Discounting the free-ride: alliances and security in the postwar world', *International Organization*, vol.49, no.1, Winter 1995, p.47.

34 A plan to form a confederal union with a common defence and foreign policy. The emphasis was on organised cooperation at the state level. Heads of Government would meet about every three months and there would be a single European Assembly comprising delegations from national parliaments.

35 Howorth, Jolyon, 'France and European security 1944-94: re-reading the Gaullist "consensus"', *op cit*, p.27.

36 Wells Jr, Samuel F., 'Les politiques étrangères de Mitterrand: bilan d'un premier septennat', *Commentaire*, no.43, Autumn 1988, p.655.
37 De La Rose, François (1989), *Défendre la Défense*, Commentaire Julliard, Paris, p.39.
38 Kennedy, Paul (1988), *The Rise and Fall of the Great Powers*, Fontana Press, London, p.627.
39 Lellouche, Pierre, 'France in search of security', *Foreign Affairs*, vol.72, no.2, Spring 1993, p.120.
40 Bozo, Frédéric, 'France and security in the new Europe: between the Gaullist legacy and the search for a new model', *op cit*, p.222.
41 Chevènement, Jean-Pierre, 'La France et la sécurité de l'Europe', *Politique Etrangère*, no.3, 1990, p.526.
42 Vernet, Daniel, 'The dilemma of French foreign policy', *International Affairs*, vol.68, no.4, Winter 1992, p.656.
43 Grosser, Alfred (1985), 'Un "Giscardisme" en politique extérieure?', in Samy Cohen and Marie-Claude Smouts (eds), *La Politique Extérieure de Valéry Giscard d'Estaing*, Presses de la Fondation Nationale des Sciences, Paris, p.419.
44 Davidson, Ian, 'Platform for historic ambitions', *The Financial Times*, 22 June 1992.
45 Moïsi, Dominique, 'Mitterrand's foreign policy: the limits of continuity', *Foreign Affairs*, Winter 1981/2, p.348.
46 Menon, Anand, 'From independence to cooperation: France, NATO and European Security', *op cit*, p.21.
47 Touraine, Marisol, 'La représentation de l'adversaire dans la politique extérieure française depuis 1981', *Revue Française de Science Politique*, vol.43, no.5, October 1993, p.815.
48 Winand, Pascaline (1997), *Eisenhower, Kennedy and the United States of Europe*, Macmillan, Basingstoke, p.250.
49 Flynn, Gregory, *French NATO Policy: The Next Five Years*, RAND, Santa Monica, June 1990, p.4.
50 Kolodziej, Edward A, *op cit*, p.351.
51 Jenkins, Brian and Chafer, Tony, *op cit*, p.2.
52 Ross, George, 'Chirac and France: prisoners of the past?', *Current History*, vol.96, no.608, March 1997, p.107.
53 De Gaulle, Charles, speech to the Ecole Militaire, Paris, 3 November 1959.
54 Wetterqvist, Fredrik (1990), *French Security and Defence Policy: Current Developments and Future Prospects*, National Defence Research Institute, Stockholm, p.14.
55 Bozo, Frédéric, 'France and security in the new Europe: between the Gaullist legacy and the search for a new model', *op cit*, p.223.
56 Gordon, Philip H., *A Certain Idea of France: French Security Policy and the Gaullist Legacy*, *op cit*, pp.33-4.
57 Faringdon, Hugh (1986), *Confrontation: The Strategic Geography of NATO and the Warsaw Pact*, Routledge, and Kegan Paul, London, p.201.
58 Lacouture, Jean (1993), *De Gaulle – The Ruler 1945-1970*, Harper Collins, London, p.334.
59 Gregory, Shaun (2000), *French Defence Policy into the Twenty-First Century*, Macmillan, Basingstoke, p.8.
60 McCarthy, Patrick (1993), 'Condemned to partnership: the Franco-German relationship, 1944-1983', in *France-Germany, 1983-1993: The Struggle To Cooperate*, St. Martin's Press, New York, p.2.
61 Friend, Julius W. (1989), *Seven Years in France: François Mitterrand and the Unintended Revolution 1981-1988*, Westview Press, Boulder, p.199.

62 Grosser, Alfred, 'General de Gaulle and the foreign policy of the Fifth Republic', *op cit*, p.206.
63 Howorth, Jolyon, 'France and European security 1944-94: re-reading the Gaullist "consensus"', *op cit*, p.19.

Chapter 3

Tactical Reappraisal and the Transferral of Ambitions

Towards the end of the 1970s, French officials were hailing France's perceived national consensus on security policy as a symbol of solidarity and as another sign of French greatness, with the whole mass of the population united behind the belief in France's special global mission. With the conversion of the Socialist and Communist parties to nuclear deterrence (discussed in Chapter Six), there were no longer any major divisions between the mainstream parties of the Left and Right regarding French security policy. Indeed, only the National Front would subsequently stand apart, in the National Assembly, from this political likemindedness. Whether it actually existed or not, the national consensus was now being pushed as an instrument to further raise the country's international standing. It became an end in itself, boosting the country's international *rang*. In addition, it facilitated the President's freedom of manoeuvre in determining security policy, in that this was a fundamental element of gaullism. However, it impeded the ability of the national leadership to undertake anything approaching a serious reform of policy. The myth of consensus militated against any alternatives to the *grandes lignes* crystallised by de Gaulle, rank and *grandeur*. Moreover, if there was almost universal national acceptance of the strategic goals, there was similarly a general willingness among policy-makers to almost blindly persist with a tactical approach which had been devised to cope with the structural pressures of the 1960s; an approach which was based on non-dependence and the promotion of the French exception. This was to have particularly serious implications with the end of the bipolar Cold War security environment in 1989-91.

This third chapter follows French security policy from de Gaulle's departure from Presidential office through to the end of the Cold War. First, it considers how the General's security policy legacy translated to the France of the 1970s and 1980s, concentrating on the roles played by Presidents Pompidou and Giscard and, in particular, François Mitterrand, who acceded to the Elysée in 1981. Attention will focus on the continued emphasis on the *force de frappe* as the embodiment of French *singularité* and world standing. Then, it will be noted that, far from pushing for an end to the bipolar international system, France's leaders and planners learnt to exploit the situation to their own considerable advantage. Policy was gradually revised until the French position could be seen to be one that was a firm advocate of the status quo as the best means by which national *rang* and *grandeur* could be ensured and augmented. Second, it examines French policy-makers' re-evaluation of France's place within the international system and the consequent shift of attitudes towards the then EC so that the latter came to be perceived as the primary instrument by which French global objectives were to be achieved in the future.

Linking to the volume as a whole, this chapter highlights the almost automatic retention of *rang* and *grandeur* as the principle strategic *raison d'être* of French security policy. On this at least there appeared to be a genuine national consensus. France would continue to behave like an agent that could manipulate, and act independent of, the international structure in which it was placed. However, it became clear that if the country was to continue to be in a position to resist structural pressures, then it would have to turn to other countries for assistance. This realisation marked the first step towards the tactical reappraisal that was to find full expression in the mid-1990s. And throughout all this, French national leaders gave the impression of being proactive, demonstrating that France was both resolved and able to determine its own destiny. And this was as much for the domestic audience as for the rest of the international community.

Gaullism Post-De Gaulle: Something Tangible?

Referring to gaullism, Maurice Couve de Murville asked:

> [s]hould one regard it as a unique episode which ... has no future because it was so closely linked to the will, the fame, the very existence of the person who was both its initiator and its symbol; or should one on the contrary see it as the foundation of a durable French foreign policy because it effectively addresses the problems of the modern world as well as the national interest and particular genius of France?[1]

Couve de Murville clearly lent towards the latter interpretation, seeing de Gaulle's political beliefs as that which had saved France from decline and restored its standing as one of the world's leading nations. Certainly, de Gaulle enabled a relatively weak country (in comparison to the superpowers) to *feel* strong again. Indeed, to a significant degree, the term gaullism came to personify the quest for national *rang* and *grandeur*.

The General's legacy clearly had a major impact on the decision-makers succeeding him. This view has been supported and expanded by Gordon:

> Whatever one thinks of the particular road France has taken in its European and alliance policies since the 1960s, it is clear that those policies have been determined to a great extent by the Gaullist worldview and that they would have been very different had de Gaulle not come to power in 1958 ... De Gaulle shaped French policy in ways that probably cannot be reversed, and it would be wrong to see his tenure as merely one more episode, albeit a remarkable one, in the recent history of France.[2]

Hence, French security policy would remain largely unaltered during Georges Pompidou's five years at the Elysée. The new President was himself inexperienced on defence matters and he chose close associates of the General as his Prime Minister and Defence Minister. And it was Michel Debré, Prime Minister under de Gaulle, who was the main figure behind the drafting of the 1972 *Livre Blanc sur la Défense*, a document, as Gregory observed, that couched the defence debate almost exclusively in Gaullist terms.[3] One explanation for this, Gregory adds, was the widely held perception among French security policy-makers that deviation from Gaullist ideas would equate to abandoning the belief in France's greatness, with the result that national *grandeur* would be lost. 'According to this view, Gaullist ideas have persisted because the French have not been prepared to face their objective circumstances and have preferred the projected image, some might say delusion, offered by de Gaulle'.[4] This continuity was characterised by renewed French efforts to forge a (west) European identity that could deal with the US as an equal partner. Partially as a result of this initiative, these years saw the fledgling steps by the EC towards the adoption of what became a common foreign and security policy; in December 1973, the EC Nine released a communiqué confirming their wish to see Europe speak with one voice on major world issues. This year also saw vigorous, but ultimately unsuccessful, French attempts to revive the Western European Union as a vehicle for political and military cooperation between Paris and its European partners.

Pompidou was succeeded by Valéry Giscard d'Estaing, also from the centre-right of the French political spectrum, and who likewise favoured the gaullist parameters, based on independence, for French security policy. But this should be qualified by the acknowledgement that, in the National Assembly, Giscard was dependent on the support of the Gaullist party. The ardent belief of the latter in its late founder's legacy on military and defence matters was matched outside the Assembly by the wider strategic community across *l'Hexagone*. In these circumstances, Giscard had little political scope for innovation that would disrupt the Gaullist orthodoxy in French security policy. Nevertheless, like Pompidou before him and Mitterrand after, he would not match the extent to which de Gaulle had pushed for non-alignment or equidistance between the superpowers. However, memories of de Gaulle's attempts at forming an international triumvirate to manage and guide world affairs were revived by Giscard's efforts to forge a similar arrangement, this time with the inclusion of West Germany, in 1979. Only one summit was held however, and the project was subsequently abandoned in the face of an international outcry from those excluded.

De Gaulle's doctrine for security policy, appealing as it did so directly to French sensibilities, had developed something of its own momentum and political force by the mid-1970s. It came to be perceived as an end in itself, as an integral part of defence policy. No national leader felt able, or indeed inclined, to openly denounce it; to do so would have been to prompt a potentially thoroughly divisive and destructive debate. There was also the sense that to shatter the illusion of consensus, in addition to being unpatriotic, was to undermine nuclear deterrence. Moreover, there was the significant political risk of becoming associated with an actual or perceived failed new policy initiative. As Frears saw it:

[b]ecause the symbols manipulated by de Gaulle – French independence, French nuclear power, France with a rank in the world – are an important part of French national

cohesion, the legitimacy of the regime and of French national pride rediscovered, the Gaullist consensus on how a President should conduct himself in foreign affairs and defence is an important constraint.[5]

Furthermore, France's inherent external vocation meant that approaches to security policy whereby France largely disengaged itself from international affairs, recalling all armed forces to the Hexagon, or in which the *force de frappe* was disbanded, never received serious consideration.

Hence, the General had guided French security policy in directions that were inherently difficult to modify. Firstly, because the approach was deemed sensible by public opinion, or at least was uncontested, because it implied national greatness and privileged global status and secondly because it embraced traditional ideas associated with France's destiny and global mission. In addition, this legacy was sufficiently imprecise to allow the General's successors significant margins of manoeuvre. De Gaulle had hung resolutely to certain key principles but had displayed considerable pragmatism in their application. The 1970s and 1980s were thus not to see an open and wide-ranging debate on security policy in the French political arena. The fabled consensus around the security policy inaugurated by de Gaulle, which was always more myth than reality, acted as a block on policy adaptation, it stifled debate and denied the respective leaderships the independence to adopt their own policy initiatives.

However, it was becoming apparent that, to some extent, the gaullist myth was by now becoming overbearing, shackling the General's successors to a set of tactical policies that were increasingly inappropriate given the evolving international situation.[6] But as this realisation took hold the avoidance of public discussion became even more crucial. The political elites refrained from constructive debate concerning security policy even if this meant that certain decisions would not be made. Gaullist-style rhetoric and references were used to paper over the illusory nature of the consensus. The remarks of Michel Pinton for example, at the time Secretary-General of the centre-right UDF party, calling into question the validity and utility of the country's nuclear deterrent were widely condemned. And this was not so much for their content but for the fact that Pinton had broken ranks and challenged the basis of cross-party support for traditional gaullist policies.[7] The predominantly common stance adopted by President Mitterrand and Prime Minister Chirac during the Fifth Republic's first period of *cohabitation*, in the late 1980s, can equally be seen in this light. But the force of the gaullist legacy could not prevent, largely private, divisions appearing among the political class and the military concerning aspects of security policy, although not the overriding *grandes lignes*: notably, strategic deterrence, tactical weapons, the place of conventional forces, France's role in the defence of central Europe and the concept of a west European defence identity. Giscard, for example, was willing to involve France in the defence of western Europe and to consider moving towards the tactical nuclear doctrine of 'flexible response'. He followed Pompidou, in being repeatedly prepared to sacrifice French aspirations for independence so as to safeguard the stability of the Western alliance. While the *grandes lignes* of security policy remained unchallenged, disagreements did emerge as to the best tactics now to be adopted for their perpetual realisation. A growing distinction could be made between those who counselled maintaining a strong link with the US, the Atlanticists, and those who favoured a more nationalist, Eurocentric, approach.

Mitterrand

François Mitterrand stands as one of the enigmas of the Fifth Republic. His long-time foreign affairs advisor and now French Foreign Minister, Hubert Védrine alluded to the man's many sides, saying that hundreds of people could tell you about *their* Mitterrand.[8] On the face of it, the new President seemed ideally equipped, in 1981, to challenge Gaullist taboos, to bring in Socialist idealism. Moreover, the French people would eventually grant him a double-*septennat* – plenty of time to forge one's own legacy. As a presidential candidate in 1965, for example, Mitterrand had attacked the notion of an independent French nuclear capacity. Yet by 1977 he had persuaded the Socialist Party, with its powerful pacifist and antimilitarist factions, that if it had pretensions of ever acceding to national power then it had, for reasons of electoral expediency, to endorse the concept. Meanwhile, his Communist allies, who helped him win the 1981 election, had relegated their pro-Soviet sympathies in favour of a fierce loyalty to the military tenets of Gaullism. Moreover, Mitterrand would unequivocally be in favour of a strong defence for France. In this, he was possibly driven by the double determination to erase the possibility of the humiliation of 1940 being repeated and to detach the Socialists from all links to pacifism. Hence, no radical transition of security policy would take place; it would remain closer to Gaullism than to anything else.[9]

Mitterrand consistently accepted de Gaulle's tactical security parameters: the independent nuclear deterrent, the ruthless pursuit of French interests abroad and the *entente* with West Germany. He matched de Gaulle's determination to preserve France's capacity to decide for itself its foreign policy. Equally, he refused to accept that French policy should behave as if Europe was divided into two blocs. French security policy continued to promote notions of a 'third way' in international politics. In this way, the whole tactical stance of claiming national distinctiveness, of setting France apart from other countries and of broadcasting the French exception, was largely retained as a tool for the fixed strategic objectives. And he had a keen sense of political strategy and was forever conscious of balances of power. Equally, Mitterrand developed, to a greater degree than either Pompidou or Giscard, into a leader acutely aware of France's world standing, historical mission and national destiny. Soon on entering office, he declared '*la France peut éclairer la marche de l'humanité*'.[a] [10] If anything, the *grandes lignes* of French security policy, as crystallised by de Gaulle, would be sought with even greater vigour.

---

[a] 'France can light up the march of humanity'.

To this end, during Mitterrand's second *septennat*, despite the announcement, on his re-election in 1988, of a thorough review of foreign and defence, French security policy altered remarkably little. As if in a time warp, he echoed the General's defence gospel. Serious choices within the defence budget were repeatedly avoided even though there was a widening gap between objectives and economic realities. According to Howorth, the force of economic and industrial imperatives behind France's arms exports has been such that, 'all Presidents of the Fifth Republic have constantly found themselves swept along in directions they had not intended as a result of the inertial thrust of the military-industrial complex'.[11] One of the most graphic examples of this was the process by which Mitterrand, a fervent advocate of European defence cooperation who had been actively seeking to cut the defence budget, was forced to abandon France's commitment to the five-nation European fighter aircraft project and to embrace the astronomically expensive French-built Dassault *Rafale*. This was an aircraft unsuited to assisting France's allies in a conflict on the plains of central Europe, having been designed as a weapon to defend the national territory. The development process consistently failed to meet deadlines and went massively over budget.[12] However, it should be acknowledged that Mitterrand's task was being made harder by the fact that changes were occurring in all key areas of defence policy simultaneously. Moreover, the President's significantly deteriorating health during this second term in office should be noted, undoubtedly having as it did a bearing on his behaviour. Indeed, several observers have subsequently pointed to a marked conservatism in French security policy at this time.[13]

A further consideration is the fact that Mitterrand was the first President of the Fifth Republic to have to deal with a majority in the National Assembly comprising his political opponents. However, this period of *cohabitation* (1986-8) would only serve to further illustrate the broad consensus on security policy across France's political spectrum. Seemingly, the Government and the Opposition were much closer in their definition of national security interests than in most other west European states. Everything was subordinated to the pursuit of *rang* and *grandeur*. Prime Minister Chirac's five-year Defence Programme Law of 1987, for example, largely mirrored the Socialists' policies while increasing planned expenditure. Mitterrand's foreign policy meanwhile, as Commander-in-Chief of the armed forces, was seen to be closer to that of de Gaulle than was that of Chirac's gaullist government, as responsible for the nation's defence. Indeed, Mitterrand gave up all pretence of neo-gaullist neutralism so as to adhere to a more fundamental gaullist tactical principal, namely the restoration of a balance of power in Europe. And he stuck much more closely than Chirac to symbols of national independence (indeed, Chirac edged closer to an Atlanticist stance). Hence, the reaffirmation of the doctrine of a full strategic response to any tactical nuclear attack, the denial to Washington of air space to facilitate its attack on Libya in April 1986, and the refusal to extend France's nuclear cover to West Germany (Chirac had expounded the possibility). But there was broad agreement on the basics: the primacy of the strategic nuclear force, perpetuation of the means for a continued global role and the continuity of French military principles. However, the Right did place greater emphasis on the 'single military space' and the capacity to deliver a nuclear warning to any aggressor, and this was opposed to Mitterrand's emphasis on the national sanctuary and the rejection of any battlefield role for nuclear weapons.[14]

Mitterrand, meanwhile, felt the need to do what he could to bolster what he perceived to be a faltering NATO. He came to acknowledge, to a degree never seen with de Gaulle, just how much France and Europe needed the United States. NATO was able to include the French Second Corps, based at Baden-Baden in south-west Germany, as a mobile reserve for its Central Front. The level of cooperation became such that Bozo was able to write, '*[u]n retour de la France au sein des structures militaires intégrées n'apporterait aucun changement sur le plan strictement militaire*'.[b][15] As early as 1981, during the so-called 'second Cold War', Mitterrand had been displaying his credentials as a full member of the Western bloc, recalling, in a conversation with Henry Kissinger, French solidarity with Kennedy's United States at the time of the Cuban Missile Crisis, and stating that he would do likewise in a similar situation. His France would continue to pursue an independent foreign policy, but would automatically stand side by side with its partners as soon as the West faced a direct threat to its integrity.[16] And the fact that there was no official explanation or presentation of France's close links with NATO meant that there was no mass popular outcry at the compromising of de Gaulle's policy. Even much of the political class remained oblivious.[17] However, Mitterrand categorically resisted all attempts to bestow the Alliance with any competence beyond the collective defence of the territory of its members. At the same time he was working to bring about reform of the Alliance's mechanisms. But as the Cold War 'thawed' in the mid-1980s, with Gorbachev assuming control in Moscow, French diplomatic efforts to push the 'third way' and to promote the French exception could be renewed.

The Transferral of Ambitions

Nevertheless, France's security policy-makers were having to come to terms with the limitations of France's global status, with sub-Saharan Africa being the only main exception (discussed in Chapter Seven) and become increasingly overt in the tactical transferral of their ambitions to western Europe. To this end, serious thought and effort were now put towards the creation of a European security and defence identity (ESDI). It was being acknowledged by the leadership in Paris that continued national *grandeur* and *rang* could only be guaranteed by operating in concert with west European partners. It remained to be seen if the political elites would take this to its full conclusion and downplay the hitherto flaunted French exception.

Deep concerns among French security policy-makers concerning growing West German pre-eminence (the latter was for example enjoying a substantial trade surplus with France by the early 1980s) were to be a major motivational factor behind this transfer of national ambitions to the European level. The reasoning in Paris was that

---

b   'The return of France to the integrated military structure would bring no change to military planning'.

Europe's structures had to be moulded to French designs before mounting German, particularly economic, power eroded France's position altogether. In the meantime, West Germany's blossoming *ostpolitik* had, from the start of the 1970s, revived the country's traditional vocation as a privileged partner of eastern Europe. But conversely, France was equally motivated by fears of its neighbour sliding towards pacifism and neutralism, and thereby encouraging other west European states to do likewise. This would have left France dangerously vulnerable in any future central European conflict and would have resulted in there being increased influence in the region for the Soviets. More seriously, West German neutralism would be the first step towards what had been de Gaulle's nightmare scenario, the next steps being German reunification leading to German hegemony. At the same time, Paris would have been horrified at any West German moves along the lines of France's withdrawal from the integrated military structure of the Atlantic Alliance. It was appreciated that France's own defence policy only made sense so long as other states, principally West Germany, did not pursue a similarly nationalist line. Equally, close cooperation with Bonn was essential to French designs for a new autonomous European security order. The *rapprochement* with the US was equally largely prompted by this desire.

It had been de Gaulle's firm conviction that France was uniquely placed to play a decisive role in transforming the European system. Bozo even argues that the necessity to forge Europe into an autonomous politico-strategic entity was the General's primary motive, rather than the restoration of France's *grandeur* and independence.[18] In the second half of the twentieth century, a strong and consolidated wider confederal western Europe was to be increasingly seen by the planners in Paris as the only vehicle by which France's elevated global rank could be preserved and subjugation under American hegemony be avoided. In a sense, France could only continue to be France through Europe. The country's fate lay in what happened beyond its borders. De Gaulle had been firm in his belief that his, and subsequent, administration should do all in its power to determine the course of these events. Hence, for instance, Mitterrand canvassed for a strengthened European diplomatic identity in the face of the apparent Reagan-Gorbachev *rapprochement* of the mid-1980s that threatened to leave the Europeans sidelined. In addition, the General had been keen to steer European integration in a direction that would preserve the nation state; he desired something like a modern-day Concert. Such an arrangement could prevent the consolidation of the American-Soviet domination of world affairs.

In order to realise the power base fundamental to the role they aspired to, French security policy-makers, aware from the 1950s and 60s of France's material and demographic shortcomings, were acknowledging that it would have to pool its resources with those of its European allies and allow itself to be integrated into a unified European intergovernmental political union. From the Schumann declaration of May 1950, proposing the European Coal and Steel Community, to the December 1969 Hague Summit, proposing the completion and deepening of the European Community, French politicians and negotiators had defined the issues and largely defined the European agenda. But from this time on, the notion of a French Europe was on the wane. Cole, for example, refers to the EC gradually adopting the German, as opposed to the French, economic model.[19] The country's leaders thus had to search for what Moreau Defarges described as 'a flexible compromise between independence and solidarity, sovereignty and integration'.[20] France had become too small for its ambitions and had to turn to Europe to take over its mission. Europe had to now act as a surrogate for France's lost empire and become what France should have been. French greatness, rank and autonomy of action could only be preserved by cooperation with France's neighbours. The latter had to be manipulated to make of western Europe what France could no longer make of itself. The EU, according to O'Neill was to become 'a platform for wise and pragmatic French statesmanship, rather than a community of partners of equal weight and mutual interests'.[21] As Hayward explained:

> [a]ccusations of French nationalism ignored the fact that because France alone defended her own and Europe's independence, the French were the real 'Europeans'. Destined by history and geography to be the motive force of Europe, Pompidou[c] claimed in 1967 that France was 'not its administrative, technical or institutional but its ideological motive force'. The ideology was that of national independence, conceived increasingly within a European framework; an extension that was tolerable only so long as France was able either to get her own way on all major points at issue or remain free to opt out or veto any proposals to which she objected.[22]

But French motives went beyond these practical considerations. There was, principally, an enormous self-belief. In the words of Grosser, as the:

> [p]remier pays continental à prendre conscience de la possibilité d'avoir une politique indépendante, la France a en quelque sorte pour mission d'assumer une fonction que ses partenaires européens n'ont pas comprise. C'est à la France de définir ce qui est bon pour l'Europe.[d] [23]

France, it was claimed, encapsulated all of Europe's future global ambitions. There was a genuine conviction among French political elites that their vision for Europe was what was best for their partners. This notion stated that Europe would exist only if it is self-defined, and if it acquires the means to be autonomous. And, of course, such an approach at the end of the Cold War enabled French leaders to be at the centre of the west European security debate at a crucial stage in European construction. For its leaders, France simply had to be heavily implicated in all the major discussions affecting the continent.

Hence, Europe was treated by the General's successors as the key. For Giscard, this meant restoring Europe's level of global influence. Hence his attempts at securing common EC stances on world problems like energy, the Middle East or the Soviet invasion of Afghanistan. There was widespread acknowledgement inside French

---

[c]   The then Prime Minister.
[d]   'first continental state to be aware of the possibility of having an independent policy, it is kind of France's mission to assume a role that its European partners have not understood. It is for France to determine what is good for Europe'.

political circles that the country's security concerns had to be perceived in terms of the wider context. For the most part, this wider context was essentially western Europe and it implied some form of collective security based on a significant degree of interdependence. Whatever entity emerged would act as a counterweight to the hitherto dominant, and now burgeoning, American influence. Equally, French planners perceived that it would provide the Atlantic Alliance with renewed credibility and effectiveness. This was what had driven de Gaulle. He had never lost faith in France's inherent greatness, in its *singularité* and the imperative of freedom of action, but he appreciated that these could only be maintained by closer interaction with France's neighbours. For Doelnitz, '*[t]ous les gouvernements de la Cinquième République se sont efforcés de transposer sur le plan européen les exigences nationales en matière d'indépendance*'.[e] [24] This solidarity with west European partners would be demonstrated by Mitterrand's support for Margaret Thatcher's Britain in the conflict with Argentina over the Falkland Islands. Foreign Minister Cheysson remarked that the French President's response was instinctive; even though Mitterrand did not want to appear as the defender of anachronistic European imperialism, Britain was an ally.[25] He led the rest of the EC in applying an arms embargo against Argentina. Mitterrand, of course, was well aware that France was potentially exposed to similar crises given the spread of its dependencies around the globe.

The French leadership can only have been delighted, in 1987, at the WEU Hague Declaration that adopted a common platform on European security interests. But the grand project of European integration and the development of some form of credible European security entity appeared to run counter to the abundant rhetoric proclaiming specificity and independence. For example, official pro-European statements were increasingly running aground on the public inability to give a definitive response to the question as to whether French nuclear forces would be launched in the defence of West Germany in the event of war.[26] Moreover, planners were conscious that the pro-European policy should not be interpreted as encouraging any supranational character for the EC. But the two stances did not necessarily contradict each other. Michael O'Neill described Mitterrand's approach as encouraging 'ideas of European integration as the most appropriate way of maintaining France's ambition to stay at the forefront of international affairs, whilst simultaneously keeping at bay the Gaullist nightmare of a federal Europe'.[27] To this end, French leaders became skilled at manipulating France's allies into pursuing policies favourable to France. They had, according to Jonathan Eyal, the 'remarkable ability ... to portray their country's national interests as Europe's fundamental imperatives'.[28]

A European Security and Defence Identity

Having made his own stark assessment of the geostrategic situation, Mitterrand was to adopt a more European, as opposed to national, tactical concept of French defence. The revival of the old 1963 Elysée Treaty with West Germany was a move in this

---

[e]   'Each government of the Fifth Republic tried hard to transpose to the European level the national demands as regards independence'.

direction. As was the creation, in 1983, of the 46,000 *Force d'Action Rapide* (FAR),[f] which, while making France better equipped for modern conventional warfare, was also an attempt to demonstrate French ambitions for the European defence identity and to bind West Germany to this vision. Moreover, by using the FAR, French leaders would not be faced with the decision whether or not to reintegrate their forces into the command structure of the Atlantic Alliance. The new force also symbolised a determination to continue to defend the country's former colonies. For Gordon, the creation of the FAR was a classic example of the desire of French leaderships to show a firm interest in European solidarity while sticking resolutely to the pretence as well as the reality of national autonomy.[29] It was unclear, however, whether the new force would be capable of playing an important military role.

In the meantime, the reactivation of the WEU, in 1984, served to raise Franco-German defence interests to a European level. In contrast to the official French line on American-led NATO, commitment to the WEU, with the necessary partial loss of sovereignty that this entailed, was tolerated because it did not lead to subordination. Similarly motivated moves were to follow: in April 1986, Mitterrand and West Germany's Chancellor Kohl announced a study on the usage of the FAR within the Federal Republic, and on the expansion of joint military exercises. Mitterrand also announced that, prior to giving any authorisation for the use of French pre-strategic nuclear weapons on West German soil, he would consult with the West German Chancellor, time and circumstances permitting. However, ambiguity remained as to whether France's military commitment to West Germany extended to France's nuclear forces, if it did not then the FAR was just a token force for Europe. Then, in 1988, on the twenty-fifth anniversary of the original Elysée Treaty, Kohl and Mitterrand launched the Franco-German Defence and Security Council, building on the success of the 1982 Commission on Security and Defence.

However, Mitterrand's Presidential tenure did coincide with a quiet, but not inconsiderable, move away from French military isolation to a greater openness towards, and willingness to cooperate with, France's NATO partners. Perhaps this was, in part, an acknowledgement that, since 1966, successive French Administrations had been unable to forge anything approaching an autonomous European security dynamic with France as the motor. On his arrival in office, Mitterrand certainly appeared willing to put great effort into revitalising and reforming the Alliance from within. And observers pointed to his initially firm stand against the Soviet Union making him, temporarily at least, one of the US' staunchest allies;[30] although this may have represented an attempt to allay the fears of France's partners following his appointment of four Communist ministers in the first Socialist government. The President was certainly conscious of being seen to be making suitably pro-Western noises and gestures.

---

[f]   'Rapid Reaction Force'.

To this end, it would be fairly uncontroversial to state that Mitterrand's astonishing January 1983 speech in front of the West German Bundestag, in the middle of a hard-fought West German general election campaign, favouring the deployment of US Cruise and Pershing II nuclear missiles on German soil, at a time when the West Germans were displaying distinct pacifist leanings, placed France most definitely within the Western bloc. The speech was all the more remarkable for its political expediency, because the President was backing Germany's Christian Democrat party (CDU) rather than his supposed political brothers in the Socialist Democratic Party (SPD). The fear in Paris was that an electoral triumph for the German Left would substantially augment the influence of West Germany's growing peace movement. Paris could not allow its independent nuclear capability to be questioned by its powerful neighbour in Bonn. Furthermore, it was essential to French security policy that American forces remain stationed inside the Federal Republic, thereby perpetuating the binding of Bonn to the West and maintaining the obligation of Washington to come to the defence of western Europe. For Mitterrand, without a balance of forces, East and West, in Europe, everything else would remain blocked; namely, Paris' relations with Washington, Bonn and Moscow.[31] Reagan, for one, would write to thank Mitterrand for the speech. Of course, it was relatively easy for Mitterrand to call on west Germans to accept the missiles that France itself had refused.

But Mitterrand would firmly oppose American President Reagan's Strategic Defence Initiative (SDI). In the short-term, the latter, he feared, would endanger the improving East-West dialogue. In the longer-term, Mitterrand believed SDI could compromise the strategic unity of the Atlantic Alliance by encouraging American isolationism. He was thus instrumental in the setting-up of EUREKA, a European response to SDI. At the same time, the French President was constantly working for a common European defence, his instrumental role in the reactivation of the WEU has already been mentioned. This move could be interpreted as a convenient side-step of the thorny legal issue of France's relations with NATO. Mitterrand felt confident that France's allies had by now accepted that while France was a loyal member of the Atlantic Alliance it would not be returning to the Organisation's integrated military command.[32] Hence, French diplomacy continued to transmit conflicting messages, playing out the perceived role as arbitrator between the two superpower blocs.

But, despite a certain *rapprochement* with the Atlantic Alliance, Mitterrand would not acquiesce to a full military reintegration. Although he did not actually like NATO as an organisation, he was not actively looking for it to disappear. Indeed, in June 1987, he declared that it was not the mission of France alone to protect West Germany and western Europe, this was the mission of the Alliance.[33] In this, he was adopting an ultra-gaullist stance. He was driven both by the reactive concern of containing German power and the proactive vision for an autonomous Europe. West German Foreign Minister Genscher, speaking in 1984, criticised Paris' NATO stance, claiming that France was not meeting its European and Atlantic responsibilities.[34] But it should be noted that France was not the only Alliance country to place constraints on its membership. Denmark and Norway, for instance, did not allow NATO bases on their territory, Denmark, Iceland, Norway and Spain would not allow the positioning of nuclear weapons on their soil, and Spain remained outside the integrated military command. Equally, it should be acknowledged that French armed forces regularly participated in joint exercises with their NATO counterparts. Nevertheless, there was the sense that Mitterrand, having come some way towards NATO would go no further. Speaking in 1988, he declared that '*notre autonomie de décision se définit particulièrement à l'égard des organes militaires de l'OTAN. Cessons, je vous prie, toute spéculation à ce sujet. Il n'est pas question pour nous de changer de statu*'.[g] [35] In addition, an ESDI that led to a fully autonomous European foreign and security policy would be subject to far greater French influence than would any developments that continued to rely on NATO and the US.

Economic Realities

Budgetary constraints were to take on a primary importance in the 1980s when Mitterrand and the Socialists, according to Howorth, '*endossèrent finalement le manteau gaulliste au moment précis de l'histoire où la défense à bon marché (avec grandeur) n'était plus une option viable, ni financièrement, ni stratégiquement*'.[h] [36] Economic realities by themselves, regardless of any geostrategic considerations, were playing a crucial role in almost *forcing* French policy-makers to abandon the go it alone approach to security policy. De Gaulle had left the French with the legacy of having to fund a global role, an independent nuclear force, and an independent national armaments industry, while simultaneously contributing to the conventional defence of western Europe. This was no longer possible now that the Americans were reducing their military commitment to the region thereby placing a greater burden on the Europeans, and now that the French economy was in depression. Moreover, technological costs were far outstripping the rate of inflation. Defence spending was being maintained by the Socialists at a time when the economy was stagnant and other budget sectors were being trimmed back. But Mitterrand was not the first French leader to defer the taking of key and tough budgetary decisions with regard to defence. And there was a prevailing mind-set among the political elite that the economy would soon be restored to a state of healthy growth.

In addition, the leaders of the Fifth Republic had consistently been prepared to forego the potential benefits of an unrestricted market for defence procurement. But the exponential rise in the cost of technology and the sharp drop in French arms exports combined to place mounting pressure for an end to the isolation of the defence industries from external competitive pressures. In addition, according to Ruiz-Palmer, 'the more the French military establishment grew in capability and sophistication in

---

[g] 'our autonomy of decision is defined, in particular, in relation to NATO's integrated military structure. Let us stop all speculation on this point. There is no question of us changing our status'.

[h] 'took on the gaullist mantle at the very moment in history when cheap defence (with grandeur) was no longer a viable option, neither financially nor strategically'.

the 1970s and 1980s, the more that almost boundless diversification in missions and means was creating the budgetary conditions which would eventually make the relative decline of French military power an unavoidable feature of the 1990s'.[37] Circumstances cried out for, and indeed demanded, budgetary restraint. But successive defence budgets to this end had proved unworkable. *Actual* expenditure far-out-stripped *projected* expenditure. The armed forces simply did not have the means to fulfil the role of projecting credible nuclear power while also furnishing a significant conventional capability. However, the nuclear programme, which had seen a curb on its expenditure under Giscard, underwent a significant expansion under Mitterrand. Equally, the global role was maintained and military interventions in Africa continued on a regular basis. And the Socialists, despite their supposed egalitarian, humanitarian and pacifist heritage, maintained France's active policy of arms exports. They were driven more by economic imperatives and considerations of global *rang* than by questions of morality. The commencement, in 1981, of arms sales to Sandinista Nicaragua, for example, were justified as part of a policy to entice that country away from communism through friendship and engagement rather than through the American policy of isolation and subversion. In practical terms meanwhile, the isolation of the French defence industry meant that the supply of equipment to the French armed forces could only be maintained by massive export orders to third countries.

Conclusion

In this chapter, it has been established that the principal emphasis of French security policy in the 20 years between de Gaulle's departure from office and the end of the Cold War was on continuity. Indeed, in the previous chapter it was shown how de Gaulle himself had embraced much of the security policy inaugurated by the Fourth Republic. Although each subsequent President would imprint their own personal style on policy, it was as though the *grandes lignes* were accepted by Pompidou, Giscard and then Mitterrand as a matter of course. Time was not seriously set aside for an open debate about alternatives. And this was partly explained by the institutional arrangements for security policy-making set out in Chapter One. This centralisation of authority at the Elysée served to perpetuate fidelity to the Gaullist paradigm and it acted as a bulwark against alternatives.[38]

But despite relentless efforts to retain a leading world role, France's leaders were having to increasingly acknowledge that economic imperatives and geostrategic realities; in practice, France as the agent perhaps did not have as much freedom of manoeuvre within the world system as had been claimed by its leaders. Official responses in Paris to the Soviet invasions of Czechoslovakia in 1968 and Afghanistan in 1979, for example, illustrated the true extent of French impartiality between the superpowers. On these occasions, anti-American rhetoric was swiftly dropped and attitudes towards the Soviet Union (read Russia), the traditional ally, hardened. But instead of modifying and toning down their ambitions for *rang* and *grandeur*, perceived as fundamental elements of France's very existence, to reflect the newly emerging realities, France's leaders transferred them to western Europe. Hence, security policy-makers were having to de-emphasise France as the autonomous actor unimpeded by the nature of the international system; this approach was becoming increasingly less tenable. Western Europe had to achieve what France could no longer achieve by itself. And it is important to note that this significant tactical shift away from non-dependence had begun before the end of the Cold War.

A further significant observation is that by the end of the 1980s, French security policy had completed its transformation from being actively and ambitiously revisionist (seeking to break-up the Cold War bipolar bloc system) to the conservative promotion of the status quo, with France seemingly enjoying considerable influence and standing in the Cold War geopolitical environment. To a large extent, pragmatism had replaced ideology, and accommodation had replaced vision. The position of standing outside the military structure of NATO and calling for a more cohesive European identity in the security and defence field now seemed to have come of age. French security policy-makers became progressively more interested in defending their perception of France's specific interests and position in the context of a durable East-West balance, as opposed to promoting fundamental modifications to European security structures; structures for which there simply were not the economic resources and which were constrained and defined by the predominance and predictability of Cold War considerations and challenges. This pragmatism was illustrated by a growing realisation among French leaders that the defence policy could only be effective so long as their Western allies, in particular West Germany, did not follow a similarly nationalistic line.[39] Moreover, Giscard had actually conceded that France could not count on remaining free in the event of the rest of western Europe not remaining free. This meant a tactical reliance on the Atlantic Alliance until such time that Europe was in a position to realise the French vision and construct political organs from which a European defence would emerge. At the same time, emphasis in Paris shifted back towards the development of conventional forces.

Notes

1   Couve de Murville, Maurice (1971), *Une Politique Etrangère 1958-1969*, Plon, Paris, p.478.
2   Gordon, Philip H. (1993), *A Certain Idea of France: French Security Policy and the Gaullist Legacy*, Princeton University Press, Princeton, p.6.
3   Gregory, Shaun (2000), *French Defence Policy into the Twenty-First Century*, Macmillan, Basingstoke, p.18.
4   *Ibid*, p.21.
5   Frears, J.B. (1981), *France in the Giscard Presidency*, Allen and Unwin, London, p.126.
6   Menon, Anand, 'Continuing politics by other means: French defence policy under the French Fifth Republic', *West European Politics*, vol.17, no.4, October 1994, p.81.

7   Menon, Anand (1996), 'The "consensus" on defence policy and the end of the Cold War: political parties and the limits of adaptation', in Tony Chafer and Brian Jenkins (eds), *France: From the Cold War to the New World Order*, Macmillan, London, p.159.
8   Védrine, Hubert (1996), *Les Mondes de François Mitterrand: A l'Elysée 1981-1995*, Fayard, Paris, p.74.
9   Moïsi, Dominique, 'Mitterrand's foreign policy: the limits of continuity', *Foreign Affairs*, Winter 1981/2.
10 Mitterrand, François, quoted in Védrine, Hubert, *op cit*, p.27.
11 Howorth, Jolyon (1993), 'The President's special role in foreign and defence policy', in Jack Hayward (ed), *De Gaulle to Mitterrand: Presidential Power in France*, Hurst and Co., London, p.180.
12 Lewis, J.A.C., 'Fitter, leaner forces for multi-polar world', *Jane's Defence Weekly*, 11 June 1997.
13 A view expressed by, for example, Jean-Yves Haine, Maître de Conférences, Centre d'Etudes des Conflits, Paris Institut d'Etudes Politiques, in an interview with the author, Paris, June 1996.
14 Gordon, Philip H., *op cit*, p.152.
15 Bozo, Frédéric (1993), 'La France, l'Europe et l'OTAN', in Pierre Pascallon (ed), *Quelle Défense pour la France?*, Institut des Relations Internationales et Stratégiques/Dunod, Paris, p.174.
16 Védrine, Hubert, *op cit*, p.184.
17 Bozo, Frédéric (1991), *La France et l'OTAN: De la Guerre Froide au Nouvel Ordre Européen*, Masson, Paris, p.159.
18 Bozo, Frédéric, 'La France, l'Europe et L'OTAN', *op cit*, pp.170-1.
19 Cole, Alistair (1998), *French Politics and Society*, Prentice Hall, Hemel Hempstead, p.236.
20 *Ibid*, p.227.
21 O'Neill, Michael, 'The pursuit of a grand illusion', *European Brief*, vol.3, no.1, October 1995, p.24.
22 Hayward, Jack, *op cit*, pp.243-4.
23 Grosser, Alfred, *op cit*, p.193.
24 Doelnitz, Tristan (1993), *La France Hantée par sa Puissance*, Belfond, Paris, p.210.
25 Favier, Pierre and Martin-Roland, Michel (1991), *La Décennie Mitterrand: Les Epreuves*, Seuil, Paris, p.382.
26 'Paris takes a European line on defence', *The Financial Times*, 28 June 1985.
27 O'Neill, Michael, *op cit*, p.22.
28 Eyal, Jonathan, 'France freezes as Europe melts', *The Independent*, 3 December 1994.
29 Gordon, Philip H., 'The Franco-German security partnership', in France-Germany, 1983-1993, *op cit*, p.145.
30 Smouts, Marie-Claude, 'The external policy of François Mitterrand', *International Affairs*, vol.59, no.2, Spring 1983, p.161.
31 Védrine, Hubert, *op cit*, p.235.
32 Housego, David, *op cit*.
33 Védrine, Hubert, *op cit*, p.726.
34 Genscher, Hans-Dietrich, quoted in Favier, Pierre and Martin-Roland, Michel, *op cit*, p.256.
35 Mitterrand, François, in a speech at the Institut des Hautes Etudes de Défense Nationale, Paris, 11 October 1988.

36 Howorth, Jolyon (1987), 'Budgets et choix stratégiques: la politique de défense sous François Mitterrand', in Stanley Hoffman and Sylvia Malzacher (eds), *L'Expérience Mitterrand: Continuité et Changement dans la France Contemporaine*, Universitaires de France/Basil Blackwell, Cambridge, p.389.
37 Ruiz-Palmer, Diego A., *French Strategic Options in the 1990s*, Adelphi Paper 260, Brasseys/IISS, Summer 1991, p.16.
38 Gregory, Shaun, *op cit*, p.22.
39 Taylor, Trevor (1988), 'European institutions and defence', in Jonathan Alford and Kenneth Hunt (eds), *Europe in the Western Alliance*, Macmillan/IISS, London, p.182.

Chapter 4

The International Order Transformed: France Becomes a Global Peacekeeper

From the reactions of France's political elites to the evolving security environment that emerged out of the Cold War, it was clear that the inherent national ambition for global status and elevated rank had not been diminished by the demise of the bipolar order. This chapter will consider France's military excursions in the new era, highlighting something of a shift from unilateral actions, emphasising French *spécificité*, to participation in multinational operations mandated by the UN. These were to constitute the new justification for the global role. Particular attention will be given to the second Gulf War and to the crisis in former-Yugoslavia (France's continued military intervention in the internal affairs of francophone Africa will be considered in Chapter Seven). These overseas experiences would be instrumental in accelerating the ongoing shift in French security policy away from *singularité* towards, what this volume terms, 'normalisation'. In the Gulf, France's shortcomings as a supposed Great Power were exposed. In Bosnia, France's promotion of the WEU option was largely ignored by its European allies and French forces were ultimately be subordinated to NATO (read American) command structures. Outside of sub-Saharan Africa, where French forces were pre-positioned, it lacked the capacity for anything approaching a significant force projection. French options had also been constrained by the traditional reliance on National Service. Indeed, as Menon notes, 'France, for all its desire to act as an effective counterweight to the United States, proved increasingly unable to wield the influence it so desired over international affairs'.[1] Nevertheless, the unquestioned dominance of the *grandes lignes* required that France participate in these multinational excursions, even if this meant subordination to American command structures.

The New Raison d'être of French Military Intervention Overseas

Bertil Lintner observed that France had 'renewed its pursuit of a more powerful role on the world stage ever since a reunified Germany began asserting itself'.[2] For what France feared almost above all else in the new post-Cold War world was international marginalisation, both politically and geographically. Gregory alerts us to the paradox of French officials having repeatedly criticised the post-World War Two settlement, from which France's leaders had been excluded, and having promoted the transitory nature of ideological differences, being almost totally unprepared for the challenges and opportunities of the post-Cold War era.[3] In particular, the general devaluation of nuclear weapons as symbols of national status implied that Paris had to search for new ways to legitimate its pretensions of *grandeur, rang* and, on a more practical level, its continued possession of a permanent seat at the United Nations Security Council (UNSC). Hence, there was a clear determination among the security policy-makers to find a post-Cold War role for the country. And there was an open preparedness to back this up with military muscle. There was never the sense, for example, that French leaders would adopt the Norwegian model and become quiet, behind the scenes, diplomatic mediators. The French armed forces, meanwhile, faced with the prospect of a possible 'peace dividend' reducing military expenditure, were anxious to establish for themselves a new mission capable of justifying current force levels.[4] But because the new international order was not an order as such, peppered as it was by conflict and instability, it was hard to define a relevant and meaningful mission other than the vague pursuit of peace and stability.

Whereas Mitterrand had seemed reluctant to concede that the Cold War system, which France as the agent had hitherto succeeded in manipulating to its own diplomatic advantage, was over, French security policy-makers began, as Menon observed, to learn that the new scenario also offered favourable opportunities. 'Regional conflicts free from the ideological overlay that the superpower confrontation had conferred on all struggles were not subject to Gaullist strictures concerning the dangers of being dragged into an all-out global conflict by American adventurism'.[5] Participation in multinational peacekeeping operations became a principle element of French post-Cold War foreign policy. Instead of being completely overshadowed by their giant neighbour and being driven to the margins of world affairs, the policy-makers in Paris carved out for France a role as a medium-sized power willing to use force abroad in the sorts of conflict that looked set to proliferate across the globe. Involvement in multinational operations on behalf of the UN and the international community became the principal conduit by which national significance would, once again, be demonstrated. Here was the justification for the country's continued global role and retention of a permanent seat at the UNSC as it attempted to maintain its international status, *rang* and a semblance of independence. Invoking the past and promoting the nuclear capability were, by themselves, no longer sufficient.

De Gaulle had initially been dismissive of the utility of the United Nations as an international organisation.[6] He deemed it to merely be another instrument of America's attempt at global hegemony. This was especially the case, notes Gregory, after the early 1950s when the United States succeeded in transferring power for 'maintenance of peace' issues from the UNSC to the General Assembly and thereby devaluing the utility of France's UNSC veto, one of the symbols of French international stature.[7] Moreover, he resented what he saw as UN interference, led by the newly empowered General Assembly, in French internal affairs, namely decolonisation. Paris was also angry at the idealist and supranational agenda of UN Secretary General Dag Hammarskjöld. This was particularly manifest with the UN's 1960 intervention in the Congo for which France refused to make any financial contribution, believing the operation to be outside the provisions of the UN Charter. Relations then deteriorated even further, to the extent that de Gaulle's administration refused to converse with the

Secretary General, due to the latter's opposition to the French military action in Bizerte, Tunisia.[8] Moreover, de Gaulle believed that he could detect signs of the UN's supranationalisation.[9]

However, the General was to modify his views, learning to use the Organisation as a means to boost France's international standing. He worked to promote the principle, as enshrined in the UN Charter, of non-intervention in a state's internal affairs. This gave legitimacy to his firm belief that France alone should be responsible for the decolonisation of what remained of the empire. Then, having divested itself of its colonies, France needed other ways to express its power and influence, and the UN came to be seen as one, if limited, potential channel. From the mid-1960s, the General began to use it as a suitable forum through which France could cultivate its new popularity with the 'non-committed' (30 out of the then 127 UN member states were francophone), Third World countries. French representatives could thus, for all practical purposes, rely on the unqualified support of a not insignificant voting bloc within the UN General Assembly, and indeed inside other world organisations. The country's permanent UNSC seat was thus exploited as a symbol of its status as a world power. Pompidou, as President, would expand on this, presiding over an ever greater French participation in UN mechanisms. Giscard and Mitterrand, likewise, were to echo de Gaulle's conviction in the organisation's utility for furthering France's global vocation. In 1984, the latter announced '*[l]a France est le pays aujourd'hui le mieux reçu et le plus populaire, parce qu'on sait que la France ... apparaît comme le pays le mieux compris, le plus aimé de l'ensemble des pays du tiers-monde*'.[a] [10] Nevertheless, the traumatic legacy of France's involvement in the UN's mission in Lebanon (UNIFIL – launched in 1978), where the international force was impotent in the face of Israel's reoccupation of the south of the country in 1982 and where its troops were brutally exposed to the terrorist tactics of some of the local belligerents, would mean that new UN commitments were refused by France's leaders for over a decade.

De Gaulle, in the early 1960s, had suspected the UN of acting as a tool of American hegemony. But by the early 1990s, Mitterrand was showing every endeavour in placing France at the very centre of UN proceedings, making it a driving force as the Organisation relaunched itself in response to the 'new world order'. Even back in 1982, Mitterrand had sought to further what he determined to be French interests by deploying French forces as part of the aforementioned multinational intervention force in Lebanon even though this required extremely close cooperation with the US. His reasoning was that, in the circumstances, this was the best means to boost France's international credibility and regional influence; to have remained aloof from the operation had simply not been an option. The UN was thus now of considerable use to French security policy-makers as they pursued *la patrie*'s global vocation. One could now observe a remarkable French activism inside the now unfrozen UNSC. This became the conduit by which pronouncements were made in the name of France on all major crises and issues around the world. The UN was now

---

[a]   'France today is the country the best received and the most popular because people know that France seems to be the country the best understood and most liked by all Third World countries'.

being utilised by Paris as a power multiplier. References, for example, to the national nuclear capability, the relevance of which in the post-Cold War security environment was questionable, could thus be dropped. Such references would, however, regain temporary prominence in 1995-96 for the duration of Chirac's series of nuclear tests carried out in the south Pacific.

Under the UN Charter, the Security Council had been given primary responsibility for the maintenance of international peace and security; France's leaders now enthusiastically upheld this mission in the new post-Cold War environment. Defence Minister Léotard put it like this:

> *[l]a France entend participer, dans la mesure de ses moyens, aux opérations de maintien de la paix. Elle sait que son histoire, sa culture, sa langue lui confèrent une responsibilité singulière, celle d'une des quelques nations du monde á vocation mondiale. Ce sont cette volonté et cette certitude qui témoignent de la pérennité de son rang de grand pays.*[b][11]

This renewed enthusiasm for the UNSC and multilateralism was simultaneously a means by which the hegemonic position of the US could be tempered. There were now claims that France was the principal humanitarian power in the world. Prime Minister Juppé, on coming to office in May 1995, was of like mind. 'Through imagination, determination, and a desire to hold its rank in the world, France can affirm itself as it wishes to be – a great world power'.[12]

The extent of France's new backing for the UN was such that Foreign Minister Dumas announced, in September 1992, that his country was ready to place a force of 1000 men at the permanent disposal of the UN Secretary General for peacekeeping operations.[13] Prime Minister Rocard, meanwhile, declared that France, always under the auspices of the UN, intended to be present immediately that the rule of international law had to be upheld and as soon as human lives were in danger.[14] This enthusiastic and generous provision of national forces to international peacekeeping/humanitarian operations would provide the French with an increased margin of political manoeuvre. First, it demonstrated that France truly was a global actor of some significance. Second, it enabled French representatives to be present at negotiations aimed at finding a resolution to the respective conflict. French interests could, in this way, be safeguarded and promoted. Moreover, French casualties suffered on behalf of the international community would demonstrate France's global stature and give it greater leverage via an emotional hold on its international partners.

Once it became clear that UN peace support operations could be used to promote France's international role, these operations became the principal element of the country's defence orientation. The UN hence came to play a central role in the definition of French foreign policy. This self-perception as a major power accounted for French willingness to take on a largely disproportionate share of the UN's

---

[b] 'Within its means, France will participate in peacekeeping operations. It knows that its history, culture and language bestow upon it a singular responsibility; namely that of one of the few nations in the world with a global vocation. It is this will and certainty which testify to the durability of its rank of great nation'.

peacekeeping burden. From 1991 (when France ranked fifteenth among countries contributing to UN military operations), French forces were to be continually at full stretch, especially given that successive governments had been steadily diminishing the conventional capability for many years. For example, of the 60,000 troops deployed by the UN around the globe at the end of 1992, the largest contribution, 10,000, was provided by France. Of the 13 UN operations underway in 1993, eight had the participation of French forces. This new-found tactic, helped to make 1994 the high-water mark of France's global vocation in terms of personnel deployed outside Western Europe (in *Dom-Toms*, sub-Saharan Africa or on behalf of the UN): over 40,000, or around ten per cent of the country's total forces. Of the 13 UN operations underway in 1993, eight had the participation of French forces.[15] Even by mid-1995, French personnel still represented some nine per cent of the UN's military operatives. By this time, the French leadership was heavily committed to the NATO operation in Bosnia. Military deployment on behalf of the Atlantic Alliance thus came to rank as an equal demonstration of a will to be associated with the major multinational operations.[16] In recognition of evolving geopolitical picture, the 47,000-strong FAR was created specifically to give France the global capacity to participate in these operations. It was to be an instrument in the country's continued bid for *rang*. At the same time there was greater emphasis on the country's global vocation. The first of these larger post-Cold War multinational operations to which France subscribed was the relief of Kuwait.

The Second Gulf War

Around no other commodity than oil, and in no other region than the Middle East, could such an international coalition have been built as that which launched *Operation Desert Storm*. France's subsequent role in the crisis provided a graphic and timely illustration of the significant shortfall between the ambitious and confident rhetoric of France's national leaders and the actual resources the country had at its disposal. On reflection, despite pretensions to *grandeur* and *rang* which prompted an almost automatic participation in the international effort to liberate Kuwait, the French were to have only a minimal impact on the military operation and the ensuing political negotiations. However, as Chartouni-Dubarry pointed out, the experience would correspond to French aspirations for the new post-Cold War world: the rehabilitation of the UN in a world order that was not bipolar or unipolar but which was fluid and which had French leaders at the very centre of the relevant decision-making authority.[17]

Iraq's invasion of Kuwait in August 1990 was the first real test of the new post-Cold War order. On the face of it, France had no fixed legal or historic obligation to the Kuwaitis. No matter, the rapid and massive American response to the Iraqi aggression presented the planners in Paris with numerous dilemmas. In considering these dilemmas, Mitterrand, who from the outset pursued a high profile, considered France's interests in a global context. His initial practical decision was, unilaterally, to despatch the aircraft carrier *Clemenceau* to the Persian Gulf (albeit at a leisurely pace and with several stopovers), justifying the move on the basis of France's special responsibility to uphold international law as a permanent member of the UNSC.[18] The Iraqi raid on the French embassy in Kuwait City and the temporary abduction of a French diplomat was then held up as legitimisation for the 15 September decision to deploy 4,200 troops and 16 war planes to Saudi Arabia in *Opération Daguet*. It should also be noted that the United States was at this time undertaking a relentless massive military build-up in the region and that Britain (France's traditional Middle East 'rival'), only the day before, had announced the deployment of an armoured brigade. France was not going to be perceived as a weak link in what was becoming a major international undertaking.

Options were subsequently kept open by simultaneously augmenting the French military contribution to the forming international force (12,000 French troops had been placed under US command by January 1991) and raising unilateral efforts to reach a diplomatic solution. With regard to the latter, French representatives put much effort into pushing for a resolution from within the Arab community, so as to pre-empt any direct American-dominated intervention.[19] Aware that France had effectively lost any effective influence in Lebanon to Syria, Mitterrand was convinced of a national interest to preserve those various strong Franco-Arab relationships that remained; and not least to protect French industry's numerous highly lucrative arms contracts in the area. Among these, Iraq had been France's oldest and closest ally and had bestowed France with something of a privileged position. In the Elysée, relations with the Arab world were deemed a key element of French international *spécificité*. Secondly, policy-makers had to consider France's own three million-strong Arab minority (the largest in western Europe). Thirdly, the gaullist tradition of demonstrating independence *vis-à-vis* the US created a need for keeping Washington somewhat in check.

Mitterrand immediately made himself France's sole arbiter, the only *décideur politique*, in the crisis; as illustrated in Chapter One, particularly in such times of international crises, the President has the capacity to be the dominant agent within the structure of domestic French politics. To this end, he extended this control by utilising personality diplomacy. This entailed the use of high profile personal envoys like Michel Vauzelle, as opposed to members of the Foreign Ministry. These individuals were intended to implement and further a separate French diplomacy that portrayed France as a Great Power. This accumulation of policy-making exclusivity likewise extended to the use of Elysée aides such as Admiral Jacques Lanxade and Maurice Schmitt to deal directly with the military establishment and to marginalise the increasing critical Chevènement at the Rue Saint-Dominique. In the meantime, Mitterrand had already succeeded in sidelining the French National Assembly. Parliamentary authorisation for the deploying of French troops had not been legally required because no conscripts were involved. In addition, Mitterrand was able to portray the operation as a police action in support of the United Nations and hence there was no need for a declaration of war as authorised by parliament. Furthermore, the President would make most of his major pronouncements on the crisis via newspapers and television rather than in front of the Assembly. Balaj noted that Mitterrand succeeded in adding crisis management to the functions of the executive.[20] From the more conceptual stance, this was the French President acting as the dominant, almost sole, agent of any import within the domestic political structure during this crisis. At the state level, however, France, despite various solo diplomatic initiatives, would largely be a subservient, reactive, agent in the wider international structure dominated from Washington DC.

Domestic opposition to Mitterrand's Gulf War policy lacked political weight, but nevertheless it was to transcend party lines both within the government and across the wider body politic. Jean-Marie Le Pen, for example, as leader of the *Front National*, actually labelled himself pro-Iraq. He argued that firstly none of France's vital interests were at stake; that secondly France was not obliged to play the role of global *gendarme* and that thirdly the Socialists had led France into all of its wars in the twentieth century. Furthermore, he stated that '[w]e are not an ally of the country that was attacked; in fact, most of our interests are linked to the country that was attacking'.[21] And the FN was joined from the other end of the political spectrum by the PCF in interpreting French participation as serving solely to protect the regional investments of American oil companies.[22] Elsewhere, a faction of the RPR, led by de Gaulle's son, Philippe, interpreted the Western effort as an irresponsible American adventure. Meanwhile, Jean-Pierre Chevènement, a founder member of the Franco-Iraqi Friendship Society, resigned as Defence Minister decrying French subservience to American imperialism. And opposition was fairly unanimous from the Green and ecological lobby. Although it would be only the Greens, of all the political parties who would actually promote pacifism. Meanwhile, there were reports of national disquiet at a French foreign policy which sent soldiers to die for the authoritarian Emir of Kuwait, while seemingly having done nothing to support the Lebanese Christian Maronite army led by General Aoun as it was ousted from Lebanon by Syria.[23] Nevertheless, popular support for the President's policy stayed relatively high, at over two thirds.

Only France and the UK, among the west European states, sent ground troops to the Gulf, while Italy contributed aircraft. Although, in response to a UNSC Resolution, WEU ships were sent to the Persian Gulf to conduct mine-clearing operations and to enforce the embargo on Iraq. Both countries' leaderships, however, distanced themselves from efforts to fashion a common EC response to the crisis. A WEU Council, for example, was not called until three weeks into the crisis; such was their anxiety to protect the UNSC as the primary political organ in the crisis. Implicit in French actions was thus the international marginalisation of Germany. The perception in Paris was that the international response to the crisis was managed by de Gaulle's old cherished Directory: the triumvirate of France, Britain and the US.[24] Both governments in Paris and London were very aware that their status as permanent members of the UNSC placed on them a special responsibility to make a major contribution to the management of the crisis. Moreover, behind their actions was the realisation that a failure to live up to this responsibility might result in a loss of this increasingly challenged status.[25] Put simply, having accepted the inevitability of military confrontation, the French had to have a direct and significant role. Mitterrand frequently made references to France's international duty. France, he declared, 'must be worthy of its responsibility as a major power'.[26] *Desert Storm* was to represent the country's largest military deployment overseas since the withdrawal from Algeria some 30 years earlier.

On 24 January 1991, having initially opposed all pursuit of the conflict beyond the liberation of Kuwait, Mitterrand, for the first time, commanded French planes to bomb Iraq. Failure to have acted in this way would, it was perceived, have left France morally, militarily and diplomatically discredited. According to Howorth, '[h]ere was an issue', Mitterrand felt, 'which spoke to the very heart of France's world influence, in which the chaotic claims of history and geography, of rights and aspirations, of force and persuasion, of pragmatism and ideology were central'.[27] Lellouche agreed, '[r]ester à l'écart aurait fait de nous un voyeur et non plus un acteur de l'Histoire'.[c] [28] The sense of *rang* was always a central feature of French policy during the crisis. And it was to impose itself on other principles, like, for instance, independence from American tutelage. Furthermore, this inherent belief in France's global mission overrode growing domestic financial considerations as epitomised by a shrinking defence budget. All obstacles had to be overcome in order that France be present and play its part in this unprecedented international coalition.

As noted in Chapter Three, the rationale among French security policy decision-makers was beginning to be that, rather than through displays of *singularité*, France's global rank could best be maintained by influence over its partners within organisations like the UN and the EU, and by proving to be a strong link in ad hoc operations like *Desert Storm*. In addition, the French leadership was eager to demonstrate the country's capacity for action in the wake of its widely perceived marginal and passive role in the aftermath of revolutions in eastern Europe and during German reunification. Mitterrand had been concluding that the ongoing evolution of the international system was making things harder for France as a global actor. An operation of this type afforded an opportunity to restore international standing and to demonstrate a special distinctiveness, even if the latter was in the throws of being progressively downplayed. Furthermore, French rhetoric, if not actions, was guided by the desire to uphold international law, and thus the restoration of Kuwait as a sovereign state. Mitterrand believed that France had to support the UN, and hence the United States.

In one sense, direct military collaboration with the US and other Western allies (which lost all ambiguity with Chevènement's resignation) marked a watershed for French foreign policy. French forces were actually placed under direct American command for the first time since World War Two, while US tanker planes, necessary for the refuelling of the B-52 bombers (themselves allowed to use French air space), were permitted to use French airfields as bases. And Mitterrand justified this policy shift by pointing out that these B-52s were part of the same international coalition, and were serving the same interests, as those French personnel on the ground in the Gulf.[29] But at the same time, it was nothing new for French forces to be standing at the side of their Western allies in some ad hoc multinational configuration during an international crisis of these proportions. The risks of antagonising traditionally friendly Arab states, particularly in north Africa, were outweighed by the prospects of a key diplomatic role in the formulation of a post-war Middle East peace process. Mitterrand considered that France's standing among the Western powers mattered a great deal more than

---

c   'to remain in the margins would be to make us watchers of and not actors in history'.

sentimental links with the Third World, even though France's Arab links were one of the principal tenets of French exceptionalism. Here too, French *singularité* was losing its prominence as a security policy tool.

Yet the French exception had not been totally discarded. Prior to the launch of *Operation Desert Storm*, French diplomats were constantly seen to be going the furthest to reach a diplomatic solution to the crisis, in the name of what Mitterrand described as 'a logic of peace'.[30] Strenuous efforts were also made to forge some form of linkage between the crisis and some wider resolution of the Middle East crisis as a whole. The outcome was intended to be some stable security structure extending from Morocco to Oman. And having already somewhat isolated himself diplomatically by calling for more time to be given for the economic sanctions imposed on Iraq by the UN to work, Mitterrand was to again break ranks with the rest of the coalition by announcing that French forces would not utilise chemical weapons and by promoting the role of the UN for the subsequent peace settlement. In addition, while the fighting lasted, France would 'fulfil its engagements loyally', but after the cease-fire 'we will once again be ourselves'.[31] Mitterrand acknowledged the US to have been the principal Western player in the crisis, but contended that France had been able to modify some of the American decisions. This was to play up France's importance. France, in the words of the President, had performed its role and held its rank.[32] For Gordon, 'French participation in the (Gulf) war and cooperation with the United States can be explained as much by a French desire to avoid "marginalisation" as by any resignation to a minor or subordinate alliance role'.[33] Nevertheless, and despite efforts to the contrary, France, along with the other European participants, was widely perceived to have been pushed to the sidelines by the US. Lellouche questioned what level of influence France could then possibly hope to enjoy in the post-war negotiations given that its forces on the ground in the Gulf only represented some three per cent of the American deployment. Essentially, the President was trying to buy a place at the top table with just 12,000 troops. In such circumstances, he added, it was hard for Mitterrand to claim that France was the world's third military power.[34]

The fallout in France from this action was hugely significant. For Laird, '[n]o factor has been of greater significance in pushing the French over the barrier to discussing the necessity for change than the Gulf War'.[35] And Heisbourg cited the latter as having as deep an impact on French foreign and security policy as the war leading to Algerian independence in the early 1960s.[36] While French political elites had still been talking of retaining nuclear deterrence as the central focus of defence doctrine, this operation highlighted the unsuitability of French defensive arrangements for the new non-nuclear, high technology, brand of warfare. The French war effort was, for example, seriously hampered by severely restricted military intelligence; by an inadequate capacity for force projection; and by outdated tactical aircraft (notably the Jaguars and Crusaders – while the new Mirage 2000Ns had not been configured for conventional operations).[37] A further significant constraint was the limited troop availability. From the outset, Mitterrand had chosen not to deploy conscripts into the combat zone. As a result, France's contingent would ultimately be drawn from some 47 different regiments – the Chiefs of Staff even had to resort to the deploying of professional non-frontline personnel like cooks and doctors based in Germany). From an army of some 280,000 personnel that was bestowed with the FAR (specifically created for 'out of area' operations) and despite one of the highest levels of defence expenditure in the West, France was only able to contribute a maximum of 12,000 troops to *Desert Storm*. Only the French naval contribution demonstrated anything resembling the cherished and long-sought elevated global *rang*.

French policy-makers had not envisaged, and thus had not prepared for, a scenario in which they would have to deploy overseas against a well-equipped army as part of a coalition comprised mainly of professional forces. With this in mind, there seemed to be genuine surprise as to how well the British and American forces had been able to integrate to positive effect during the operation. As a result, attitudes softened, at least partially and among some influential circles, towards the utility of NATO. Furthermore, Marshall observed, the war had brought 'the jaw-dropping revelation that being outside NATO's military structure limited France's influence. That, plus the waning of the Soviet threat, has helped to bring it back towards NATO'[38] (discussed in Chapter Five). The war in the Gulf was also to have something of a psychological impact among the French leadership. On one level of analysis it was said to demonstrate that France's national security still had to be interpreted within a global context. On another, it raised the level of awareness concerning disturbing potential occurrences in the developing world such as the proliferation of nuclear, chemical and biological weapons; the spread of ballistic missile technology; and the widening demographic gap with the developed world. Moreover, nuclear deterrence had worryingly been seen not to work in this particular conflict. For Blunden, '[i]mplicit in the emphasis on threats from the South was the need to move closer to the "North"'.[39]

The confrontation between the international community and Iraq has simmered ever since *Desert Storm*. Occasionally, it appeared as though renewed armed conflict was once again a possibility. Over the winter of 1997-8, for example, there was a face-off concerning the remit of UN weapons inspectors inside Iraq, and significant American and British forces were once more preparing for military strikes on Iraqi targets. French policy, meanwhile, maintained a certain distinctiveness from the 'anglo-saxon' line. The Socialist Government repeatedly voiced its opposition to the military solution. There was continuity with the previous centre-right administrations' emphasis on improved trade relations with Iraq and the easing of international sanctions. As French policy towards Iraq illustrated, autonomy of action was retained by policy-makers, but it was downplayed.

Bosnia

The European Community was still in the process of negotiating an economic package with the Yugoslav government, in the spring and summer of 1991, when the federal consensus behind the government collapsed, under pressure from Croatia and Slovenia, on 23 June. And then, initially at least, the Yugoslav crisis was somewhat sidelined in Western capitals by concerns over events in the former Soviet Union and over the ratification of the Maastricht Treaty of European Union. Moreover, the now EU struggled to present a united front, although it did agree to impose an arms embargo in July. The member states were still habituated to conducting international relations on a predominantly bilateral basis. Franco-German disagreements over the crisis in Croatia then served to impede the cohesiveness and effectiveness of the EU's response, with the French worried that German influence in the Balkans, backed by Austria, would be extended.

Mitterrand wanted Yugoslavia to remain intact but transformed, seeing it as a possible element of stability in the new Europe, and as an obstacle to the creation of a German dominated *Mitteleuropa* – Croatia and Slovenia having formerly being part of the Austro-Hungarian empire.[40] Once again, he could be seen to be favouring preservation of the Cold War status quo rather than accepting the emergence of new forces across the European continent. However, the Elysée clearly would not go so far as to authorise the use of force in order to hold the disintegrating Yugoslavia together. Garde criticised this preoccupation with the maintained integrity of Yugoslavia as a mistaken analysis of the situation, describing the country as an artificial construct.[41] For French traditionalists, the policy compromised France's reputation as the country of liberty, as the guarantor of human rights and the right to self-determination.[42] And yet, other elements of French political culture and historical experience hardly predisposed French policy-makers to welcome the dissolution of multinational states. France's imperial heritage, its initially fierce resistance to decolonisation and its sacred concept of 'the one and indivisible republic' made it especially hard for its leaders to remain inactive as an internationally recognised state fell apart.

From the outset, Mitterrand and his foreign policy advisors were determined that France would assume what they perceived as its international responsibilities. Indeed, it was not really conceivable that the French policy-makers could do anything but assume a significant role for their country despite there being neither serious economic interests at stake nor any diplomatic, judicial or military obligation to the region. France's status as a permanent member of the UNSC, its culture, its tradition as an interventionist power and the near-global nature of the weaponry at its disposal, all conspired to push France to the front line in the conflict.[43] The country's leaders' inherent quest for *rang* and *grandeur* meant they simply could not contemplate any other course of action. Moreover, French public opinion, usually ambivalent about foreign policy issues, became relatively and uncharacteristically animated over the Bosnian question, most especially in the wake of the revelations about the Bosnian Serb concentration camps that prompted a massive public and political demand for intervention. The Sarajevo Party would even poll ten per cent of the votes at France's subsequent 1995 election for the European Parliamant. The widespread view was that France *had* to do something. As James Gow saw it, '[w]hatever French rhetoric may suggest, in practice France has shown itself committed to international operations in a way which makes it hard to imagine Paris not, with special considerations, associating themselves with an intervention such as could have been in Bosnia'.[44] Later in the conflict, President Chirac would allude to the words of de Gaulle when he described French soldiers as sacrificing their lives 'for the sake of a particular idea of France, a France that stands firm in times of trial, a France that refuses to surrender to fatalism and irresponsibility'.[45]

Only Le Pen's *Front National* consistently opposed the intervention. Although that is not to say that elsewhere in French society the consensus was complete. As Howorth described it:

> [p]oliticians from virtually right across the spectrum have been passionately committed to intervention, while others, again from right across the spectrum, have been equally passionately opposed. The same has been true of military officers. Intellectuals tend to have divided themselves into those pleading a particular cause (Serbian, Croatian, anti-communist, humanitarian, or whatever) and those seeking a complex and extremely elusive global solution. The press, rather astonishingly, has been largely at sea, confining itself to regular lamentations about how dreadful the situation is. Church leaders have attempted above all to maintain ecumenical unity, but everybody has been aware that, not far beneath the surface, has lain the sensitive issue of Croatian Catholicism and the memory of the Ustashe period. Significantly, only the National Front as an organisation has taken an overtly pro-Croatian stance.[46]

Even in February 1994, French public opinion largely backed France's role in the crisis; 58 per cent (against 28 per cent) approved the continuation of the French presence on the ground in Bosnia, while 55 per cent (against 35 per cent) would have accepted further French losses.[47] Nevertheless, in the years since the stabilisation of the crisis via the Dayton Peace Accord (discussed below), the French Administration has been subject to some serious domestic criticism for its perceived failure to sufficiently seek international justice for the countless instances of human rights abuses committed by the various parties in the conflict.[48] Here again was a public expression of France's claimed inherent vocation as the guarantor of the rights of humanity.

But Mitterrand was adamant that the French could not act alone.[49] At the same time, his Elysée was concerned to minimise potential interference from Washington and Moscow. After the experiences of the Gulf and Somalia, they did not wish to once again be perceived as being led in an international crisis. In September 1991 the French leadership, as Chair of the UNSC, proposed the creation of an emergency European (WEU) force, under Chapter VII of the UN Charter, declaring itself prepared to bear the lion's share of the military burden. Mitterrand was particularly keen to get the WEU directly involved, wanting it to prove its effectiveness as the military instrument of the EU. But France's west European partners would not live up to the expectations in Paris. There was no agreement on a European force deployment. The UK (not wanting to give the WEU a prominent role ahead of the Atlantic Alliance, as well as out of fear of Balkan entanglement) vetoed this option in the UNSC, and Denmark, the Netherlands and Portugal similarly used their vetoes in the WEU. There was, hence, a general reluctance to be seen to be acting without the US. The Elysée's subsequent frustration at its inability to harness European assets in the crisis was considerable.

The UNSC did, however, agree to Resolution 713 that imposed an arms embargo on the whole of former-Yugoslavia. And by February 1992, with the impotent EU having handed over responsibility for resolving the crisis to the then CSCE and the UN, French representatives were pressing for the sending of a UN peacekeeping force. UN Resolution 743 subsequently provided, in March, for the creation of the 14,000-

strong UNPROFOR (United Nations Protection Force in the former-Yugoslavia) in Croatia. Western leaderships, not least the one in Paris, were by now facing considerable significant popular demands for action in the face of the heavy media coverage of the Serb sieges of Vukovar and Dubrovnik.[50] In response to the subsequent civil war in Bosnia, French representatives then urged for the deployment of UN forces here also, but this was rejected. Yet in June the UNSC did agree to send a 1000-strong force to protect Sarajevo airport. The UN then deployed troops throughout Bosnia in October and declared an air exclusion zone via Resolution 781. At each step, France stood at the front of the queue of contributing states, providing the largest national contribution to UNPROFOR. And French efforts to bring about a permanent resolution to the conflict were unmatched by any other country, consistently taking the political and diplomatic lead at the UN. It was important to the French policy-makers that France be seen to demonstrate its commitment to UN peacekeeping, a crucial element of the country's renewed claims to a global role. Perhaps also, Mitterrand was seeking a UN mandate for France to become the high-profile protector of Sarajevo.[51] As the crisis evolved and deteriorated, UNPROFOR was, in June 1992, replaced by UNPROFOR II. This was a multinational force of 15,000 troops, of whom, eventually, some 4500 troops would be French. Significantly, the French contingent was placed within a NATO force. This marked the final recognition by the decision-makers in Paris that there would be no lead role on the ground for the WEU and nor would there be the marginalisation of the Atlantic Alliance. At the same time, French platforms formed part of a combined NATO/WEU naval taskforce in the Adriatic with the brief to ensure the strict enforcement of the embargo passed by the UNSC: specifically, Resolution 820.

France was heavily criticised for what appeared to be its pro-Serb stance. Yet Védrine claimed that the approach was more pro-Yugoslav.[52] Nevertheless, the leadership would not describe Serbia, a historic ally and traditionally key element of French geopolitical interests, as the aggressor until the Lisbon European Council in the November, when it had to acknowledge the reality of the situation. It subsequently began to set the pace in the UNSC on sanctions against the Bosnian Serbs. And there was even a call, prior to any deployment of humanitarian forces on the ground, by Foreign Minister Juppé for decisive air strikes as a pre-emptive move against the Serbs. Once the West had intervened militarily, according to Wood:

> France was not averse to supporting some use of force but only within limits that would not antagonise the Serbs to the point where French peacekeepers on the ground might be endangered. Thus, the French government attempted to balance its foreign policy between enough support for the US to maintain a good working relationship and enough resistance to forceful military intervention to preserve its ability to influence the Serb leadership.[53]

The use of force to protect the delivery of relief supplies, but not to attack Serbs, was subsequently endorsed in Paris.

Mitterrand, backed by his Canadian and British counterparts, favoured a major UN involvement in the command and control of any peacekeeping mission. He opposed the control of the Yugoslav operation by NATO's integrated command for fear that acceptance would have been interpreted as France rejoining the Alliance's integrated military structure. The Organisation's efficacy as an instrument of execution for the UN was acknowledged, but the President denied that it should have some role in policy formation. For Beylau:

> *[t]radition gaullienne oblige. Paris ne veut pas apparaître comme étant á la remorque d'une Alliance atlantique dont il a quitté le commandement intégré. La France cherche donc á sauvegarder les apparences sous la houlette d'une ombrelle Onu clairement affichée. Même si les militaires français sont bien conscients que seul l'OTAN peut fournir les moyens d'une opération de cette envergure.*[d][54]

But one consequence of the UN's inclusion was an extension of the chain of command, rendering it increasingly cumbersome. In any event, despite French claims that the command structure should be run by the UN, the reality on the ground was that it was a NATO operation in all but name. Although the initial troop commitments to the UN were made through the WEU, operations were organised by a core from NATO Northern Army Group Headquarters – Forward.

Despite this, French representatives remained at the forefront of the allies' decision-making process. One initiative, in June 1993, resulted in the UNSC passing Resolution 836 which, in principle, provided for strengthened means for UNPROFOR to deter any aggression against five Muslim enclaves and Sarajevo. The French commander of UNPROFOR had just made an emotional and desperate outburst decrying the lack of means at his disposal, stating that the humiliation to which his men were being subjected to had reached unacceptable levels.[55] Moreover, legislative elections in France had just produced a centre-right government under Edouard Balladur. The latter had believed that French troops had been too exposed to risk, and that the burden assumed by France in the conflict was too great; indeed, he leaned towards disengagement.[56] In desperation at the perceived failures of both the European and UN-led attempts at resolving the crisis, French policy-makers would eventually change tactics. Following a mortar attack on a Sarajevo market January 1994, Foreign Minister Juppé actually turned to NATO's Atlantic Council in an attempt to get some decisive action.

The fact that France had thousands of its troops on the ground in the former-Yugoslavia was necessarily a primary factor in its policy regarding the crisis. Hence, its leaders, in conjunction with the British, consistently rejected American calls for the lifting of the arms embargo against Bosnia for fear of an even greater bloodbath with the UN forces caught in the middle. Then, the continued and largely needless loss of life among the French contingent, 43 French peacekeepers had been killed during the conflict between the start of the operation in 1992 and July 1995, inevitably resulted in loud noises emanating from Paris concerning a full French withdrawal from the

---

[d] 'Gaullist tradition requires it. Paris does not want to appear as if it's being towed by the Atlantic Alliance whose integrated command it had left. Thus, France looks to preserve the image of being under the leadership of a clearly defined UN umbrella. Even if the French military was well aware that only NATO had the capability for an operation of this scale'.

region.[57] Indeed, over a third of the French contingent in the Balkans had already been withdrawn in May 1994. In April 1995, France called an emergency session of the UNSC where it threatened to pull out all its troops unless the UN devised better protection. The move was subsequently interpreted as a French bluff aimed at shocking all parties to restart the stalled peace negotiations.[58] This approach was retained by the incoming Chirac/Juppé administration, in May, which made it clear from the start that the 4,800-strong French contingent would not remain in Bosnia in the absence of substantial progress towards a political solution. This administration was now using its troops as a bargaining chip. At the same time, it pushed strongly for a fundamental review of the whole Yugoslav peacekeeping operation.

On the ground meanwhile, the sense of impotence was growing. In June 1995, a sizeable number of French troops were among the hundreds of UN personnel taken hostage by the Bosnian Serbs as a guarantee against further NATO air-strikes against Bosnian Serb targets. These latter had been launched, at the behest of the UN, because the Bosnian Serbs had taken heavy weapons into UN exclusion zones in the face of renewed attacks by Bosnian Government forces. The French army was the traditional and symbolic instrument of the sovereignty of *la grande nation*. This perceived, almost unprecedented, humiliation of French and other allied forces, as transmitted by the media around the globe, prompted the first real public outcry against involvement since the original deployment of French forces. French popular opinion was reminded of the national trauma suffered after Diên Biên Phu during the 1950s *débâcle* in IndoChina.[59] Chirac, with his own military past, was particularly sensitive to the hapless position of the French peacekeepers.

The new President's arrival at the Elysée coincided with a serious deterioration of the situation on the ground in Bosnia. In addition to the hostage crisis there was also the question of the supposed UN safe havens, the status of which was being increasingly challenged by the Bosnian Serbs. Chirac felt he had to get things moving, as national honour was at stake. Indeed, it has been claimed that Mitterrand, faced with similar circumstances, would have been just as decisive.[60] One response was the creation, with the United Kingdom, of a 12,000-strong rapid reaction force, later joined by Dutch elements, to reinforce the UN in Bosnia and, in Chirac's own words, to 'prevent our troops from being humiliated';[61] the decision was ratified by both NATO and the EU. This new force was to be backed by heavy weaponry, hardly traditional peacekeeping equipment. UNPROFOR was hence moving even further away from its stance of neutrality and pure defence with the sole aim of providing humanitarian aid. France and its partners appeared to be increasingly downplaying their UN mandate and edging towards anti-Serb peace enforcement. As Alain Joxe noted, '*[l]'aide humanitaire suppose une attitude de stricte impartialité, alors qu'une opération militaire exige des objectifs politiques clairement définis*'.[e] [62] Certainly, there was confusion as to just what the mandate for the new force should be. One possible task was a scheme, revived by the French, to secure and keep open supply routes feeding Sarajevo and the Muslim enclaves. While the new French Defence Minister,

---

[e]   'Humanitarian aid assumes strict impartiality, whereas a military operation requires clearly defined political objectives'.

Charles Millon, stated that the force's mission would be based on the 'four Rs': regroup, reinforce, respond and respect.[63] Speculation was rife that the force was actually being put in place in order to facilitate the withdrawal of the whole UN operation, although this was vigorously denied by official sources. The tougher rhetoric emanating from the Western powers was partly matched on the ground at the end of June 1995 when French soldiers on Mount Igman, outside Sarajevo, became the first UNPROFOR troops in Bosnia to resort to artillery fire. The next month in the same area, French troops actively engaged Bosnian-Serb forces by retaking a strategic bridge. The statements coming from Paris were particularly remarkable because they made no reference to any linkage between the new force and either Eurocorps or the WEU. Nor, for that matter, was NATO mentioned.

As for the EU, there was, by this time, no doubt that as an institution it had lost all but minimal influence in the crisis. And the French had assisted in this sidelining, channelling, instead, almost all their diplomatic efforts through the five-nation Contact Group (Britain, France, Germany, Russia and the US), established in April 1994. This was an ad hoc arrangement, along the lines of a temporary Concert, which functioned without any legitimising international mandate. And in ultimately ceding the leadership role in the brokering of a peace settlement for the Bosnian crisis (Dayton) to the US, French policy-makers were inevitably, after months of their own painstaking diplomacy, humbled. While the Americans had stood wavering on the sidelines, the French had been able to occupy a prominent position within the international community's response to the crisis. The Dayton accords significantly lowered France's profile. Although the French did try to salvage some prestige by having the formal signing ceremony in Paris, with the accords supposedly then becoming the Elysée Peace Treaty. The ploy failed, in that the agreement is still referred to as Dayton. However, it has been argued that Chirac was acting in the belief that the future of the Atlantic Alliance depended on the outcome of the crisis in Bosnia. To this end, so the argument goes, he attempted to urge tougher action by the allies so as to boost NATO's credibility.[64]

The Bosnian experience prompted disillusionment in Paris with the UN's ability to lead the international community, and a corresponding further acknowledgement of NATO's worth. Concerning the latter, French policy-makers appreciated the higher profile accorded in the management of the crisis to the intergovernmental North Atlantic Council, as well as to NATO's Military Committee.[65] These moves implicitly downgraded the role played by the integrated military command (SHAPE) of which France was not part. Hence, Franco-NATO relations at the political level witnessed a dramatic improvement. The French leadership was bound to be more receptive to an Alliance structure with a strengthened intergovernmental element and weakened integrated military apparatus. Moreover, first-hand observance of the British forces in Bosnia demonstrated that participation in an integrated, American-dominated operation did not automatically imply the loss of autonomy and identity. The experience could actually be a positive one for medium powers like Britain and France.

Conclusion

The cumulative impact of France's numerous military excursions overseas in the first post-Cold War years was, this chapter has argued, to be crucial to the ongoing reassessment of security policy tactics. When Michel Debré, writing in 1991, asked whether France still existed he would encapsulate a view that came to be widely held in the wake of the reactive nature of the Bosnian and Gulf excursions and the frequent subservience to American policy goals.[66] Debré, one can assume, had been deliberately alarmist, but was nevertheless correct in noting that the whole character of the country's claimed global mission had been transformed. French forces could not, for example, now operate alone in an operation of any size; partners were a pre-requisite. The nature of the international system had changed to the extent that France was no longer in a position to act alone as an agent in pursuit of its fundamental security policy objectives. But this did not require that the *grandes lignes* be abandoned; tactics simply had to be adjusted in order to exploit the new opportunities. To this end, the experiences in the Gulf and, in particular, Bosnia revealed that greater cooperation with NATO, and participation in American-led operations were not so detrimental to French interests as many had assumed. After these engagements in particular, and given the growing prominence of economic imperatives, France's leaders drew the following conclusions: independence, autonomy of action and reliance on French *spécificité* no longer best served French interests, and these were to be substituted in favour of multilateralism. This new rationale would be reflected in the efforts of French policy-makers with regard to the European Security and Defence Identity.

Notes

1   Menon, Anand (2000), *France, NATO and the Limits of Independence 1981-97*, Macmillan, Basingstoke, p.61.
2   Lintner, Bertil, 'Not neighbourly', *Far Eastern Economic Review*, 30 November 1995, p.20.
3   Gregory, Shaun (2000), *French Defence Policy into the Twenty-First Century*, Macmillan, Basingstoke, p.37.
4   Tardy, Thierry, Institut de Relations Internationales et Stratégiques (IRIS), in interviews with the author, Paris, July 1996.
5   Menon, Anand, Lecturer in Politics of the European Union, University of Oxford, in an interview with the author, Birmingham, May 1996.
6   Moreau Defarges, Philippe, 'La France et l'ONU: le ralliement', *Relations Internationalese et Stratégiques*, no.9, Spring 1993, p.112.
7   Gregory, Shaun, *op cit*, p.170.
8   Urquhart, Brian (1995), 'Un regard extérieur sur 50 ans de présence française', in André Lewin (ed), *La France et l'ONU (1945-1995)*, Collection Panoramiques, Condé-sur-Noireau, p.119.
9   Grosser, Alfred, 'Le rôle et le rang', in *La France et l'ONU (1945-1995)*, *op cit*, p.66.
10 Mitterrand, François, in an interview on French national television with Anne Sinclair, Dominique Bromberger, Michel Colombès, Paul-Marie de la Gorce, André Mazières and Michel Tatu, 18 December 1984.

11 Léotard, François (1995), in Preface to *De Sarajevo á Kigali: Deux Années D'Interventions Extérieures de l'Armée Française Fin 92-Fin 94*, Ministère de la Défense, Paris, p.3.

12 Juppé, Alain, quoted in 'A prime minister for France', *The Economist*, 20 May 1995, p.43.

13 Moreau-Desfarges, Philippe, *op cit*, p.121.

14 Rocard, Michel, quoted in Torrelli, Maurice, 'Les missions humanitaires de' armée française', *Défense Nationale*, vol.49, March 1993, p.65.

15 *The Military Balance 1994-95*, IISS/Oxford University Press, 1994, p.45.

16 Tardy, Thierry, 'French policy towards peace support operations', *op cit*, p.65.

17 Chartouni-Dubarry, May, *France and the Gulf War*, IFRI Report, Paris, February 1992, p.13.

18 'La France souhaite que le problème soit reglé au sein de la communauté arabe', *Le Monde*, 11 August 1990.

19 An aim set out, for example, in the statement by President Mitterrand of 9 August 1990, Service de Presse de la Présidence de la République, Paris.

20 Balaj, Barbara S., 'France and the Gulf War', *Mediterranean Quarterly*, vol.4, no.3, Summer 1993, p.108.

21 *Ibid*, p.100.

22 Utley, R.E. (2000), *The French Defence Debate: Consensus and Continuity in the Mitterrand Era*, Macmillan, Basingstoke, p.181.

23 'Still in step, mostly', *The Economist*, 27 October 1990, p.29.

24 Grosser, Alfred, *op cit*, p.67.

25 Deniau, Jean-François, 'Le rang de la France', *Le Monde*, 7 September 1994.

26 Mitterrand, François, quoted in 'Mitterrand vows to pursue peace plan until last dawn', *International Herald Tribune*, 19 January 1991.

27 Howorth, Jolyon (1993), 'The President's special role in foreign and defence policy', in Jack Hayward (ed), *De Gaulle to Mitterrand: Presidential Power in France*, Hurst and Co., London, p.184.

28 Lellouche, Pierre, 'Mitterrand ou l'art du zigzag', *Le Figaro*, 9 February 1991.

29 Mitterrand, François, during a televised interview, quoted in 'L'épreuve cruelle de vérité aura lieu. Il faut que les Français y préparent leur esprit', *Le Monde*, 9 February 1991.

30 Mitterrand, François, in a speech in Oslo, 28 August 1990, quoted in 'Les positions de la France depuis le début de la crise', *Libération*, 10 January 1991.

31 Mitterrand, François, quoted in Marnham, Patrick, 'Not quite as American as pomme tarte', *The Independent*, 26 February 1991.

32 Mitterrand, François, quoted in Colombani, 'Le rang de la France', *Le Monde*, 5 March 1991.

33 Gordon, Philip H. (1993), *A Certain Idea of France: French Security Policy and the Gaullist Strategy*, Princeton University Press, Princeton, p.179.

34 Lellouche, Pierre, *op cit*.

35 Laird, Robbin (1992), 'The renovation of French defence policy', in Stuart Croft and Phil Williams (eds), *European Security without the Soviet Union*, Frank Cass, p.102.

36 Heisbourg, François (1991), 'La France et la crise du Golfe', in *L'Europe Occidentale et la Golfe*, in Nicole Gnesotto and John Roper (eds), WEU Institute for Security Studies, Paris, p.17.

37 It has also been suggested that Mitterrand initially did not deploy more advanced aircraft so that France could not be associated with any subsequent raids deep into Iraqi territory and with the destruction of Iraqi infrastructure; Paris' image in the Arab world still

retained political significance. See, for example, Cohen, Samy, 'Le Président chef des armées', *Pouvoirs*, no.58, 1991, p.34.

38	Marshall, Andrew, 'Old rivals unite in a military embrace', *The Independent*, 5 June 1995.

39	Blunden, Margaret, 'France after the Cold War: inching closer to the Alliance', *Defense Analysis*, vol.9, no.3, 1993, p.262.

40	Canivez, Patrice (1994), *Questions de Responsabilité: La France et l'Idée d'Europe Face a la Guerre dans l'Ex-Yougoslavie*, Colibri, Paris, p.23.

41	Garde, Paul, interview in *Le Point*, 3 June 1995, pp.67-8.

42	Boulmer, Michel, 'Les errements de la politique française', *Le Monde*, 27 March 1993.

43	Gnesotto, Nicole, *The Lessons of Yugoslavia*, Chaillot Paper 14, WEU Institute for Security Studies, Paris, March 1994, p.23.

44	Gow, James, *op cit*, p.31.

45	Chirac, Jacques, quoted in Dejevsky, Mary, 'Chirac spells out role of French force', *The Independent*, 2 June 1995.

46	Howorth, Jolyon (1994), 'The debate in France over military intervention in Europe', in Lawrence Freedman (ed), *Military Intervention In European Conflicts*, Blackwell, Oxford, p.114.

47	IPSOS-Le Point survey, quoted in Lasserre, Isabelle, Laporte, Benoît and Roche, Marc, 'Sarajevo: les Français pour la manière forte', *Le Point*, 12 February 1994, p.28.

48	'Des intellectuels dénoncent le "manque de détermination" de la France en ex-Yougoslavie', *Le Monde*, 20 December 1997.

49	Mitterrand was to dominate France's Bosnian policy until the overwhelming legislative victory of the Centre-Right in March 1993.

50	Védrine, Hubert (1996), *Les Mondes de Mitterrand: a l'Elysée 1981-1995*, Fayard, Paris, p.612.

51	D'Orcival, François, 'Chirac au pont de Vrbanja', *Valeurs Actuelles*, 3 June 1995, p.21.

52	Védrine, Hubert, *op cit*, p.630.

53	Wood, Pia Christina., 'France and the post-Cold War era: the case of Yugoslavia', *European Security*, vol.3, no.1, Spring 1994, p.141.

54	Beylau, Pierre, 'Bosnie: veillée d'armes', *Le Point*, 7 May 1993, pp.37-8.

55	Colomès, Michel, ' L'OTAN: le révélateur yougoslave', *Le Point*, 8 January 1994, p.31.

56	Tréan, Claire, 'Sursaut français en Bosnie', *Le Monde*, 9 June 1995.

57	Borger, Julian andDuval Smith, Alex, 'French threaten Bosnia pullout', *The Guardian*, 17 April 1995.

58	'Helmet blues', *The Economist*, 22 April 1995, p.46.

59	Colomès, Michel, 'Bosnie: la première épreuve de Chirac', *Le Point*, 3 June 1995, p.59.

60	Cot, Michel (Général de l'Armée), Président de Grope de Réflexion, Fondation pour les Etudes de Défense, and former French UNPROFOR commander, in an interview with the author, Paris, July 1996.

61	Chirac, Jacques, quoted in Eagar, Charlotte, 'Stench of war shrouds city as sniper takes its toll', *The Observer*, 11 June 1995.

62	Joxe, Alain, interviewed in 'Le mariage manqué du blindé et du sac de riz', *Le Nouvel Observateur*, 18 November 1993, p.37.

63	Block, Robert, 'Fighting talk may mask subtle campaign of bluff', *The Independent*, 7 June 1995, p.15.

64	'A Gaullist defiance', *Newsweek*, 31 July 1995, p.17.

65 The military committee comprises the respective armed forces chiefs of the Alliance's member countries and meets at least three times a year; crucially for France, it comes under the control of the North Atlantic Council (a political, rather than military, body).
66 Debré, Michel, 'La France n'existe plus', *Le Figaro*, 7 October 1991.

Chapter 5

West European Security Architecture Re-evaluated

Chapter Three has already demonstrated how, in the face of national limitations, French security policy-makers came to acknowledge that France by itself was no longer in a position to attain the sacrosanct strategic *grandes lignes*. To scale back the scope of these strategic objectives to a more realistic level would have been one option, but this was never really seriously considered by the decision-makers in Paris. Instead, France's leaders gradually turned to the country's west European partners. These would be harnessed in order that France, in a European guise, could continue to claim greatness and an elevated global standing. Hence, the tactical focus was on western Europe to help France achieve what it no longer had the means to achieve by itself. This theme is taken up and followed through the first decade of the post-Cold War era. It is clear that, through the 1990s, France lost some of its ability to manipulate, and act independent of, the structural constraints of the international system. These years would thus see several French reassessments of Europe's security architecture as serious attempts were made to foster closer military cooperation with France's west European partners. Three phases will be highlighted. Initially, French representatives continued to push their model of an autonomous European security and defence entity. France's military experience in Bosnia (as described in Chapter Four) combined with a general lack of west European enthusiasm for the French model then prompted a significant *rapprochement* with NATO as the only realistic home for the European security and Defence Identity (ESDI). Finally, and with a certain amount of surprise among the policy-makers in Paris, the agenda appears to have come full circle in that significant progress has been made in recent years to make the EU a credible, functioning, military actor with a discernible European Security and Defence Policy (ESDP).

Re-evaluation of Europe's Security Architecture

Persistence with the French Model

For many in the French security policy-making apparatus, the ability of the United States to throw its weight around in the early years of the post-Cold War era often appeared to amount to intimidation and diktat. Their response was a mixture of loud displays of France's own importance and continued efforts to unite Europe around

Paris as a counterweight to Washington. In light of the end of the new global security environment, French leaders attempted to argue that since NATO had fulfilled its primary objective of deterring Soviet aggression, then west Europeans should prepare themselves for an American withdrawal from the continent by building up their own defence capability. The Organisation seemingly no longer had a *raison d'être*. And these reticent attitudes towards the Alliance were driven in no small part by the fact that this was an organisation 61 per cent funded by the US, with the French contribution being only some nine per cent.[1] Hence, there remained hostility towards the Atlantic Alliance among French political circles. France had, for example, been attempting to use its influence in the 1980s to steadily move the reactivated WEU away from a position as the European pillar of NATO towards one as an integral part of the European political union. Other perceived attacks on the Atlantic solution would follow.

Nevertheless, French strategic planners would continue their reappraisal of European security begun towards the end of the 1980s. To this end, Valance was able to acknowledge the *'aveu que nous avons transposé à l'échelle de l'Europe les rêves ancestraux de la "grandeur" française, et l'abandon de l'espoir d'une Europe unie et puissante sous domination française'.*[a] [2] Vernet noted that all the principal political groupings across the French political spectrum, save for the Communists and a few staunch guallists, had been in favour, for instance, of a review of France's NATO status but that no one was prepared to take the responsibility of making the first move.[3] The possibility of normalising relations with NATO was finally broached, in April 1990, at Mitterrand's summit meeting with US President Bush at Key Largo. Simultaneously, French officials had been holding exploratory talks with their British, German and American counterparts about NATO reform and a possible French 'return'. The subsequent report was, however, rejected by the Elysée.

For Mitterrand, the overriding necessity had now become the need to contain the future power of the reunified Germany. The Key Largo initiative was soon dropped, the reasoning being that French strategic autonomy would be too severely compromised within an Alliance subservient to an American-German axis.[4] This was part of the motivation as French representatives subsequently conducted something akin to a guerrilla campaign against the reform of NATO that would allow it to expand its area of competence. This campaign reached its height in 1992. The establishment of the Eurocorps (see below), independent of NATO, was at least partly for this purpose. Although Defence Minister Joxe, among others, stressed that there was no intention of the latter constituting a European army.[5] At the same time, the decision to withdraw the bulk of French forces from Germany (again, see below), the refusal to take part in the establishment of multinational units and cross-stationing arrangements and the continued rejection of joint Allied consultations on nuclear strategy all seemed to indicate a preference for the national choice.

---

[a]   'admission that we have transposed the ancestral dreams of French grandeur to the European level, and abandoned the hope of a French dominated unified and powerful Europe'.

The French negotiating position, equally resisted any extension of the Alliance's remit to collective security initiatives in central and eastern Europe, such as the NACC (North Atlantic Cooperation Council), and opposed any close working relationship between NATO and the then CSCE. Hence, any calls for the expansion of NATO's mandate, beyond the strict limits of the Washington Treaty's Article V, were rejected. This was spelled out by Mitterrand at NATO's July 1990 NATO summit in London, and was graphically illustrated by French opposition to any official role for the Organisation in the second Gulf War and to any specific out-of-area mission for its Rapid Reaction Corps. Then, Paris insisted that NATO reform would have no bearing on the progress of the EU's parallel Intergovernmental Conference (IGC), on the agenda of which was the move towards forging ESDI. Thus, from the French viewpoint, NATO's role should have been restricted to one of mutual defence and the preservation of the geopolitical balance in Europe; there should have been no political component. This was why French negotiators opposed the creation of NACC, perceiving it as a second pan-European security organisation that still left the continent without a fully functioning mutual defence organisation. They had generally eschewed the collective approach to global security, favouring instead a looser, ad hoc coalition-based approach that did not involve unequivocal commitments.

Meanwhile, Mitterrand's July 1990 announcement that all 50,000 French troops, save for those dedicated to the Franco-German Brigade (subsequently made part of Eurocorps), would be withdrawn from German soil by 1994 left the French military searching for a new European role that did not imply direct subordination to NATO (the troops that remained in Germany did so under the terms of a bilateral agreement outside of the NATO apparatus). The establishment of the Eurocorps, which had swiftly evolved into a fighting force of some 45,000 troops from five states, partly served to fill this vacuum. As in the years following the Second World War, French policy-makers were again proposing a European alternative to a potentially dominant German national army. From their perspective, the Eurocorps was initially a means to tie Germany into a structure that was answerable to Europe, outside of NATO and distanced from any direct contact with the US.[6] But, in an agreement signed in January 1993 after protracted negotiations and, no doubt, vigorous German lobbying, the Eurocorps was made available to the Atlantic Alliance in the event of an attack on one of its members. It had, incidentally, already been put at the disposal of the WEU, particularly for peacekeeping operations, and to the UN for humanitarian operations. The Corps could henceforth be employed on the basis of the Alliance's Article V; that is to say, as a main defence force or, more likely, as a rapid reaction force. But the Corps could only be commanded by the above institutions on the following conditions: the preliminary agreement of the contributory governments, that the mission had been predefined according to a plan approved by the contributory governments, and that the mission plan was followed. These conditions were especially important to the French, being outside NATO's integrated military command. But did not the operational agreements formulated with NATO mean that they were making significant steps towards returning to the Alliance's integrated military structure, even if it was by the back-door? This was denied in Paris. But the Franco-German Brigade, for instance, as part of Eurocorps, was deployed, in 1997, as part of NATO's SFOR (Stabilisation

Force) in Bosnia. As noted in Chapter Four, the Bosnian experience followed that of the Gulf, with Paris ceding part of its traditional and sacred independent military capability to multinational commands.

However, French policy-makers began to finally accept what almost amounted to political isolation within Europe as regards their plans to breathe real life into the WEU as a viable European security organisation, while simultaneously acknowledging the limitations of the Eurocorps or any other separate European military operation of reasonable size. The Germans, for example, were showing major reluctance to be seen as attempting to supplant NATO with the WEU. In this crucial sphere, the Franco-German axis did not appear to be functioning as cohesively as in other areas. Lellouche later pointed to what he saw as a crucial French error at this time. By seemingly placing the WEU and 'Europe' in opposition to NATO, Paris gave the impression, whether in Bonn, London or Washington, that it was attempting to break the Alliance and push the Americans away.[7] France's smaller west European partners, meanwhile, appeared to have greater suspicions with regard to a Europe that would inevitably be dominated by a Franco-Germano-British directory than towards a Europe still largely beholden to the US, particularly in the security and defence field.[8] Furthermore, no other west European government was willing to commit itself to the extra financial costs that the creation of an effective alternative to NATO would entail. Moreover, generally falling defence budgets within EU member states made the grand project untenable.[9] The prospect of a significant downgrading of the American military presence in western Europe had not had the effect of encouraging European governments to take on a greater share of their security burden. As Baumel acknowledged, '*[n]ous souhaitons l'émergence d'un pôle de sécurité et de défense européen, mais nous sommes presque les seuls à le souhaiter réellement*'.[b] [10] And unfortunately for French security policy-makers, the post-Cold War paradox was that they were striving to fashion a common foreign and security policy for the EU at a time when increasingly diverse external threats were appearing at an alarming rate. What was once a conceivable strategic solidarity among west European states now seemed decidedly uncertain. The fact that French diplomacy had devoted the majority of its resources to the promotion of the European politico-military process meant that the relative lack of real progress in this direction could be seen as a significant blow to French post-Cold War security policy ambitions.

The France of the 1990s was suffering from not being at the West's principal security decision-making table, that is to say from its absence from NATO's military decision-making structures. The habitual rhetoric denouncing calls for reintegration had served to diminish French influence in the European security debate. Allies unable to discern, and sometimes distrustful of, France's leaders' actual intentions became increasingly receptive to Atlanticist options. At the same time, France's ever expanding international peacekeeping role required much more concerted coordination with allies. Equally, this role was making French officials aware that the greater exposure of French troops to active service necessitated a French presence on the

---

[b]   'we desire the emergence of a European security and defence pole, but we are virtually the only ones to really wish it'.

respective NATO committees where the fate of French lives was being determined. And it was clear that only NATO would have the capacity to counter any military attack on the territorial integrity of western Europe, however unlikely this latter scenario actually was. Aware of this, French representatives made recurring calls for NATO reform, believing that the Organisation had ceased to adequately meet the new security and strategic challenges. At the same time as France's supposed guerrilla campaign against NATO, Mitterrand had been breaking certain supposed gaullist taboos regarding the Alliance. As noted in Chapter Four, French forces were subordinated to American command during the Gulf War and American B-52 bombers had been permitted to use French airfields. In 1992 Mitterrand accepted that the Alliance could play a role in international peacekeeping, and, in January 1993 (as noted above), that it could have command of the Eurocorps for such operations, as well as in wartime.

It has been claimed that the French saw these gestures as representing their only means to anchor Germany to the Western camp. And that once the reunification question was settled, French efforts were refocused on limiting the impact of NATO reforms and on building up the roles of the EU and the WEU. This meant, essentially, having the WEU as the military instrument of the European Council. But as Bozo pointed out, the latter two organisations, just like NATO, were very much products of the Cold War, and so it was difficult to interpret France's defence of them as anything but an attempt to preserve an international structure that served French interests; namely as a check on potential German might.[11] Conversely, Yost pointed to a number of French statements that implied that the retention of French forces in Germany, or indeed the stationing of other European forces inside France, 'would only make sense in a European structure based on new foundations, not on political premises remaining from World War II or the Cold War'.[12]

While Mitterrand remained in office, France could never formally reintegrate itself into the military structures of the Atlantic Alliance.[13] Despite all of his moves towards *rapprochement* with the Alliance, he could only go so far and no further. His carefully thought-out pronouncements on the matter were suitably ambiguous so that they simultaneously demonstrated support for NATO while not precluding the emergence of a European organisation that could ultimately substitute the North Atlantic club.[14] By never fully embracing the adaptation and redefinition of NATO in order to perpetuate its dominance of west European security architecture into the post-Cold War era, the President retained valuable room for manoeuvre. And it is perhaps conceivable that he was conscious of not leaving a legacy as having betrayed a supposed basic, if illusory, tenet of Gaullist security policy – autonomy from American hegemony. For whatever reasons, successive Socialist administrations serving under Mitterrand were only willing to take small and inconspicuous steps towards reintegration. The President adamantly opposed any formal reintegration, believing the arrangement functioned well as it was; a view (as shown in Chapter Four) he felt was particularly vindicated by the experiences of the Gulf War. To note here is that this intransigence on the part of the President on this matter went against the repeated advice of the Defence Ministry. Furthermore, the latter's stance was backed by the respective wings of the armed forces that were all pushing the NATO card (even the army, in the wake of its experiences in the Gulf and Bosnia, was increasingly coming round to the idea of some form of reintegration).

Some French observers had argued that, in the post-Cold War environment, a general conventional conflict in Europe had now been made implausible and that therefore military integration of the NATO-type had lost its whole *raison d'être*. Some went further, claiming that with NATO having realised its primary objective of deterring Soviet aggression, western Europe should prepare for an eventual American withdrawal from the region by building up its own defence capability.[15] But NATO did not confine itself to its Cold War mandate, let alone wind itself up, having seemingly run its course. The French were surprised to observe the Organisation act with renewed vigour as it underwent relatively swift and effective reform, showing itself ready and able to operate in the changed security environment by broadening its remit. In May 1991, for example, the Alliance bestowed itself with an 'out-of-area' role and created a Rapid Reaction Corps, under British command and comprising Belgian, British, Dutch and German troops, to enact this new function. This appeared, for the time being at least, to scupper French hopes for the emergence of some form of European army outside of the NATO apparatus. According to Lansford, the ineffectual nature of the now OSCE and the WEU when placed in comparison with the evolving NATO precluded the creation of a whole new security organisation and persuaded Mitterrand's successor, Chirac, that French choices would be made within the confines of the existing security architectural framework.[16] Given the latter acknowledgement, and given the nature of the new security environment with the proliferation of international military interventions, French planners inevitably came to focus on scenarios that increasingly touched upon France's relations with NATO. For Lawrence this implied that 'gaullist notions of a dignified independence would have to be qualified by the logic of alliance'.[17]

But the basic principle of French policy remained that west European integration via the EU would be incomplete unless it was to include defence and security matters. The popular myth still existed that fuller cooperation with NATO's integrated military command structure would inevitably entail a diminishing of national sovereignty. Pierre Joxe, while Defence Minister, stated that France could not conceive of integrating important elements of its defence in some larger entity unless there was the affirmation of a genuine European will.[18] However, as the 1990s progressed, the reappraisal of France's position within the European and global security environments gathered pace and assumed an ever greater weight of logic. French defence circles began to increasingly push strategic doctrine and force structures away from their stereotyped Gaullist stance, which had begun to unravel, towards active participation in the construction of a European pillar within the Atlantic Alliance.

Tactical Adjustment: NATO or Bust

It had become abundantly clear that France's European partners were not yet prepared to construct a common defence structure autonomous of NATO for risk of alienating an increasingly introspective United States. These countries had become accustomed to waiting and relying on the Americans to provide leadership and to take the initiative. Mitterrand's concerted attempts at persuading them to favour creating an independent European security entity had, for now at least, failed. Pfaff went so far as to claim that the west Europeans had now missed the opportunity to take control for themselves of the post-Cold War European order.[19] In addition, the 'cause' of an autonomous ESDI continued to suffer from the military impotence of Germany due to the constitutional block on German troops being deployed abroad in combat zones. If Germany was unable to fully commit to the French design for Europe's security architecture and was thereby revealing an imbalance in the crucial Franco-German security relationship, then there was little credibility for an ESDI outside of the Atlantic Alliance. In addition, the British, whose participation would be crucial if the French ESDI model was to be capable of anything more than evacuating EU citizens from some far-flung war-torn capital were totally opposed to European military solutions outside of the NATO framework. To this end, in 1991, they had joined with the Italians to propose the relocation of the WEU inside the Atlantic Alliance. With the exception of the Communists and some of the Gaullist old guard, agreement emerged across the French political spectrum that, at the very least, France's relations with NATO should be subject to review. However, noted Vernet, as always there was a uniform reluctance to be seen to be making the first move to reform a principal element of de Gaulle's security policy.[20]

As this adjustment was taking place, French attitudes towards the US itself were shifting. Rather than fearing American hegemony in Europe rendered unjustifiable by the end of the Cold War, there was now genuine concern that the Americans may pull out of the continent altogether before the Europeans had had time to fill the vacuum. At the same time, the attitude of the Americans towards some form of European defence and security identity had become more receptive. While President Bush had been anxious to protect American leadership in Europe, the Administration of his successor, Bill Clinton, proved far more enthusiastic for some sharing of the role with the Europeans, and did not see a form of European identity as a challenge to the US' position. And this not least because an enhanced burden-sharing by the Europeans would alleviate some of the domestic budgetary pressure. And a certain warming of American attitudes towards the French maverick was inevitable in the aftermath of the Gulf War and the Bosnian crisis where it had proved a willing and capable partner.[21] In addition, and not least because of the part played by France in these crises, American policy-makers could finally point to some actual potential for ESDI and realised that this concept could possibly evolve into something tangible. On a more practical level, NATO had reformed its patterns of deployment so that most national forces remained in their home countries unless in time of crisis. This potentially provided greater scope for French political acceptance of increased cooperation between French and American conventional forces, building on the experience of the Gulf War. And, as noted in Chapter Four, with regard to the Bosnian crisis, French security policy-makers can only have been pleased to see the political North Atlantic Council given greater participation in operation planning.

At the same time, the EU's Common Foreign and Security Policy (CFSP), a wholly European initiative formalised in the 1992 Maastricht Treaty of European

Union, had shown little sign of getting off the ground. Indeed, expectations of the CFSP among member states were being significantly downgraded. Europe's response to the wars in former-Yugoslavia provided, for Bozo, a graphic illustration: *'les espoirs français de voir l'Union européenne jouer un rôle majeur dans cette crise devaient très vite se heurter aux réalités opérationnelles'.*[c] [22] The outbreak of hostilities in former-Yugoslavia had been supposed to mark the 'hour of Europe', when the Europeans would show themselves capable of balancing American military power and finally take in hand the security of their own strategic arena. But the crisis proved too great a challenge as the first major debut of the EU's CFSP or for the ability of the WEU to assume collective military responsibility. By the time the Dayton Peace Accord had been forced through by American pressure, the EU, through its envoy Carl Bildt, and the UN, had been all but excluded from the principle decision-making processes. The credibility of the EU/WEU, and the UN, as definitive security organisations took a series of potentially fatal blows. This was the defining moment when the planners in Paris could discern categorically that their European partners lacked the political will to realise the ambitions they had for Europe. The bottom line was that these countries did not have sufficient confidence in Europe's ability to act alone against major security threats. European forces, for example, dominated the composition of UNPROFOR, and yet each contingent had been deployed in a national capacity and was paid for out of the respective national budgets; in addition, all air operations had been conducted by NATO.[23] Indeed, the French leadership was becoming increasingly worried about a possible renationalisation of security policies in Europe, a trend it hoped to avert by throwing France fully back into NATO and working for a rejuvenation of the Organisation.

The reaction of many of France's west European partners to the temporary resumption in 1995 of nuclear testing in the south Pacific (rather clumsily, and presumably inadvertently, timed to coincide with the fiftieth anniversary of the nuclear bombing of Hiroshima and Nagasaki, and the tenth anniversary of the sinking of the *Rainbow Warrior*) was a further ominous sign for the future of a common European foreign and defence policy. Ten EU member states voted for a UN Resolution denouncing France's actions (Germany, Greece and Spain abstained, and the UK voted against). The concurrent French offer to Europeanise their nuclear force was met more by scepticism than support in the other European capitals. For the foreseeable future, French aspirations for a Europe built largely to French designs, in which Paris would pull the strings in order to preserve national *grandeur* and to assert the country's elevated global *rang*, would have to be put on hold. France's plans for Europe were becoming unravelled.

Over a period of several years, French security policy had been shifting from the aggressive pursuit of a distinct European defence identity towards a more conciliatory and pragmatic attitude regarding NATO. For Bozo at the time, *'[l]e retour de la France à une politique activiste d'indépendance stratégique européenne n'est donc*

---

[c] 'French hopes of seeing the European Union play a major role in this crisis were to quickly come up against operational realities'.

pas aujourd'hui une option credible'.[d] [24] If military policy was to continue to provide France with the benefits it once had, policy adaptation was now a necessity. This was backed by a determination not to be marginalised in Europe. Increasing store would thus be placed on the successive NATO declarations (London 1990, Rome 1991, Brussels 1994 and Berlin 1996) affirming a European defence and security identity within the Alliance. There was the reluctant acknowledgement of the need to offset and balance German strength by moving closer to Britain and the US.[25] As early as March 1991, it was announced that France would participate in NATO's Strategy Review Group, although Foreign Minister Dumas (never the most pro-American French politician) cautioned that the move changed nothing in France's relations with NATO.[26] In the same vein, Mitterrand announced that he had decided to allow France, from the turn of the century, to participate in NATO's Air Command and Control System. Then, during 1993 and 1994, three permanent French missions were established at standing NATO commands. And in Bosnia, thousands of French troops on the ground had been placed under NATO control. It was clearly imperative that France's Defence Minister and Chief of Staff now sat on, and had an influential voice in, those committees determining the fate of French forces especially given the rising number of French casualties and fatalities.

Defence Minister Pierre Joxe had already hinted, in September 1992, at greater French participation in NATO's politico-military activities. This meant a possible return to the Defence Planning and Military Committees. The same year, Paris accepted that NATO could undertake actions of collective security on behalf of the then CSCE or the UN. At the January 1994 NATO summit in Brussels, the French and Germans, as noted above, consented to the subordination of Eurocorps to NATO for Article V operations. François Léotard, as French Defence Minister, attended a NATO defence ministers' meeting in Seville in October 1994. The 1994 *Livre Blanc* on defence produced by the centre-right Balladur government then went as far as to say that henceforth the Chief of Staff could participate in the Alliance's Military Committee whenever the deployment of French troops was at issue or whenever French interests were at stake.[27]

Pragmatism of the kind frequently displayed by de Gaulle was required. For Quatremer, 'the "European defence identity" will be built within NATO or will not be built at all'.[28] NATO was being acknowledged by the leadership in Paris as fundamental if ESDI was to evolve into anything more than a hazy, vague, concept. This being the case, it had to end its relative isolation in the European security dialogue. Antagonism in this domain was now proving counterproductive. French negotiators had to help forge Europe's new security shapes via NATO reform before France's favourable strategic position of the Cold War was finally eroded. For Vernet, 'France, which had for a time entertained the notion of a European defence identity that was allied to and complimented the United States, but which was independent, has just made a double acknowledgement: the Europeans have neither the financial means nor the political will to be independent. With our principal partners integrated in

---

[d]   'France's return to an active policy of European strategic independence is not today a
       credible option'.

NATO, it is in NATO that the "European defence identity" has to be asserted'.[29] Moreover, it was now clear that the countries of central and eastern Europe were looking to the Atlantic Alliance, rather than to the OSCE or the EU/WEU for security guarantees and that the significance and scope of the Alliance's military and political activities was set to increase. The interpretation of the Chirac/Juppé Administration in Paris was that, in pan-European terms, the French had to be on the inside of all aspects of NATO to have any real influence in the Europe of the future. France's special status with regard to the Alliance no longer served a useful purpose. In addition, there was the fear that if France did not actively involve itself in key organisations like the Alliance then Europe would be more inclined to assume a Germanic form. Chirac made a simple calculation. France had to sacrifice a measure of, often notional, national sovereignty for the reality of continued influence. But, noted de Montbrial, this did not mark the abandonment of France's European ambitions: 'Europe will exist only if it is self-defined, and if it acquires the means to be autonomous. Hence, Paris earnestly desires preservation of a strong Atlantic alliance, but one whose European pillar is on an equal footing with the American pillar'.[30]

In December 1995, Foreign Minister de Charette announced, with certain provisos, France's full return to the non-integrated military bodies of the Alliance (save for the meetings of the Nuclear Planning Group)[31] and a commitment to improve working relations with SHAPE.[32] Chirac reiterated French demands that the Americans cede some of their leadership in the Alliance in favour of the Europeans, that there be more of an equal partnership. '*La France s'est rapprochée de l'Alliance pour la voir évoluer dans une double direction: redéfinition de sa mission, à l'heure de l'après-guerre froide, et renforcement de l'identité européenne au sein de l'organisation*'.[e] [33] Prime Minister Balladur, in late 1994, had asked 'must the Europeans constantly wait for an American decision in order to know what they can do in the area of security? ... The Europeans must be able to take decisions and act on their own'.[34] Meanwhile, Chief of the Defence Staff Admiral Jacques Lanxade stated that '[t]he matter at issue today is not to set up a military organisation responsible for Europe's defence instead of NATO, but to establish the structures required to allow us Europeans to act in an autonomous way if need be'.[35] Thus it was abundantly clear that the French were expecting that the functioning of the Alliance would be transformed to allow for greater European autonomy.

After initial reservations, France finally approved American proposals for Combined Joint Task Forces (CJTF). This was a concept by which a wholly European force would be able to use NATO's (read the US') logistics and communication and intelligence facilities without operating under a non-NATO (non-American) command. The reasoning here was that there would be instances in the future when the Americans would not want to directly respond to a particular international crisis but when the Europeans would want to mount a collective response but for the lack of military hardware. Given the virtual American monopoly in these areas, the French

[e] 'France has drawn nearer to the Alliance in order to see it evolve in two directions: the redefinition of its mission for the post-Cold War era, and the strengthening of the European identity within the Organisation'.

had previously claimed that this represented an effective US veto on such operations, and on any further development of a distinct European security and defence identity. And this reticence was much stronger at Mitterrand's Elysée than at Balladur's Matignon. Yet there were even signs that both were slowly coming round to accepting the idea that NATO itself should be ready to undertake military operations outside its own area.[36] France thus intimated at rejoining the Atlantic Alliance's command structure partly so as to promote the CJTF concept through which, theoretically, the Europeans would gain greater flexibility and autonomy when faced with out-of-area issues. This was thus a useful framework for bringing the French closer to their allies without challenging the taboo of reintegrating its military command into the NATO structure. In exchange for French cooperation on NATO's continued core functions, the signing of the Alliance's New Strategic Concept in its entirety and the reluctant adherence to the creation of the NACC, the US recognised the growing role of a European defence identity. Moreover, the reasoning in Paris was that, in the future, NATO integration would soften, thereby making it more acceptable. More initiatives like the less-doctrinal CJTF would emphasise cooperation rather than integration.[37] NATO would henceforth operate under a much looser, ad hoc, arrangement. Indeed, this reasoning was a major element of Chirac's argument in the face of domestic criticisms. He denied French moves with regard to NATO constituted *un retour* because the Organisation itself was no longer the same entity it had been during the Cold War. Rather, it was NATO that was moving closer to the French vision of the global security environment.

NATO's June 1996 Berlin summit marked the formal ratification of the CJTF concept, and it also marked a further narrowing of the divide between France and the Alliance's military structures.[38] Paris declared that a true European security pillar would emerge within NATO, with the capacity to undertake operations independent of the north American member countries. But in effect, there was no real guarantee that this would happen. Many of the official French comments were based more on hope and speculation than any degree of certainty. In a sense, the French negotiating team had paid in advance for an unfinished product, the final nature of which was uncertain. Many among the political elite did not see any reason why France should compromise its sovereignty when it had already obtained from NATO, at two successive summits, recognition of a separate European identity within the Alliance without having had to make any major concessions on sovereignty and status.[39] Former Defence Minister Quilès, for one, believed that all the possibilities for ESDI within the EU/WEU had not yet been fully explored.[40] Ironically, it was the Socialists who were now decrying the lack of public debate on the matter, who were criticising Chirac's initiative as a betrayal of gaullism.

Chirac's opponents were stressing that France did have a choice regarding the Alliance, that to have maintained the relationship as it was would have been a positive step. In this way, the argument went, France could look to reform the Alliance from the outside. For Quilès, the supposed Europeanisation of NATO did not amount to the French aim of a European defence. Rather, this move by Chirac represented a French capitulation, effectively making the US the sixteenth member of the European Union.[41] Dabezies, meanwhile, deplored what he saw as the loss of a key element of French *spécificité.*[42] And Védrine referred to the banalisation of France as an international actor, a trend that would have been complete but for the country's nuclear weapon capability.[43]

Certainly from their rhetoric, the Administrations in Paris and Washington appeared to have signed up to different documents. The former seemed to have a vision of the Alliance as some form of looser collective security organisation with the capacity for variable geometry and hence something significantly different to its traditional integrated military format. In addition, French representatives continued to press for political, as opposed to the existing military, control over NATO's operations. They thus pushed for an increased role for national governments and for the NAC. However, considerable doubts were raised about American preparedness to supply NATO assets for an European operation run from a headquarters they would not control (any decision for deployment would require a unanimous vote in the NAC, thereby giving any member state an effective veto).[44] This could be described as an American double-veto on European CJTFs, on determining the mission, and on allocating the resources. Then there was an apparent dispute over the allocation of NATO commands between the US and Europe. When asked in an interview whether France tended to confuse its own objectives with those of Europe, French Foreign Minister de Charette replied:

> [w]hen leaders of influential European countries like Germany or France travel around the world, they carry Europe on the soles of their shoes, so to speak. I do not mean by that that every time France speaks, it expresses the point of view of Europe. France has its own foreign policy, which it alone defines, but like the other European countries, it bears part of Europe's collective responsibility.[45]

Moreover, if ESDI was to be forged within the Atlantic Alliance, just where did this leave French plans for an enhanced political and military role for the EU?

But this *rapprochement* with NATO was not the radical policy shift that it may have seemed. For one thing, the 1994 defence *Livre Blanc* invoked the same requirements claimed in 1966: namely, the right of France to deploy its troops as it wants, national control over its territory, the independence of its nuclear forces, and the freedom to determine for itself the conditions for its security and to choose the appropriate course of action unilaterally in times of crisis.[46] For another, it was more the logical continuation of a trend that had emerged over recent years, under both Socialist and centre-Right Administrations. The move was simply part of a wider strategy for Europe. For Moïsi:

> *[e]n poursuivant un processus de normalisation des relations de la France avec l'OTAN, Jacques Chirac ne fait que prolonger, de manière plus spectaculaire, une réflexion et une action déjà menées par ses prédécesseurs. Il ne s'agit certainement pas*

d'une rupture révolutionnaire, de la violation d'un tabou, mais d'une évolution graduelle, légitime et réaliste.[f][47]

Moreover, as noted earlier, French national leaders had, in practical terms, almost clandestinely maintained the level of France's military commitment to the Alliance. There were hence significant disparities between the political rhetoric, claiming complete autonomy, and the military situation on the ground.

At the same time, French perceptions had undergone something of a transformation. The Yugoslav experience, in addition to once again demonstrating the limits to French power, had significantly altered official perceptions of Europe's security architecture, and especially of NATO. Moreover, for Beyleu, *'[l]'OTAN est en pleine évolution, et la France ne peut se permettre de demeurer trop en marge d'un militaire indispensable à la gestion des crises où elle est impliquée'*.[g][48] And it should be stressed that the guiding objectives of French security policy remained *rang* and *grandeur*, not independence. The latter, in the form of non-dependence, had only ever been a tactical device employed in response to a certain set of circumstances. It was perfectly coherent for France to now change tack by downplaying independence given the new security environment. Pfaff likewise observed a simple reappraisal of the geopolitical situation. This was 'old policy in a new guise ... France has come back to NATO because NATO has been reactivated as agent of Western policy in Bosnia. Since 1990 the alliance had lacked a post-Cold War mission. Now it provides the only game in town'.[49] And this is not to rule out further tactical shifts in the future with regard to the Alliance. The *rapprochement* was thus a calculated, tactical, response to a particular set of circumstances.

It may also partly be the case that the shift in French policy towards the Alliance could be attributed to the efforts of a Germany eager to appease its neighbour but anxious not to alienate the United States. This was encapsulated by the December 1996 adoption at Nuremburg of a common Franco-German strategic concept. In this, Paris accepted that in the short to medium-term, a European defence identity would be forged within NATO to which it would return so long as measures were put in place to give greater visibility to the Alliance's European component. Bonn, for its part, agreed that the WEU, in liaison with the European Council would become the judicial base for the future ESDI and gave its support to French efforts to Europeanise the Atlantic Alliance.

Meanwhile, France could even be seen softening its opposition to the strengthening of the now OSCE. The latter became the preferred option among French policy-makers for future progress in pan-European security. This could, in part, be attributed as an attempt to tie in Russia to the European security community, a traditional goal of

---

f   'In pursuing a normalisation of relations between France and NATO, Jacques Chirac is only prolonging, in a more spectacular fashion, a stance and policy already practised by his predecessors. It certainly does not represent a revolutionary rupture, the violation of a taboo, but a gradual, legitimate and realistic evolution'.

g   'NATO is in full evolution, and France cannot allow itself to stay too much on the fringes of a military tool that is indispensable for the crises in which the French are involved'.

French European policy. Prime Minister Balladur's proposed pan-European Stability Pact of April 1993, for instance, implied greater competence for the Organisation. Moreover, this initiative broke with previous French proposals by providing for the continued involvement of the US and Canada in European security. But then perhaps this could be interpreted as an attempt to forestall the expansion of American-led NATO's remit, both in terms of geographic reach and in the range of its activities. President Chirac spoke at the end of 1996 of a real reinforcing of the OSCE's capacity to act as a pan-European security organisation, including bestowing it with an international judicial character.[50] Equally, opposition to plans to give the OSCE's Conflict Prevention Centre something more than just a technical role was withdrawn, provided that it did not become a future European Security Council.

The triumph of a Socialist-dominated left-wing coalition at the June 1997 legislative elections, after President Chirac's surprise dissolution of the National Assembly, perhaps inevitably, placed Chirac's whole adaptation of security policy in doubt, particularly the *rapprochement* with NATO. Lionel Jospin, as the new Prime Minister, was, for instance, known to fear the subordination of French nuclear forces to decisions taken within the Atlantic Alliance. Crucially, no formal reintegration of France and NATO took place at the latter's July 1997 Madrid summit. One thorny issue was Washington's veto, despite vociferous French lobbying, of the Romanian, principally, and Slovenian candidacies for NATO membership. The weakness of France's negotiating leverage within the Alliance, and that of its European partners, had been blatantly exposed. At the same time there was the ongoing Franco-American dispute concerning the allocation of a senior European military officer to the head of NATO's southern command based in Naples. But with regard to latter question, the key factor appeared to be the change of government in France that left Chirac somewhat politically isolated. On the reallocation of commands at least, French negotiators now had to await the reorganisation that would accompany the extension of Alliance membership to the Czech Republic, Hungary and Poland. But then, the new Defence Minister, Alain Richard, stated in the following December that the re-balancing of responsibilities within the Alliance between the US and the Europeans had, to date, failed to meet French requirements.[51] Even the most Atlanticist French leaders, including Chirac who was now constrained by *cohabitation*, could not commit to a full re-integration with the Alliance until the French model for its reform had been accomplished; only a fully Europeanised Alliance would allow France to be a major player in determining its future orientation.

It seems clear that Chirac and his advisors overestimated the welcome and the accompanying concessions to their demands that they would receive from its NATO partners. The amount of leverage that France was able to exert was not that significant; not least, notes Menon, because after decades on the outside of fora like the Military Committee, French officials simply did not fully grasp the negotiating culture. The hitherto successful tactic of promoting the French exception, of portraying France as distinct from the rest of the Alliance, through 'grand gesture politics' counted for little once they were trying to operate on the inside of these integrated structures.[52] Yet, there seemed no real alternative but to pursue the *rapprochement*. Besides, France was committed to maintaining its military role in the former-Yugoslavia (the strategic objectives of French security policy dictated that withdrawal was not an option) and this meant remaining inside the respective NATO operations. The reality of the situation was acknowledged by Richard who stated that the view of the new government converged with that of the President concerning the eventual reintegration of France into NATO's military structures.[53] On this matter, the talk in Paris at the end of 1997 was now of *insertion* of French forces (into the Alliance), as opposed to their *intégration*. And France's membership of the Alliance was described as *solitaire* but *solidaire*.[54] However, Vernet wondered how France could claim to be both inside and outside the Alliance at the same time.[55] Even if the French perceived that there had been insufficient progress towards ESDI within the Alliance, economic and geopolitical imperatives dictated that NATO was the best and only viable multilateral option for the furtherance of French *rang* and *grandeur*, not only within Europe but also in the wider world. This could likewise have been one of the conclusions drawn, by pessimists, from the EU's June 1997 Amsterdam European Council at which little practical progress was made in building on the vague provisions of the Maastricht Treaty for a fully developed CFSP and ESDI within the Union. Indeed, the French stressed their commitment to maintaining the dialogue with the Alliance regarding reintegration. And the Socialists did not reverse the centre-right's policy of having the Defence Minister and the armed forces Chief of Staff attend NATO conclaves such as the Military Committee. But this was not to say that the picture would not change and that French policy-makers would not institute another tactical shift in pursuit of the *grandes lignes*. As 1997 drew to a close, NATO represented the best tactical choice for the French ambitions. The extent of the transformation of French tactics was revealed with the 1998-9 Kosovo crisis. Here, there were no flamboyant displays of the French exception nor where there desperate calls for a Europe-only solution. Instead, almost the entire French strategic community made an early and explicit commitment to the Alliance's war aims, and this even in the absence of any UN mandate. But external forces were now at work that would prompt a further tactical shift in French security policy with regard to ESDI.

Full Circle: the French Model Revived

Events moved so quickly that the June 1999 Cologne European Council approved a potentially landmark document that formally pledged the Union to a common policy on security and defence aimed to bestow it with the capacity for autonomous action in crisis management, backed by credible military forces. To this end, the 15 foreign ministers announced their intention to absorb the WEU, including its satellite centre, into the EU. By so doing, they were committing the EU to assuming responsibility for peacekeeping and conflict resolution. Six months later, the Helsinki European Council launched the Franco-British driven process by which the EU will, by 2003, have at its disposal a Rapid Reaction Force (RRF) of 50-60,000 personnel. This force was set to operate in accordance with the principles of the UN Charter and to be deployable within 60 days and capable of staying in place for at least a year. And, crucially, the member states formally committed themselves to providing the material assets and necessary budgetary provisions for these ambitious goals to become reality. The Reaction Force was not to constitute a standing European army, but it was to have its own planning staff.

In all this, the relationship between this newly militarised Union and NATO remained a key issue, particularly for the leadership in Paris. Initially after Helsinki, French negotiators were reluctant to give the Alliance a major input in the discussions pertaining to the CSDP beyond informal contacts. But in April 2000, Jospin's government suggested holding meetings of EU and NATO officials to discuss key issues relating to the establishment of the former's crisis management capability. Almost for the first time, the EU membership was moving away from rhetorical references to 'identity' and 'architecture' and was actually talking about practical commitments and the necessary concrete steps. Hence, the possibility of a 'common defence policy', as mentioned in the Maastricht Treaty, began to be talked about as something both concrete and realisable. These moves, combined with the various initiatives underway among European defence industries (elaborated in Chapter Six), seemingly indicated that France's European partners had finally come round to the original vision of its leaders. As Gnesotto observed, '[t]hat all countries of the Union – whether large or small, from the north or south, NATO members or not belonging to a military alliance, having an interventionist tradition or not – now subscribe to the political and operational aims set out at Cologne and Helsinki, is certainly a major political revolution'.[56]

Security and defence is in the process of becoming the third *grand projet* of European integration, after the common market and the single currency. Indeed, more progress has arguably been made since 1998 in the forging of a European defence than in the previous 50 years. But this could not seriously be attributed directly to French diplomacy, although the limited *rapprochement* with NATO has clearly had an impact. Rather, the principal explanations lay in a convergence of different events and processes. First, there were changes in the German stance, and this was followed by the even more significant radical policy shift across the English Channel. Added to this there was the impact of yet another perceived failure for an autonomous and credible ESDI with the 1998-9 crisis in Kosovo. In addition, one can point to an evolving reappraisal by certain EU members of their neutrality and changing attitudes among the membership towards the Union's role in the world. It is also conceivable that French leaders were not the only ones to be exasperated at the apparent stalling of the Europeanisation of NATO in terms of military operability, as opposed to the strengthening statements of NATO support for ESDI as a principle.

Germany was going through something of a personal journey with regard to ESDI. First, the fallout from the Gulf War and the impact of events in Bosnia had served as the catalysts for a momentous constitutional change that allowed German troops to be deployed abroad in a conflict situation. Second, France's rapprochement with NATO's integrated military structures, despite its ongoing problems, and the concomitant warming in Franco-American relations, eased tensions among German policy-makers. They were reassured that French ambitions for ESDI were not now a direct challenge to the rationale for NATO. They thus felt comfortable pushing ahead with European defence cooperation because the perception was that this would serve to reinforce the Alliance.

Much to the surprise of the French, Prime Minister Blair, largely in response to conclusions drawn from the Bosnian crisis with regard to the new state of American interests, announced, in October 1998, a major reorientation of British policy on European defence. An immediate outcome from this dramatic and momentous shift, once French security policy-makers had recovered from the shock, was the Franco-British St Malo summit declaration of the following December. This stated that 'the Union must have the capacity for autonomous action, backed up by credible military forces, the means to decide to use them and a readiness to do so, in order to respond to international crises'.[57] In May 1999, British Foreign Minister Cook expressed the desire that the EU be able to mount its own peacekeeping missions and humanitarian operations without relying on the US.[58] These moves amounted to calls for European autonomy in the conduct of military operations and finally ended the Franco-British contradiction – two countries with fairly symmetrical worldviews and similarly impressive military capabilities but with opposing stances on ESDI. France continued to work closely with Britain, although Howorth pointed to a certain division between the two concerning the WEU's Article V, the collective defence guarantee. For Britain, this was essentially a non-issue given the mutual defence guarantee provisions of NATO's Article 5. But French leaders saw its retention as fundamental to any future European Security and Defence Policy (ESDP) for the Union. However, Howorth noted, the French were largely isolated on this point.[59]

Then the whole Kosovo experience, and particularly the minimal European contribution to the 78-day air campaign and the subsequent ground operation, finally rammed home to west European leaders the limits of the military weight they could collectively bring to bear in any given crisis situation. While Britain, for example, was able to offer 15,000 troops, in July 1999, towards an intervention force, Germany, with the biggest armed forces of any EU member state, could only muster 5,000 (the first occasion since World War Two that German combat troops were actively involved on the ground in a conflict zone). Nevertheless, it can be no coincidence that after this bitter lesson, and with the change of policy in London, that EU leaders subsequently opted, in Helsinki and for the first time, to establish an autonomous European force for crisis management. There was, for Graham, a general conviction that Europe must 'move rapidly to acquire the means to act independently of the US since the EU has increasingly a different set of priorities from that of Washington and may become willing to intervene where the Americans are reluctant'.[60] One tangible product of this new political will was the NATO-endorsed deployment, in spring 2000, of Eurocorps, itself, after the Franco-German joint decision of May 1999, being transformed into a rapid reaction force by its participating countries, to Kosovo as the new operational headquarters for the military side of the allied peace and reconstruction operation. Here, significantly, were EU operational assets being successfully utilised within a NATO mission; this was the first instance of a non-NATO military force taking control of an Alliance operation. This focus on practicalities was repeated in November 2000 with the crucial pledging conference for the RRF. The Union then sought to maintain this new-found momentum. One such effort was associated with the Portuguese Presidency in the first half of 2000 and was a commitment to the establishment of a civilian crisis management capability. The 2001 Swedish Presidency then assumed the baton.

It is too soon to fully evaluate the impact on French strategic objectives of the appointment, in late-1999, in accordance with the 1997 Amsterdam Treaty, of the EU's first High Representative for Security and Foreign Affairs – Javier Solana, former NATO Secretary-General. However, it is unlikely that Solana, or any successor, would simply act as the mouthpiece for French foreign policy. One can speculate that in order for France's European partners to fully commit to an autonomous ESDI within the Union it would have to have impartial leadership, just as the Commission is headed by a President that is unbiased towards any particular member state. And perhaps, importantly for some member states, this appointment mitigates against a Franco-Germano-British domination of this policy field. Nevertheless, the leadership in Paris retains its longstanding objective, since the transferral of ambitions of the 1980s, of forging the EU into not only a regional, but also, ultimately, a global security actor.

Conclusion

This chapter has mapped out France's reaction and adjustment to the new post-Cold War security environment. This response, which initially could be described as faltering, would gain in clarity and firmness of direction. These years have been characterised by an almost unprecedented level of debate on security policy among the political elites and other observers, and yet the *grandes lignes* remained resolutely unaltered. Perhaps this was not surprising given the cultural/historical legacy described in Chapter One. This debate focused on form rather than substance, on tactics rather than on ultimate objectives. After the experiences of the Gulf War and Bosnia, in particular, and given the growing prominence of economic imperatives, France's leaders drew the following conclusions. France now required Europe to help realise its national ambitions and it had to become far more responsive to the vagaries of the now transformed international system. In the mid-1990s, the French leadership came to acknowledge that, for the foreseeable future, ESDI would have to be crafted within the Atlantic Alliance. Chirac thus made not inconsiderable moves towards re-integration into NATO's integrated military structures. Independence, autonomy of action and reliance on French *spécificité* no longer best served French interests; tactics had to be adapted. But then, although largely due to external factors, the ESDI debate moved full circle and the European Union is now seemingly in the process of bestowing itself with a credible and functioning common defence and security policy. An autonomous and functioning ESDP centred on the EU is thus now emerging. France's leaders could only have been delighted at this rapid turn of events. If their EU partners can now deliver in terms of defence expenditure, then it is possible that French desires for European defence initiatives that are not subject to an American veto and run by American diplomacy might be realised. Whitney, for one and in accordance with

French strategic objectives, saw the Helsinki decision concerning a rapid reaction force as an indication that the Union now intends to become 'a strategic player that the United States and other countries will have to reckon with'.[61] But as has been highlighted, this 'progress' cannot be attributed to France as the decisive, dominant actor within the European security structure. Rather, ESDI appears, at the beginning of the twenty-first century, to be adopting the French model largely because of factors outside of French control.

Notes

1 Merchet, Jean-Dominique, 'La défense dépense tous azimuts', *Libération*, 5 June 1996.
2 Valance, Georges (1990), *France-Allemagne: Le Retour de Bismark*, Flammarion, Paris, p.285.
3 Vernet, Daniel, 'The dilemma of French foreign policy', *International Affairs*, vol.68, no.4, Winter 1992-3, p.661.
4 Blunden, Margaret, 'France after the Cold War: inching closer to the Alliance', *Defense Analysis*, vol.9, no.3, 1993, pp.261-2.
5 Joxe, Pierre, in a speech to the Western European Union's Parliamentary Assembly, quoted in *Europe*, no.5744, 5 June 1992.
6 Vernet, Daniel, 'The dilemma of French foreign policy', *op cit*, p.658.
7 Lellouche, Pierre, 'La France et l'OTAN', *Relations Internationales et Stratégiques*, no.7, Autumn 1992, p.97.
8 Patry, Jean-Jacques, 'L'OTAN dans l'oeil du cyclone', *Défense*, no.67, March 1995, p.12.
9 The combined defence budgets of the EU15, at the end of 1996, could only match half of that undertaken by the US; Lagarde, Dominique, 'OTAN: la bataille d'Europe', *L'Express*, 5 December 1996, p.85.
10 Baumel, Jacques, 'La France et l'OTAN', *Relations Internationales et Stratégiques*, no.7, Autumn 1992, p.107.
11 Bozo, Frédéric (1995), 'France and security in the new Europe: between the Gaullist legacy and the search for a new model', in Gregory Flynn (ed), *Remaking the Hexagone: The New France in the New Europe*, Westview Press, Boulder, p.216.
12 Yost, David S., 'France and west European defence identity', *Survival*, vol.33, no.4, July/August 1991, p.333.
13 A view confirmed by the President himself on many occasions. See for example, his televised broadcast on nuclear dissuasion, Elysée Palace, Paris, 5 May 1994.
14 Gregory, Shaun (2000), *French Defence Policy into the Twenty-First Century*, Macmillan, Basingstoke, p.41.
15 Riding, Alan, 'Paris moves to end isolation in NATO', *International Herald Tribune*, 30 September 1992.
16 Lansford, Tom, 'The question of France: French security choices at century's end', *European Security*, vol.5, no.1, Spring 1996, p.47.
17 Freedman, Lawrence (1989), *The Evolution of Nuclear Strategy*, Macmillan/IISS, Basingstoke, p.323.
18 Joxe, Pierre, opening speech at a conference entitled 'A New Strategic Debate', Paris, 29 September 1992.
19 Pfaff, William, quoted in Fontaine, André, 'Diplomatie française: Jacques Chirac et l'ombre du Général', *Politique Internationale*, no.70, Winter 1995-6, p.84.

20 Vernet, Daniel, 'The dilemma of French foreign policy', *op cit*, p.661.

21 Gregory, Shaun, *op cit*, p.69.

22 Bozo, Frédéric, 'La France et l'Alliance: les limites du rapprochement', *Politique Etrangère*, vol.60, no.4, Winter 1995, p.866.

23 Gnesotto, Nicole, 'La défense européenne au carrefour de la Bosnie et de la CIG', *Politique Etrangère*, vol.61, no.1, Spring 1996, p.117.

24 Bozo, Frédéric, 'La France et l'Alliance: les limites du rapprochement', *op cit*, p.874.

25 Woollacott, Martin, 'The great Atlantic drift away', *The Guardian*, 10 February 1995.

26 Quoted by Claire Tréan in 'La relation de la France à l'OTAN n'est pas modifiée, affirme M. Roland Dumas', *Le Monde*, 23 March 1991.

27 Beylau, Pierre, 'La France revient', *Le Point*, 24 September 1994, p.20.

28 Quatremeyer, Jean, editorial in *Libération*, 17 January 1996.

29 Vernet, Daniel, 'L'OTAN fait une place à l'Europe en son sein', *Le Monde*, 4 June 1996.

30 De Montbrial, Thierry, 'French "exception" yes, and it isn't likely to fade away soon', *International Herald Tribune*, 14 September 1995.

31 It should be noted, however, that, in January 1996, France did announce its willingness to discuss nuclear issues within NATO but while retaining full independence with regard to the development, production and use of nuclear weapons.

32 'France increases its participation in the transformation of the Alliance', *NATO Review*, vol.44, no.1, p.16.

33 Frachon, Alain, 'M. Chirac revendique un "partenariat plus égal" entre l'Europe et les Etats-Unis au sein de l'OTAN', *Le Monde*, 2 February 1996. See also, Rhodes, Tom, 'Chirac pushes for more balanced Atlantic alliance', *The Times*, 1 February 1996.

34 Balladur, Edouard, in a speech to the Western European Union's Parliamentary Assembly, quoted in *Atlantic News*, no.2675, 2 December 1994.

35 Lanxade, Jacques, 'French defence policy after the White Paper', *RUSI Journal*, vol.139, no.2, April 1994, p.18.

36 'The defence of Europe: it can't be done alone', *The Economist*, 25 February 1995, p.21.

37 A view likewise supported by Jean-Yves Haine, Maître de Conférences, Centre d'Etudes des Conflits, Paris Institut d'Etudes Politiques, in an interview with the author, Paris, June 1996.

38 In addition to the formal launching of the CJTF, the Berlin summit endorsed commitments to giving substance to the European defence identity within the Alliance, and to structural reform of the Alliance in response to the new global security environment.

39 These summits had, however, not produced a clear division of labour between the Alliance and any concurrent project; hence the European identity was more rhetoric than practice.

40 Quilès, Paul, cited in *Les Echos* (editorial), 17 January 1996.

41 Quilès, Paul, 'Défense européenne et l'OTAN: la dérive', *Le Monde*, 11 June 1996. See also, Desaubliaux, Patrice-Henry, *Figaro*, 6 June 1996.

42 Debezies, Pierre, *op cit*.

43 Védrine, Hubert, former external affairs advisor to François Mitterrand and current French Foreign Minister, in an interview with the author, Paris, July 1996; Messmer, Pierre, *op cit*.

44 See for example, 'A new NATO', *The Economist*, 9 December 1995.

45 De Charette, Hervé, 'A new dialogue between equals', *Time*, 27 January 1997.

46 *Livre Blanc sur la Défense 1994*, Union Générale d'Editions, Paris, 1994, p.67.

47 Moïsi, Dominique, 'De Mitterrand à Chirac', *Politique Étrangère*, vol.60, no.4, Winter 1995, p.855.
48 Beylau, Pierre, 'OTAN: la France revient', *Le Point*, 24 September 1994, p.30.
49 Pfaff, William, 'The ill-grasped logic behind France's "return" to NATO', *International Herald Tribune*, 31 January 1996.
50 Chirac, Jacques, quoted in Frachon, Alain, 'La France peine à imposer sa conception de la sécurité en Europe', *Le Monde*, 4 December 1996.
51 Richard, Alain, quoted in Rosenzweig, Luc, 'Les ministres de la défense de l'OTAN approuvent la réforme des commandements alliés', *Le Monde*, 4 December 1997.
52 Menon, Anand (2000), *France, NATO and the Limits of Independence 1981-97*, Macmillan, Basingstoke, 2000, p.85.
53 Richard, Alain, in a radio interview, quoted in, Desaubliaux, Patrice-Henry, 'Le test de la défense', *Le Figaro*, 10 July 1997.
54 Isnard, Jacques, 'Solitaire mais solidaire', *Le Monde*, 4 December 1997.
55 Vernet, Daniel, 'La France toujours à la recherche d'un arrangement avec l'OTAN', *Le Monde*, 2 December 1997.
56 Gnesotto, Nicole, 'CFSP and defence: how does it work?', Western European Union Institute for Security Studies Newsletter, no.30, July 2000.
57 Franco-British Joint Declaration on European Defence, St-Malo, 3-4 December 1998.
58 Parker, George, 'Europe: Minister to urge less reliance on US forces', *The Financial Times*, 13 May 1999.
59 Howorth, Jolyon, 'Britain, France and the European Defence Initiative', *Survival*, vol.42, no.2, Summer 2000, p.42.
60 Graham, Robert, 'Defence: pledge on European capability', *The Financial Times*, 31 May 1999.
61 Whitney, Craig R., 'Military posture of Europe to turn more independent', *The New York Times*, 13 December 1999.

Chapter 6

The Armed Forces: Nuclear and Conventional Adjustments

Hitherto, this volume has largely ignored the impact on the military of the various tactical shifts in French security policy. And yet the armed forces have constituted the principal instrument by which the strategic objectives of rank and *grandeur* have been pursued. This chapter thus starts off by examining the origins and rationale behind the nuclear weapons programme. The priority given to the latter, combined with the decolonisation process, served to downplay the emphasis placed on France's conventional forces. As a result, they were subjected to decades of neglect and under-funding; as graphically illustrated in the Kuwaiti and Iraqi desert in early 1991. The new geostrategic order emerging out of the Cold War prompted a radical reappraisal of the utility of conventional forces. And even during the 1980s, budgetary pressures were requiring a major rethink about the traditional unilateral, autonomous approach to the conduct of military operations and the development and manufacture of military equipment. The inherent retention by the policy-makers in Paris of the *grandes lignes* in to the 1990s in the face of economic realities then appeared as something of a contradiction. But rather than comprising on the claimed global vocation, these financial exigencies have led to an overt policy of military-industrial and military-operational cooperation and coordination with France's west European partners. In addition, France is over halfway through a process inaugurated by President Chirac that is abandoning conscription and replacing it with fully professional armed forces that are better disposed to fulfilling the strategic goals. All these measures, the thrust of which, with minor reservations over the form they should take, have been largely backed by successive centre-right and left-wing governments, have been introduced in order that French leaders will still be in a position in the new century to claim, even through the guise of some European construction, *rang* and *grandeur*.

Nuclear Priorities and Conventional Sacrifice

One practical result of de Gaulle's conclusions, outlined in Chapter Two, about French national interests within the 'Cold War game' was the acceleration of the national nuclear programme. The reality was that all forms of force other than the nuclear would be so constrained by international restrictions that subordination to the US in the foreign and defence field, thereby leading to political subservience, would be inevitable. From this perspective, the French had thus to carve for themselves a nuclear niche out of the bipolar superpower rivalry in order to derive maximum political and military leverage, thereby keeping France on the top rungs of global power. Moreover, as Davidson put it, it was to become an article of faith that, as a nuclear power, France could not share or subordinate the ultimate decisions of life and death.[1] In this way, de Gaulle refused Kennedy's offer of a Polaris nuclear missile system, in the early 1960s, because he believed that the conditions attached to the offer would compromise French interests. The offer would have been gladly accepted had it been unconditional.[2] Moreover, according to Lawrence Freedman, de Gaulle was to come to perceive the American nuclear guarantee as 'a flimsy foundation for security, much inferior to a national effort'.[3] The need to defend the national territory was paramount. De Gaulle's was the only national leadership to talk of nuclear *sanctuarisation*.

Thus, throughout the 1960s, the French nuclear deterrent was an existential one, although France's existence was never in question. However, de Gaulle had to ensure that French interests would continue to be promoted to their maximum extent. Thus, according to Gordon, he would 'endow France with a powerful and invulnerable nuclear force that would make it possible for his successors – if warranted by events – not to follow quietly the policies of their protector, the United States'.[4] This stance deliberately fostered a general ambiguity about the potential targets for the *force de frappe*. And this was exacerbated by the widely discussed, although never adopted, *tous azimuts* strategic doctrine promoted by General Ailleret at the end of the 1960s. This proposal would have had France's nuclear missiles being targeted anywhere around the globe, and not just at central and eastern Europe.

There was a sense, as Gregory observes, that the past humiliations of 1914 and 1918, when France had been technically exposed, made it crucially important that France now be at the forefront of any technological and tactical advances such as nuclear weapons.[5] But, the nuclear deterrent made greater sense if seen as the ultimate political symbol and instrument of national independence from America and of global standing rather than as a military weapon directed at the USSR. Militarily, the French nuclear deterrent was not yet credible. The military only attained the ability to deliver a nuclear device in 1964 with the entry into service of the first Mirage IV aircraft, while the land and submarine-based elements of the nuclear deterrent would not become operational until the 1970s. The French nuclear component did not, hence, comprise any serious part of collective Western defence planning at this time. Nevertheless, for the leaders of the Fourth Republic, atomic weapons had been commissioned to act as support for the policy of promoting independence and boosting prestige, but within the existing framework of the Atlantic Alliance. De Gaulle, however, used the so-called *force de frappe* as an instrument for the pursuit of wider foreign policy objectives. For him, the diplomatic significance of an independent nuclear capacity outweighed any strategic importance. It was an ideal mechanism by which France could reassert its distinctive identity and demonstrate to the world its determination to regain the Great Power status lost as a result of power politics. It was used to limit the psychological damage caused by relative national decline. A France equipped with nuclear weapons would be in a position to free itself from the fear resulting from successive military defeats and would once again be in a position to take its destiny into its own hands. And de Gaulle was able to nurture a form of national mind-set that made a direct correlation between a nuclear weapons capability and permanent membership of the UNSC. In de Gaulle's own words, a Great State that does not possess nuclear weapons while others have them 'does not command its own destiny'.[6] In theory at least, this simply was not an option for France.

The combination of the nuclear arsenal, and the constraints placed on Germany, allowed France, in the words of de Gaulle, 'to ride first-class on a second-class ticket', or to punch above its weight, given its actual resources.[7] The General's successors were to share the view that the price, a considerable proportion of the defence budget diverted to the nuclear weapons programme to the detriment of conventional forces (which increasingly were to play a support role), was worth paying. As a result of the confidence in the protective shield provided by the nuclear forces and because of budgetary constraints, French conventional forces would progressively and sharply be reduced in size and strength in the years following the withdrawal from Algeria. Equally, the supply of modern conventional equipment to these forces would suffer. Writing in 1963, Raymond Aron, himself a supporter of strong national defence, decried the nuclear programme for the funds and resources it drained away from the attainment of just the minimum conventional force levels and from non-military scientific research.[8]

Despite these reservations, the retention and expansion of the autonomous nuclear weapons programme begun back in 1954 represented a central element of the perpetuation of the *grandes lignes* of security policy via the tactical choice of non-dependence. And the 'conversion' of the Communist and Socialist parties at the end of the 1970s had meant that all the major political parties supported the national nuclear deterrent as the ultimate guarantee of France's elevated global rank through independence of defence. This correspondingly left virtually no political space for the expression of opposition to French nuclear policy. The Left now deferred to its strong tradition of defending of *la patrie* that dated back to the aggressive patriotism of the Revolutionary era. Hence, the Socialists subordinated their rhetoric promoting disarmament as an aim in itself to the desire to maintain France as a great power. And this could partly be justified because they defined the nuclear deterrent as a tool to prevent war breaking out as opposed to being a tool for fighting wars.

The French leadership, like their British counterparts, refused to participate in the Superpower nuclear disarmament negotiations. Mitterrand, as President in 1987, went as far as to say that France would never reduce its nuclear capacity so long as a threat to French security remained.[9] Moreover, he pointed to the almost insignificant size of the French arsenal when compared to those of the two nuclear giants. The fear in Paris was of a bilateral Soviet-American arms limitation agreement that would legislate the French *force de frappe* into insignificance. This determination also translated itself, during the 1980s, to the need to counter the potential of the west European anti-nuclear movement. Furthermore, this meant the denial that pacifism and disarmament were necessarily the best means to ensure peace and security.[10]

For Mitterrand, the primacy of strategic nuclear deterrence was not open to discussion. He stated that French national security was centred on the nuclear capacity, and that to do away with the latter would be to leave France bereft of any army at all. And he pointed to 20 years of history, describing the *force de frappe* as '*une réalité, un prestige, un atout pour notre rayonnement'.*[a] And in November 1983 he stated on national television that he was the key element in France's nuclear deterrent: *'La pièce maîtresse de la stratégie de dissuasion en France, c'est le chef de l'Etat, c'est moi; tout dépend de sa détermination'.*[b] He then added that he was prepared to 'push the button' should it be necessary.[11] Nuclear weapons had by now become associated with national independence and security against another world war and, more broadly, with de Gaulle's successful efforts to restore France's honour and international status. Mitterrand also spoke of the anomalies surrounding the nuclear deterrent, saying it 'was made to protect national territory and to defend vital interests which are not defined in advance but whose interpretation depends on the head of state'.[12] But the 1980s did see an evolution of French nuclear strategy away from the isolationist defence of the national sanctuary. Mitterrand declared, in May 1986, the French strategic nuclear force to be an important contribution to NATO's deterrent capability.[13]

Giscard, as President, had already taken the lead in this respect by distancing himself from de Gaulle's nuclear policy in the purest sense. France, in the new thinking, could not continue to define sanctuary solely in terms of the national territory and it could not stand aside from an eventual battle in Germany. The 'two battles' strategic concept was replaced with the notion of the 'enlarged sanctuary'. He thereby broadened France's security interests to embrace its immediate neighbours and the Mediterranean basin. Thereafter, strategic defence thinking would focus on three circles. The first encompassed the Hexagon; the second took in the area around France, this particularly implied a stronger commitment to the defence of West Germany; and the third incorporated France's allies and its overseas *départements* and *territoires*. While it was clear that the first circle would have the automatic protection of the *force de frappe*, an aggressor encroaching on the outer two circles would not know when a French nuclear response would be triggered. For some observers at least, France's tactical nuclear capacity were now considered part of the battlefield armoury, rather than as the instrument for a warning shot prior to the launch of the nuclear arsenal's strategic component;[14] although this distinction was far from clear.

Giscard's administrative team challenged the hitherto dominance of the 'all or nothing' nuclear policy, arguing that a broader spectrum of military options would allow for greater flexibility of response. To this end he instigated the reform of the army to enable it to be suited to fighting alongside the forces of France's NATO allies on the plains of central Europe and he ordered a general strengthening of the country's conventional capability. This significant shift of French strategic doctrine prompted considerable controversy, not least among the Gaullist and Socialist parties, because it implied bringing France closer to reintegration with NATO's integrated military structure. Perhaps under the force of this mounting political pressure, the emphasis on the 'enlarged sanctuary' was downplayed after 1977. Significantly, in Ottawa in 1974, a NATO document, the *Declaration of Atlantic Relations*, stated that the French and

---

[a]   'a reality, an object of prestige, an asset for our emanating influence'.

[b]   'The main element of France's strategy of dissuasion is the head of state, and that's me; everything depends on his determination'.

British nuclear forces were contributing to an overall strengthening of the Alliance's deterrence capability.

As the Fifth Republic's first Socialist President, Mitterrand might have been expected to question France's retention of a nuclear capability. Such thoughts were quickly dispelled. Within days of taking office, he had announced that the ongoing nuclear test programme would be allowed to continue. In addition, a seventh nuclear-armed submarine, postponed by Giscard, was commissioned and Soviet attempts to incorporate the French deterrent into the superpower disarmament process were repeatedly resisted. Next, the new President proclaimed his wholehearted support, in the face of the Soviet refusal to withdraw the newly-deployed SS20 nuclear missiles from eastern Europe, for NATO's decision to deploy Pershing II and Cruise nuclear missiles in western Europe. But clearly, this did not extend to the Hexagon itself.

There was also a growing acceptance in Paris that some form of consultation should be promised to Bonn prior to the use of nuclear weapons on German soil in times of crisis; although there was to be no concession with regard to the French President retaining the final decision.[15] By no means was this a sign of French willingness to share the definition of targets or of the conditions for use. Yet, French leaders were feeling increasingly uncomfortable in justifying the continued deployment of *Hadès* nuclear missiles on the Plateau d'Albion (in central France). The limited range of these missiles meant that, if fired, they could only impact on German soil. In fact, this new conciliatory French position only brought it in line with those taken by the US and Britain towards West Germany 20 years earlier. But, as with Giscard, there were adjustments to national strategic doctrine. Tactical nuclear weapons were redefined as 'pre-strategic' and these were directly linked to the strategic component, thereby, so the reasoning went, placing greater emphasis on France's determination to avail itself of the latter and thus rendering the national deterrent more credible. At the same time, conventional forces were cut by some 30,000 troops so as to finance the enhancement of the strategic arsenal.

The end of the Cold War did not herald a serious and public debate on the continued utility of the *force de frappe*. Retention seemed almost instinctively obvious to France's security and defence policy-makers. As Gregory notes, those looking to justify continuity had no shortage of threats to put forward, such as: the unpredictability of Russia's domestic situation, possible further proliferation around the world, and the political leverage nuclear weapons accord.[16] This said, it should be noted that nuclear spending had actually begun to fall in 1988. Over the ensuing few years, the proportion of the defence budget being diverted to the nuclear component fell below 16 per cent, although the modernisation programme did not appear to be hampered.

Regarding the europeanisation of France's nuclear capacity, namely the participation of France in some form of European deterrent, it seems that some discussions were held with the British in the mid to late 1980s but only produced agreement on low-level bilateral cooperation. The French negotiators clearly were unable to assuage British concerns about preserving and protecting the transatlantic alliance, or more specifically the American commitment to European security. Then, in the spirit of the newly signed Treaty of European Union at Maastricht, Mitterrand began 1992 claiming the European nuclear deterrent would constitute a key element of a future joint European defence. Perhaps, this could be interpreted as an attempt to claim a continued justification for a traditional and fundamental part of France's defence, the utility of which had now come into question, by placing it in a west European context. Mitterrand's initiative was swiftly followed by a proposal from Defence Minister Joxe that the British and French nuclear capacities be combined in the name of European cooperation.[17] Although a European nuclear deterrent did not emerge, the British and the French had, by July 1993, established a permanent Joint Commission on Nuclear Policy and Doctrine. As discussed in Chapter Five, further French efforts were then seriously impeded in 1997 by the furore among France's west European partners as a result of *force de frappe* testing in the Pacific and the claims that this was on behalf of 'Europe'.

Economic Constraints and Greater Military Cooperation with Allies

By 1988, the French economy was under severe pressure and was being subjected to serious attempts at *rigeur* by the government. This clearly had implications for defence spending. The instinctive adherence to the *grandes lignes* was creating a growing set of problems. The *force de frappe* was still being prioritised, but this now required an enormous effort to keep pace with the global modernisation and expansion of nuclear arsenals. Concurrently, demands on other aspects of France's military capacity, namely retaining the ability to project force around the world, were rising dramatically. Yet, French leaders, unlike their Western partners, made little attempt to reap a 'peace dividend' in the first years following the end of the Cold War. To this end, the defence budget retained its elevated levels. While defence expenditure in Britain, Germany and the US fell by 17-21 per cent between 1985 and 1994, the figure for France actually rose by two per cent, although the rate of increase was being deliberately slowed down. In 1994, 3.3 per cent of France's GDP went on defence, compared to a NATO average of 2.5 per cent.[18] In 1996, France had the highest defence budget in Europe, standing at some 190 billion francs.[19] French policy-makers, it seems, were late in acknowledging the dominant role of the economy in security policy, holding on to the view that power came with diplomatic and military might. Former-Defence Minister Jean-Pierre Chevènement got close to the truth when he observed that, '*[a]ujourd'hui, c'est la direction du Budget qui fait la politique de défense de la France*'.[c][20] For better or worse, the planners were slow, or reluctant, to develop anything resembling a political culture driven by the markets, as opposed to notions of *rang* and *grandeur*.

As a result, France was the last Western state to draw the budgetary consequences of the collapse of the Soviet empire and the end of the Cold War.[21] Mitterrand's instinct in those first post-Cold War years was to postpone major decisions and to persist with costly, and possibly anachronistic, procurement schemes. Gregory also points us towards the domestic political situation at this time. Neither of the main political groupings vying for the imminent Presidential vacancy, to be contested in

---

[c]   'Today, it is the supervision of the Budget which makes French defence policy'.

1995, was prepared to commit itself to the necessary defence expenditure cuts for fear of being associated with the negative on employment that would ensue.[22] Eventually however, France's deteriorating position within the global market of the 1990s led first to a further slow-down in the defence budget increases, begun in the late 1980s, and then to actual defence cuts. In 1996, for example, the ongoing six-year defence programme was scrapped and replaced by a slimmed down version for 1997-2000 in which 8.4 billion francs were withdrawn. Subsequent years would each receive some 15 billion francs less than originally envisaged.[23] Indeed, 1997 was due to see the lowest proportion of GDP spent on defence since World War Two, 2.9 per cent (1996's comparative figures for the US, Britain and Germany stood at 3.7, 3.0 and 1.7 respectively).[24]

By the 1990s, France had achieved a level of self-reliance in defence manufacture of nearly 96 per cent (second only to the US among NATO members).[25] In the words of then Prime Minister Cresson, *'[i]l n'a pas de système de défense solide qui ne soit fondé sur de véritables capacités industrielles'.*[d] [26] Yet, this nationalist approach to defence procurement, which had sheltered French defence manufacturers, predominantly part of the public sector, from the exigencies of the competitive global market, such as the need to reduce costs, was now clearly producing negative results. France had been steadily producing armed forces brimming with prototypes and samples, rather than ones equipped with material of the highest quality or the best value for money compared to alternatives in the international market. France's fighting forces were, according to Yves-Marie Laulan, acting as an arms shop. Some of that on view in the shop window, principally equipment associated with the nuclear deterrent, looked impressive, but out the back the stock (such as the Crusader and Jaguar aircraft and the AMX 30 tank) looked worn and out-dated.[27] Moreover, the incompatibility of much of France's equipment with that of its allies in the Gulf War and French unfamiliarity with many of the procedures used contributed to the French military being consigned to a marginal role in the conflict. Meanwhile, the hitherto all-powerful defence lobby was losing its clout, being progressively weakened by market forces. The defence sector was being squeezed by lower post-Cold War orders, both domestically and from abroad, and by the Government's imperative to combat the budget deficit.

This squeeze was accentuated as successive governments strove to meet the EU's Maastricht convergence criteria for economic and monetary union (EMU). The latter came to increasingly dominate policy decisions. And EMU was all the more vital because the Paris political elites hoped that it would act as a shield against the impact of the globalisation of the market, against which the French franc, on its own, would, given its volatility, be extremely vulnerable. Noises emanating from Paris appeared to hint that the combination of the EU's budget deficit requirements (for EMU) and a reappraisal of the security environment implied the abandonment of certain joint military projects. To this end, the National Assembly approved a new defence expenditure ceiling for 1997-2002 which envisaged 30 per cent savings in defence procurement. The news was not particularly well received in Germany, having only

---

[d]   'A defence system not founded on a strong industrial base is not solid'.

agreed with France at the end of 1996 to harmonise the respective armaments programmes.[28] It should be noted at this point, however, that no French government in the Fifth Republic had hitherto managed to fully honour any parliamentary-approved military spending plans.[29] The new Socialist Government then stuck closely to the 1997-2002 spending plan. In the event, defence spending, excluding salaries, fell by eight per cent between 1997 and the 2000 budget; the country now spends less than two per cent of GDP on defence.[30]

Meanwhile, the exponentially rising cost of military technology was putting certain conventional and non-conventional equipment beyond the financial means of middle range powers like France, and this was also the case with command, control and information systems. A country like France, with a general political consensus behind the determination to base security policy on global *rang* and *grandeur*, could not be allowed to be left behind and marginalised in terms of military capability. Cooperation with partners was thus the only solution. This was especially the case with space technology. The policy-makers in Paris had determined that France, or Europe, should be bestowed with its own satellite intelligence capacity rather than relying on information supplied by the Americans. This was to be a new tool by which the French could claim an elevated global *rang* and perpetuate national *grandeur*. But for this, the financial support of partners was required. In the meantime, the expansion of the Atlantic Alliance eastward through its Partnership for Peace programme, with the prospect for some of these central and east European countries of full NATO membership, offered the opportunity to partially arrest this decline. NATO's new partners were now expected to ultimately acquire NATO-compatible electronic, communication and general military equipment. French industry would be in a more advantageous position to exploit this new potential market if the political leadership were to move France closer to the Alliance's permanent structures.

All these elements combined to greatly reduce the scope for de Gaulle-style political manoeuvring. And it was clear that the threats present in the new security environment required greater flexibility of response capabilities. Greater effort was thus put into promoting coordination and interoperability. As previous chapters have shown, if French security was to continue to be based on *rang* and *grandeur* it would have to turn to partners in the international system for help. As a result, French planners began active, but selective, cooperation with west European allies on several fronts. This translated itself into joint military exercises (for example, between the FAR and the British Field Army), cooperation on equipment development and the greater fusion of strategy. And this was enacted on a bilateral basis between national defence staffs. The Chief of Staff of the French Navy hence announced in April 1992 the creation of a temporary Franco-German naval force based in the Mediterranean. And the May 1994 launch for sea trials of the new nuclear-powered aircraft carrier *Charles de Gaulle* was heralded by President Mitterrand as a symbol that France intended to assure its place in a future European navy.[31] In 1995, France joined Portugal, Spain and Italy on the development of Euromarfor, a Mediterranean naval squadron, and Eurofor, a rapid-reaction ground force of up to 9,000 troops. The relevant documents signed by the participating countries referred to the aim of giving Europe its own military capacity. Both forces were thus declared 'forces available to the WEU' and as being at the disposal of the European pillar of NATO. Germany then agreed to partially fund the French spy satellite *Hélios*-1B. Although this commitment appeared less than certain by the end of 1997. In the end, the satellite was launched in December 1999. Some financial support had come from Italy and Spain, but the German Government had pulled out by this time.

Meanwhile, the governments in Paris and London had been converging their defence outlooks, a trend accentuated by their joint experiences in former-Yugoslavia. At the Chartres joint summit, in November 1994, the creation of a Franco-British Euro-Air Group was announced. This has subsequently been expanded to include Italy; with Belgium, Germany, the Netherlands and Spain also due to join. Meanwhile, the British Field Army and the French FAR drafted a partnership agreement, which included joint training and exercises. There was also the launch of the joint development of a transport plane, an attack helicopter, a transport helicopter, armoured vehicles, a frigate, an air defence system and an observation satellite. And the two countries held discussions regarding the pooling of resources to create a new navy for Europe. There already existed a relatively high degree of inter-operability between British and French maritime forces. In addition, there was talk of joint patrols and targeting by the two sets of nuclear-armed submarines. Furthermore, nuclear cooperation between the two countries had been steadily deepening over the years, principally through the Franco-British Joint Nuclear Commission. This was exemplified in October 1995 by the joint declaration that each country would be willing to use nuclear weapons to defend the 'vital interests' of the other.[32] And the French were joined by Britain and Germany in developing, independently of NATO, a joint arms procurement agency to coordinate government purchases, research and development and standardisation.

Similar developments were taking place in the French industrial sector. Prime Minister Balladur recognised the emerging nature of the global economy:

> [f]ar-reaching moves to bring about alliances and groupings of firms at European level are needed to give French and European industry the capacity to tackle increasingly fierce international competition, at a time when defence budgets are in recession all over the world. ... In many spheres the development of our skills and competitiveness will necessitate ambitious international cooperation, especially between Europeans.[33]

A long overdue restructuring of a heavily protected armaments industry based on State-aid was announced in early 1996. But this initiative lagged significantly behind similar moves by France's Western partners. For President Chirac, 'the State today no longer has any place in the management of competitive industries ... our big companies cannot live without alliances ... and modern countries cannot imagine their private companies teaming up with public companies subject to considerations that have nothing to do with the market'.[34] Particularly noteworthy was the proposed merger of the Dassault and Aérospatiale defence concerns and the privatisation of the Thomson CSF defence electronics group. One further intended outcome of this and other rationalisations was that they would serve as the foundations for larger, European, 'federations' that, not least, would be in a position to offer real competition to their American counterparts. But it was evident to most observers that these European ambitions were designed, partly at least, to foster French leadership in this field, and even to access wider funding for national projects that the government could no longer afford to bank-roll alone.[35]

However, these moves, like those concerning NATO, were stalled by the Socialists' Legislative victory in June 1997. The new government initially gave no clear signal about its intentions for the defence sector, restricted as it was by its commitment to the maintenance of the public sector. In response, François Fillon, RPR Deputy and specialist on defence matters, urged that France's defence manufacturers not be condemned to the global second division by remaining outside of pan-European alliances.[36] But the Socialists did accept the logic of a further reining-in of the defence budget. Defence Minister Richard, for example, ordered a review (which was completed by the beginning of 1998) of all armaments programmes with a view to both financial efficiency, given the constraining economic situation, and practical utility, given the transformation of the global security environment. Almost for the first time, there was a public preparedness to terminate, if necessary, entire equipment programmes. Orders for Dassault's troubled and seriously overdue Rafale fighter aircraft have, for example, been cut back. It seems likely that this project will constitute the last instance when a French government unilaterally embarks on a major equipment initiative when there is a viable multilateral European alternative. In addition, Richard did cut the allocation for new equipment by eight per cent. Meanwhile, regarding Thomson-CSF, full privatisation was rejected, but the state's stake was cut to 40 per cent. For the Socialists, this partial privatisation was, rather, 'an opening of capital'.[37] Domestic consolidation had already been boosted, in late 1998, when Aerospatiale acquired a 46 per cent share in the family run Dassault Aviation.

One indication of this new-found pragmatism came in early 1998 with a joint Franco-German-British appeal for consolidation in Europe's aerospace and defence industries. To this end, Jospin's administration, which had gradually been marginalising President Chirac's role in defence policy-making, cut the public stake in Aerospatiale in July 1998. The latter then, later that year, began the merger process with Matra, the defence arm of the privately-owned Largardère. But there was disappointment among the French leadership when, in January 1999, British Aerospace (BAe) began talks to buy Marconi from GEC (another British company) over a deal with Germany's DASA (DaimlerChrysler Aerospace). The British appeared to be pursuing domestic, rather than European, integration. Nevertheless, multinational negotiations did finally produce, in October 1999, the long-sought European Aeronautic, Defence and Space Company (EADS), comprising a merger between Matra-Aerospatiale (in which the French State retained a 44 per cent golden share) and DASA (which itself was in the process of absorbing Spain's CASA). In a move unthinkable to French leaders even five years earlier, 40 per cent of this new venture was to be floated. Defence industries had virtually been the French State's last frontier against the logic of the market and global capitalism. For better or worse, here, as in other tactical shifts, one can point to the ongoing normalisation of French security and defence policy.

Elsewhere, in early 1999, France's Giat undertook a joint venture with Britain's Vickers to produce armoured vehicles. Thomson-CSF, meanwhile, is linking up with

Britain's Racal. And BAe and Matra now have a joint missile development project. But the consolidation of Europe's defence industries has not all been a story of success. In April 1999, officials in Paris were dismayed when the British Government announced its withdrawal from the Horizon frigate project (a tri-nation enterprise involving Britain, France and Italy). Tony Blair would redeem himself in this respect, in May 2000, with the awarding of two key defence contracts to European, as opposed to American, consortia – Matra-BAe's Meteor missile and 25 of Airbus' A400M transporter aircraft. And the change of policy in France regarding public ownership of strategically sensitive businesses has been further illustrated with the decision, finally, to transform Airbus Industries from a consortium into a fully-fledged company. And the French were also, in July 2000, one of six countries (along with Britain, Germany, Italy, Spain and Sweden) to sign a treaty that implements the Letter of Intent agreed two years earlier. This lay down the framework for common rules governing closer defence cooperation. The activities covered by the agreement were security of supply, export restrictions, security of information, research and technology and the harmonisation of military requirements. It was designed to make it easier for armaments companies in different countries to work together.

Evolving Strategic Priorities and the Overhaul of Conventional Forces

As these economic constraints were increasingly dominating policy decisions, the fundamental requirement to redress the balance in French defence policy in favour of conventional forces was being widely acknowledged. For former Prime-Minister Pierre Messmer, '*[l]es nombreux conflits extérieurs, qui offensent les Droits de l'homme et menacent la paix du monde se multiplient. Les interventions qu'ils appellent, lorsqu'on les décide, réclament des moyens non nucléaires dont nous ne disposons pas*'.[e] [38] The progressive down-grading of its conventional forces during the Cold War years, and the reliance on the symbolism of the nuclear deterrent, had meant that by the 1990s France was not even in a position to prevail alone in a conventional conflict against a regional power like Iraq or Syria.[39] Essentially, with the demise in status of the nuclear deterrent, France now lacked the military capability to back up its pretensions to a world role in the new security environment. According to Touraine, '*ce n'est pas d'un outil politique dont nous avons le plus besoin, mais d'une capacité d'intervention concrète*'.[f] [40] To rectify this alarming situation, it had become patently clear that France's leaders had to make a tactical shift and seriously augment the country's conventional capability. But some observers like Yves-Marie Laulan argued that this decision was simply not taken. Rather, Laulan claimed, the French persisted '*á poursuivre des missions dévolues á une puissance á vocation mondiale avec les*

---

[e]   'The number of conflicts abroad which offend human rights and threaten world peace is increasing. When we agree to the interventions which they require, we will not have the non-nuclear capability which they demand'.

[f]   'It is not a political instrument that we need, but a real intervention capacity'.

moyens, les ressources, l'effort de défense correspondant á celles d'une puissance régionale'.[g] [41]

But there were finally moves to remedy the deficiencies in the conventional forces which had been known for some time and which were highlighted by the *Desert Storm* operation. To this end, several measures were instigated. First, the military command structure was redesigned to facilitate force projection. Second, the proportion of defence expenditure dedicated to the nuclear capability was cut further, to about a fifth of the total budget. During 1992 and 1993, the mobile S-45 missile was cancelled, production of the *Hadès* missile was frozen, two Pluton regiments were disbanded and not replaced, the production schedule for the new generation nuclear submarine was put-back and the government announced a one-year moratorium on nuclear testing in the Pacific Ocean. And third, the upgrading of the intelligence gathering capacity was made a top priority.[42] Equally, the limitations imposed on French participation in *Desert Storm* had reopened the debate concerning conscription. French law prohibited conscripts, though not volunteers, from being deployed in conflicts abroad (volunteers had to join the Foreign Legion, the Paratroops or the naval infantry). At the same time, it was being acknowledged that participation in NATO operations and exercises could provide French forces the experience they lacked with regard to training and expertise in the command and control of large-scale integrated battlefield scenarios.

With the internal debate in full swing, the 1994 *Livre Blanc* on defence highlighted France's key strategic interests. On the one hand it stressed the maintenance of peace across the European continent and its bordering regions, particularly the Mediterranean basin (French policy had consistently been placing greater emphasis on the security threats emanating from the other side of the Mediterranean) and the Middle East. On the other, emphasis was placed on ensuring the peace in, and freedom of access to areas of direct economic significance to France (principally maritime routes).[43] The oil-rich nations of the Middle East provided one such example. The nature of the threats to national security may have changed and diversified, but there was no suggestion that they had diminished. For then Prime Minister Balladur, in a forward to the:

> *Livre Blanc, '[l]a défense de la France ne se joue plus immédiatement á ses frontières. Elle dépend du maintien de la stabilité internationale, de la prévention de crises, en Europe ou hors d'Europe, qui, dégénérant, mettraient en péril nos intérêts et notre sécurité'.*[h] [44]

The *Livre Blanc* continued:

> *[a]u-delà de ces intérêts qui répondent directement á une logique de sécurité, la France a des **intérêts** qui correspondent á ses responsabilités internationales et á son **rang** dans*

---

[g]   'to undertake missions suited to a power with a global vocation with the means, resources and defensive effort associated to a regional power'.

[h]   'The defence of France no longer rests at its frontiers. It relies on crisis prevention and the maintenance of international stability, within or outside Europe; the deterioration of which threatens our interests and security'.

le monde. Ses responsabilités internationales résultent de ses obligations de membre permanent du Conseil de Sécurité, de son histoire, de sa vocation particulière.[i] [45]

The role of the army in the 1990s was thus split into three main constituents: first, to guarantee the integrity of the national territory; second, to participate in the security of Europe; and third, to conduct out-of-Europe operations either in protection of the DOM-TOMs, or under the aegis of the UN, or to secure vital lines of communication or to honour defence agreements with France's partners in sub-Saharan Africa.[46] The French thus maintained the global presence of permanent forces abroad: primarily in the Antilles (5000 personnel), French Guiana (3600), the Indian Ocean (La Réunion and Mayotte, 4000), New Caledonia (3900), Polynesia (3800), Central African Republic (1300), Chad, Côte D'Ivoire, Djibouti (3900), Gabon and Senegal (1500). In addition, there were permanent naval squadrons in the Indian Ocean and the Pacific Ocean.

It became clear that, for a country wishing a global role for itself, real armed intervention was set to be the main activity of the armed forces in the future. Moreover, the new vogue for multilateralism, heralded by *Desert Shield/Storm*, meant that elevated international standing depended on a country's ability to contribute to multinational operations on behalf of the world community. This was part of the motivation behind the emotive reappraisal of several of the basic tenets of French strategic posture. Hence, people started to question the validity of conscription, the appropriateness of command structures, the adequacy of logistics, the nature of relations with France's allies, even the relevance of nuclear doctrine.[47] Certainly, the traditional political consensus was split. One group was calling for an across-the-board cut in the defence budget, another clung to the nuclear deterrent as the major priority, while a third group pushed for greater emphasis on the capacity for conventional intervention abroad at the expense of the nuclear programme.[48]

In the face of this debate, successive national governments remained fixed in their determination not to lessen any global commitments and to retain as many capabilities as possible despite a reduction in capabilities and in the overall size of the armed forces (it was envisaged that the armed forces would number some 580,000 personnel by the turn of the century).[49] By doing so they avoided any controversial decisions. Moreover, this retention of a global military and diplomatic presence helped to disguise and compensate for *la patrie*'s lack of resources. This was one way to promote the illusion that France was indeed a great power. Furthermore, by the early 1990s, the proportion of the defence budget being diverted to the nuclear programme had fallen to around 18-20 per cent, from a figure of 25 per cent in the 1970s and 1980s. But the relatively high proportion of defence expenditure now being targeted at conventional forces created something of a false impression. First, the *force de frappe* was reaching maturity and thus had less need for research and development. Second, military downsizing had costs of its own. For example, the 1992 defence budget

---

[i] 'Beyond those interests linked directly to conventional security, France has interests linked to its international responsibilities and its world rank. Its international responsibilities come from its obligations as permanent member of the Security Council, from its history and its particular vocation'.

totalled some 245 billion francs. However, some 40 billion francs of this total was absorbed by the financing of the early retirement programme. And third, the high cost of the nationalist defence procurement policy which has already been noted.

The military shortcomings highlighted during France's role in the second Gulf War (when France struggled to deploy a force of 12,000), ever greater budgetary constraints and the realisation that participation in multinational intervention operations overseas would constitute the principal activity for the armed forces for the foreseeable future were major motivations behind the military reforms announced by Chirac and the Juppé Government in February 1996. One emphasis was on *forces projetables*, while another rested on reform of military service (the latter is discussed below). Hence the major military mission was to be a lean professional force with advanced weapons ready for rapid deployment around the world. For Lagarde, *'la professionalisation de l'armée française est directement liée à la nouvelle donne stratégique en Europe et au rôle qu'entend jouer la France dans l'Otan'.*[j] [50] The apparent gaullist doctrine that no expenditure was too great to safeguard French military independence finally appeared to have been publicly abandoned. For Chirac:

> [l]a France doit être capable de projeter dans des délais très courts, partout dans le monde où la situation pourrait l'exiger, une force significative pour que son point de vue et ses intérêts soient pris en considération dans la gestion de la crise et dans tous les aspects de son règlement définitif.[k] [51]

The significance of the downsizing and professionalisation of the armed forces was not lost on Jacques Isnard. For him, this implied that France's security policy planners no longer envisaged France acting alone in military operations of any particular size or duration.[52]

In practical terms, these reforms would require a further cutting of the armed forces from 500,000 to 350,000 personnel, with ground forces being virtually halved. The land army was due to be cut between 1997 and 2002 from 240,000 to a strength of 140,000, losing in the process around a third of its regiments. Air force and navy personnel were both due to be downsized by about 20 per cent. Equally, the number of air force fighters was to fall from 400 to 300 and the navy's blue water fleet of 100 warships and support vessels is to be trimmed to 80 by 2002. And yet this down-sizing process now sits somewhat uncomfortably with the policy, long-awaited among the French political elite, presently being pursued by the EU of forging a credible and autonomous military capacity. For anything beyond the simplest of Petersberg tasks, EU members, France included, will have to halt the trend of falling defence expenditure. Certainly, the vision, held by many, of a standing, self-supporting, European army with its own satellite, communication and deployment capacity (as

---

[j]   'the professionalisation of the French army is linked directly to the new strategic
      situation in Europe and to the role France intends to play in NATO'.
[k]   'France has to be capable of projecting, at very short notice, a significant force anywhere
      in the world where circumstances require in order that its point of view and its interests
      are taken into account in the management of the crisis and in all aspects of its
      resolution'.

opposed to its current reliance on NATO and the US) will necessitate a transformation of government attitudes across the Union towards defence budgets. Even if the French feel able to counter economic pressures and decide upon a budgetary expansion in the defence field, and there are no signs currently that they will, it is hard to envisage the other EU member states doing likewise. Indicative of these doubts is the fact that defence procurement in the EU fell by 6.9 per cent between 1996 and 2000 (as compared to a rise in the US of 4.7 per cent over the same period).[53]

Conscription

Former-President Giscard had spoken publicly in 1989 about ending conscription (formally established in 1905), and this view would be expressed on numerous occasions in the 1990s by François Fillon. These proposals were repeatedly resisted on the grounds that they represented a renunciation of the tradition of the citizen in uniform. Historically, this dated back to the *levée en masse* of 1792 and the subsequent victory over a seemingly invincible Austro-Prussian force at the Battle of Valmy that was deemed to have saved the revolution; and politically it dates from 1905. The proposals were also said to be detrimental to the nation's resolve to defend itself.[54] Moreover, it was still held to be the case, according to the *Livre Blanc*, that *'[l]e service national demeure le meilleur gage de l'attachement de la nation et des citoyens á leur défense'.*[1] [55] This document also referred to conscription as a school for good citizenship and as a paradigm of the Frenchman's national allegiance.[56] National Service thus persisted due, in large part, to the French belief system. It was a symbol of the traditional commitment of everyone to *la patrie*, the idea that each citizen wishes to play his or her part and it preserved the crucial link between army and nation. Ideas associating the people with the defence of the nation remained fundamentally important to many in French society even in the 1990s. As the *Livre Blanc* stated, *'[q]ue le peuple français demeure, tout compte fait, responsable de sa défense est le principal vecteur de l'esprit de défense qui unit l'Armée á la Nation dont elle est á la fois le prisme et le miroir – ce qui fait que l'on ne peut concevoir l'une sans l'autre'.*[m] [57]

Nevertheless, President Chirac announced in early 1996 that France would turn to a fully professional army on the grounds that the country no longer faced a ground threat and that French forces were now only involved in operations beyond the country's borders. The reasoning went that if the concept of the defence of frontiers no longer existed, then there was no further need for the resources provided by conscription. Chirac had the same urge to modernise as Pompidou, his mentor. In addition, these measures were portrayed as essential if France was to be able to project significant numbers of troops into violent theatres abroad as part of multinational peacekeeping and humanitarian operations. Here, Chirac was referring to deploying

---

[1]   'National Service remains the best guarantee of the attachment of the nation and its citizens to their defence'.

[m]   'That the French people remain responsible for their own defence is the principal element in the notion of defence which binds the Army to the Nation of which it is both the prism and the mirror – to the extent that one cannot be imagined without the other'.

30,000 personnel in one engagement while still having the capacity to simultaneously deploy a brigade (between three and five thousand troops) in one or two other theatres;[58] an option that simply was not open to an armed forces still employing conscripts. The ongoing move to a professional army was also justified on financial grounds. Close to 170,000 conscripts were serving in the French armed forces in early 1997. Chirac claimed that once professionalisation had been completed, expected to be 2002, the new product could cost approximately 15 per cent less than the existing arrangement.[59] The Socialists voiced deep concerns about the abandonment of conscription. Lionel Jospin, as Party leader, reiterated the old fear of the army being cut off from the nation.[60] It seemed likely, for example, that the disbanding of a number of regiments based in towns and cities that have traditionally been host to the military would exacerbate the lack of contact between the military and the rest of society. However, speaking as Prime Minister in July 1997, he declared his Government would not oppose the professionalisation process.[61] The Communists, however, announced their intention to vote against the change.[62] And the suddenness of the decision was questioned. Chirac's strong-arm rhetoric was leaving little room for real debate. However, Alain Peyrefitte, a Gaullist of the old guard, declared that 'the myth of the nation in arms has always outlived its practical utility'.[63] Lellouche declared that the Republic could live without it.[64] And François Heisbourg believed that the decision would have to have been made eventually, regardless of who was in power.[65]

The move appeared to imply a greater and open reliance by the national leadership on France's allies through the conduct of joint operations. The reforms caused particular concern in Bonn, which, while Paris was looking to global power projection, still clung to the notion of the conventional defence of the national territory by a conscript army. And it was uncertain, for example, what the implications would be for Eurocorps. As a standing defence force, it was seemingly being sidelined by the France's shift in favour of mobile expeditionary forces. Moreover, these moves towards a wholly professional army raised doubts as to whether France would be able, in the future, to provide enough personnel for the Corps.[66] But as illustrated in Chapter Five, Eurocorps stock has since risen with its April 2000 deployment in Bosnia. Jean-Marie Colombani, editor of *Le Monde*, interpreted the military reforms as a reduction in the field of national ambitions, as adapting to the country's limited means and as a bid to lay to rest the myth of national *grandeur*.[67] In practical terms, it was believed that a professional army would better enable France in the future to meet the international obligations its leaders had assumed for it, thereby preserving the country's elevated global *rang* and its inherent universal calling.

Conclusion

Tactical adjustments in French security policy as the strategic *grandes lignes* were retained have filtered through to the French military. The decision-makers drew the simple, if belated, conclusion that rhetorical shifts would count for nothing if not backed by practical alterations in the armed forces as the key policy instrument. The *force de frappe* was prioritised as a key element of de Gaulle's approach to the Cold War 'game'. It served as a demonstration of the French exception and of the country's non-dependence on either of the superpower blocs. But this nuclear emphasis came at a cost however, namely the sacrificing of the conventional capability. Then, with a new geostrategic order in the 1990s came a recasting of priorities. The strategic utility of the *force de frappe* has been devalued and it is to the conventional forces that the policy-makers are now looking. If the French are to retain a place at the high table of global politics they have to be able to deploy credible military missions around the globe. To retain this capability, Chirac's planners have embraced a number of significant changes; and these have deliberately reversed de Gaulle's tactic of emphasising the French exception. Cooperation with other west European militaries has been embraced at the expense of the nationalist approach to defence equipment development and procurement. This has helped to enable the defence budget to be stabilised well below the level set out in the 1995-2000 *Loi de Programmation Militaire*. The devalued nuclear capability has been reduced to a dyad, with the loss of the land-based component. The armed forces have been downsized by some 30 per cent. Finally, the traditional symbol of the nation in uniform is being dismantled as the remaining military units become fully professional. All these measures will better enable the French to continue their claims to global significance and their pursuit of their strategic *grandes lignes*.

Notes

1   Davidson, Ian, 'Gulf shakes Gaullist taboos', *The Financial Times*, 27 October 1990.
2   Védrine, Hubert (1996), *Les Mondes de Mitterrand: A l'Elysée 1981-1995*, Fayard, Paris, p.141.
3   Freedman, Lawrence (1989), *The Evolution of Nuclear Strategy*, Macmillan/IISS, Basingstoke, p.313.
4   Gordon, Philip. H., 'Charles de Gaulle and the nuclear revolution', *Security Studies*, vol.5, no.1, Autumn 1995, p.147.
5   Gregory, Shaun (2000), *French Defence Policy into the Twenty-First Century*, Macmillan, Basingstoke, p.11.
6   De Gaulle, Charles, in a speech of November 1961, quoted in Kohl, Wilfred (1971), *French Nuclear Diplomacy*, Princeton University Press, Princeton, p.129.
7   De Gaulle, Charles, quoted in Pointon, Clare, 'The French identity crisis', *European Trends*, no.2, 1992, p.39.
8   Aron, Raymond (1965), *The Great Debate*, Doubleday, New York, p.109.
9   Daniel, Jean, editorial in *Le Nouvel Observateur*, 18 December 1987, p.39.
10 Foley, James B., 'Pacifism and antinuclearism in France: perceptions of the crises of deterrence and détente', in James E. Dougherty and Robert L. Pfaltzgraff jr. (eds), *Shattering Europe's Defence Consensus: The Antinuclear Protest Movement and the Future of NATO*, Pergamon-Brasseys, Oxford, p.154.
11 Mitterrand, François, during a broadcast on French television channel Antenne 2, quoted in Cohen, Samy (1986), *La Monarchie Nucléaire: Les Coulisses de la Politique Etrangère sous la Cinquième République*, Hachette, Paris, p.15.
12 Mitterrand, François, quoted in *The Independent*, 26 May 1994.

13 Timmerman, Kenneth R., 'Defense policy shifts from isolationism toward Europe', *International Herald Tribune*, 1 June 1987.

14 See for example, Wetterqvist, Fredrik (1990), *French Security and Defence Policy: Current Developments and Future Prospects*, National Defence and Research Institute, Stockholm, 1990, p.17.

15 Wells jr, Samuel F., 'Les politiques étrangères de Mitterrand: bilan d'un premier septennat', *Commentaire*, no.43, August 1988, p.662.

16 Gregory, Shaun, *op cit*, p.74.

17 *Ibid*, p.78.

18 'France's changing view of the world', *The Economist*, 10 February 1996, p.29.

19 Routier, Airy, 'Armement: la campagne du Général Chirac', *Le Nouvel Observateur*, 25 January 1996, p.51.

20 Chevènement, Jean-Pierre, 'Chevènement: on abaisse la France', *Le Nouvel Observateur*, 15 February 1996, p.43.

21 Guisnel, Jean, '"L'exception militaire" française', in *L'Etat de La France 1994-5*, Editions de la Découverte, Paris, 1994, p.588.

22 Gregory, Shaun, *op cit*, p.84.

23 'A French projection', *The Economist*, 2 March 1996, p.25.

24 Lewis, J.A.C., 'Fitter, leaner forces for multi-polar world', *Jane's Defence Weekly*, 11 June 1997, p.71.

25 Ruiz-Palmer, Diego A., *French Strategic Options in the 1990s*, Adelphi Paper 260, Brasseys/IISS, Summer 1991, p.40.

26 Cresson, Edith, in a speech to L'Institut des Hautes Etudes de la Défense Nationale, 6 September 1991.

27 Laulan, Yves-Marie, 'La défense de la France á l'heure des choix: puissance mondiale où puissance régionale?', in Pierre Pascallon (ed), *Quelle Défense pour la France?*, Institut Français des Relations Internationales/Dunod, Paris, 1993, p.96.

28 Isnard, Jacques, 'L'Allemagne et la France cherchent à harmoniser leurs besoins en matière d'armement', *Le Monde*, 10 December 1996.

29 Lewis, J.A.C, *op cit*, p.71.

30 Graham, Robert, 'Defence: Government faces a financial squeeze', *The Financial Times* (country survey), June 2000.

31 Buchan, David, 'France unveils first N-carrier', *The Financial Times*, 9 May 1994.

32 Brown, Kevin and Clark, Bruce, 'UK and France in nuclear pact', *The Financial Times*, 31 October 1995.

33 Balladur, Edouard, in a speech to the Institute of Higher National Defence Studies, Paris, 8 September 1994.

34 Chirac, Jacques, in a Bastille Day television interview, quoted in Taylor, Paul, 'Chirac hits at left's U-turn', *The Guardian*, 15 July 1997.

35 See, for example, Gregory, Shaun, *op cit*, p.98.

36 Fillon, François, quoted in 'L'opposition s'inquiète du risque de "repli" de l'industrie de défense', *Le Monde*, 15 July 1997.

37 Whitney, Craig. R., 'France sells a third of Aerospatiale to Groupe Lagardère', *The New York Times*, 16 February 1999.

38 Messmer, Pierre, 'Quelle place pour l'arme nucléaire française?', in *Quelle Défense pour la France?*, *op cit*, p.196.

39 Laulan, Yves-Marie, *op cit*, p.93.

40 Touraine, Marisol, 'La France doit revoir son organisation de défense', *Le Point*, 17 July, 1993, p.23.

41 Laulan, Yves-Marie, *op cit* , p.92.
42 Gordon, Philip H., *op cit* , p.181.
43 *Livre Blanc sur la Défense 1994*, *op cit*, p.50.
44 Balladur, Edouard, Preface to *Livre Blanc sur la Défense 1994*, *op cit*, p.6.
45 *Livre Blanc sur la Défense 1994*, *op cit*, p.50.
46 Multon (Général d'Armée [C.R.]), Pierre, 'Armée de métier ou armée de conscription', in *Quelle Défense pour la France?*, *op cit*, p.264.
47 Howorth, Jolyon, *op cit*, p.107.
48 Schmitt, Jean, *Polémique sur le nucléaire*, *Le Point*, 17 July 1993, p.20.
49 Balladur, Edouard, in speech given to the Institute of Higher National Defence Studies, Paris, September 8 1994.
50 Lagarde, Dominique, 'Le retour de la France', *L'Express*, 5 December 1996, p.90.
51 Chirac, Jacques, in a speech to the Ecole Militaire, Paris, 23 February 1996.
52 Isnard, Jacques, 'Solitaire mais solidaire', *op cit.*
53 Latter, Richard, *European Security and Defence: Forging an EU Role*, Wilton Park, December 2000, p.8.
54 Ruiz-Palmer, Diego A., *op cit*, p.39.
55 *Livre Blanc sur la Défense 1994*, *op cit*, p.155.
56 *Ibid*, p.127.
57 *Ibid*, p.230.
58 *Une Défense Nouvelle*, Ministère de la Défense, Paris, February 1996, p.6.
59 Lewis, F.A.C., *op cit*, p.71.
60 Gonin, Jean-Marc and Pierre-Brossolette, Sylvie, 'Armée: 10 questions en suspens', *L'Express*, 29 February 1996, p.40.
61 Fortier, Jacques, 'Lionel Jospin confirme la mise à contribution de budget de la défense', *Le Monde*, 30 July 1997.
62 Merchet, Jean-Dominique and Schneider, Vanessa, 'Millon subit l'assaut des députés', *Libération*, 6 June 1996.
63 Peyrefitte, Alain, quoted in Sancton, Thomas, 'Farewell to some arms', *Time*, 4 March 1996, p.18.
64 Lellouche, Pierre, 'L'utilité militaire du service est dépassé', *Libération*, 13 May 1996.
65 Heisbourg, François, *op cit.*
66 Fitchett, Joseph, 'French-German military vision clouds again', *International Herald Tribune*, 30 May 1996.
67 Colombani, Jean-Marie, quoted in Lewis, Flora, 'In revamping its military, France moves closer to Europe', *op cit*, p.6.

Chapter 7

France in the Wider World: The Limits of Exception

Hitherto, this volume has primarily focused on France's position in, and policy towards the rest of Europe. But what of the 'global vocation' that was given so much prominence in Chapter One? How did the country's quest for *grandeur* and *rang* translate to the wider international system? This chapter examines this question by focusing on sub-Saharan Africa, France's traditional 'back yard'. It was in this region that France maintained a particularly strong post-colonial presence. This was one area in the world where French leaders were able to live the illusion and still play the great power. And Africa was key to their claim for a special role for France in the wider world as espoused by the formalisation of *la francophonie*. And yet, even here, there have been clear signs of tactical adaptation in line with the measures taken with regard to Europe. There is the sense that the French armed forces are ceasing to be deployed as the region's *gendarme*. The unilateral missions that will characterise the first part of the chapter are becoming a thing of the past. There has been a greater reluctance to intervene militarily in the affairs of sub-Saharan states. When there is intervention, it is now more likely to be as part of a multinational force. And the clear preference for the decision-makers in Paris is for regional solutions. To this end, the French have been contributing to the international effort that is enabling African states to deal with local crisis situations themselves. Hence, a downplaying of the French exception in the one region where France really could claim great power status serves to illustrate the extent of the tactical transformation underway in French security policy.

Colonial Legacies

De Gaulle's attempts to carve out a special role for France within the Cold War bipolar system were discussed in Chapter Two. However, a further aspect of this tactical approach was the early recognition that a France seeking *rang* and *grandeur* had to divest itself of its empire. By the beginning of the 1960s, colonies had outgrown their usefulness to a gaullist France posing as the champion of national independence and seeking to break down the hegemonies of the Superpowers. Moreover, Paris had been the target of heavy criticism at the UN for its colonial policy, supposedly for standing in the way of countries' right to self-determination. And the colonies had become a major and growing economic burden, acting as a constraint on de Gaulle's global aims; for the reality was that, by this time, France was largely left with only the weakest and most dependent of its colonies. As Kolodziej observed, '[c]ompelled to use force to pacify rebellious foreign populations, French self-esteem and stature abroad inevitably deteriorated'.[1] The General never faltered from his conviction in the predominant importance of France's *grandeur* and global standing. But as Gordon observed, he was not oblivious to the forces that had been released around the globe by the Second World War. For all his own political will, he appreciated that the colonies could not be contained for long, their aspirations for independence would be realised one way or another. It was therefore better for France to recognise this and incur minimum human and material costs.[2]

The policy of decolonisation was further motivated by de Gaulle's aforementioned decision to favour expenditure on the nuclear programme rather than on the maintenance of a large conventional capacity. As we have seen, this implied that France had to bring an end to its massive military presence in Algeria. A force of up to 600,000 troops had been deployed in the country for the nine years of the conflict, and clearly this had constituted a huge drain on the Hexagon's resources. Added to these more obvious problems was the opportunity cost for France, a country experiencing a shortage of labour, of having such large numbers of its young men fighting on Algerian soil. The economic consequences of the war went far beyond statistics within the defence budget. With decolonisation complete, the policy-makers in Paris were subsequently to place great store during the Cold War on France's status as a former colonial power; this was given as evidence of its rank as a great global power. And sub-Saharan Africa stood at the heart of this post-colonial policy.[3]

French leaders would still find it necessary, on numerous occasions, to directly intervene militarily and politically in the affairs of its African partners. This can partly be attributed back to the country's behaviour as an imperial power. It had been held that Africa, for its own benefit, should be given the French language and culture and the ideals of the French Revolution, and be assimilated into the worldwide French community. This approach just happened to mean that the predominant position of the French language would serve to perpetuate French influence after independence. In MacNamara's view:

> Francophone Africa has no really viable replacement for French as a *lingua franca* or as a vehicle for advanced education and international communication. African languages abound, but few are spoken widely enough to warrant their becoming the national language of a single country ... Moreover, ethnic jealousies often preclude favouring one African language over others. The absence of technical vocabulary and a broad body of literature are other shortcomings.[4]

The concept of assimilation had thus left little room for the emergence of a tradition of self-government in the colonies. This made the transition to independence all the more difficult and continued French assistance was, for the most part, readily accepted. And when, for example, Guinea, in 1958, renounced its special relationship with France, Paris swiftly cut all trade links. For Roberts, '[w]hat differentiated French decolonisation of the 1960s from that of the rest of the European experience in Africa was that it did not really happen'.[5]

Jacques Foccart is the man most closely associated with the formulation of France's African policies during the first 20 years of the Fifth Republic, and he served as advisor on African affairs to President Chirac from 1995 until his death. The publication of his memoirs in 1995 confirmed the extent to which French leaders had consistently sought to retain something close to France's old imperial influence in sub-Saharan Africa. Foccart and his agents had managed, via an elaborate network of administrative structures, the affairs of several former French colonies until the mid-Seventies. These countries duly followed France's lead at the UN. Economic links, the identity of intermediaries and the processes of cooperation would remain largely unaltered for at least two generations after independence. This was in many respects an empire in all but name. For McNulty, these were relations based on the idea of patron and client: the patron's influence resting on the client's survival, the client's survival often relying on the patron's protection.[6] And this aspect of French foreign policy would remain almost free of any democratic accountability within the Hexagon. Affairs were conducted with a virtual clandestine approach, resting on personal friendships and on corruption. Furthermore, Paris repeatedly deployed secret service operatives. The DGSE, for one, was omnipresent across the continent, providing at the very least advisors to the respective Heads of State.

Where possible, pre-independence conditions were set. The former colonies had to acquiesce to prior consultation for major foreign policy decisions; defence assistance against both internal and external threats, including the permanent garrisoning of French troops in those countries; privileged access to raw materials and strategic products (notably, Niger's uranium), a common monetary policy via the franc area and reciprocal preferential trade relations. And the policy-makers in Paris ensured that any military interventions were safeguarded by a solid legal basis. Hence, they would fall under one of two French-drafted rubrics that surpassed any other North-South military pact. The first were *accords de défense*. These were bilateral defence agreements that were conditional on French assistance being requested by the local authorities. In practice, these were usually signed when it had already been decided to intervene (eight such accords were signed with African states: the Central African Republic, Gabon and Senegal in 1960; Côte d'Ivoire in 1961, Togo in 1963; the Comores in 1973; Cameroon in 1974 and Djibouti in 1977). The second were *accords d'assistance militaire technique* (signed with the preceding eight states and with 18 other sub-Saharan states). These represented French aid in the form of the organisation, equipping and training of local police forces and national armies. But in addition to these public undertakings, secret *conventions spéciales* were instigated with Chad and Gabon in 1961 and with Côte d'Ivoire in 1962. These designated the aid that France could provide for the restoration of public order in these countries, something not covered by the other types of *accord*. In this way, troops solely responsible to the French Defence Ministry, with no jurisdiction for the Ministry of Cooperation, could be deployed in these instances almost as interior police.[7] France's military reach in sub-Saharan Africa was then extended to the former-Belgian colonies of Burundi, Rwanda and Zaire in the mid-1970s.

Another interpretation of this African policy was that although its rationale at such times may have been the protection of French nationals (by the mid-1980s, Côte d'Ivoire, for example, was host to some 50,000 while around 20,000 resided in Senegal) or economic interests (particularly oil and uranium), the decision-makers in Paris also visibly relished the occasional chance that Africa afforded them to prove France as an international power. Here was a relatively risk-free route to enhanced global status, to an elevated international *rang*. National independence had been granted, but only to subdivisions of the former-French colonial blocs. France's limited military means were perfectly adequate for operations in an Africa made up of small, artificial and weak nation-states. Whatever the reasons, the French dissolution of the two large colonial African federations produced a host of powerless and dependent states easy to manipulate. In these vulnerable countries, a small force of just 500 French troops could change the course of history. They were ideal for the small-scale interventions in which French national leaders seemed to revel. Long-term operations that would recall the humiliations of IndoChina and Algeria were to be avoided at all costs. Hence, in geopolitical terms, France was a power to be reckoned with in the region and could claim to be an alternative leader to the two superpowers. Moreover, no other external power should feel at home in France's equivalent to the US' backyard. This regional hegemony, it was claimed, clearly placed France apart from, and indeed above, the status of an 'average' middle-sized European power.

The rationale for military interventions in Africa evolved from the early post-colonial efforts at stabilising regimes to defending francophone states from external threats. Once the Soviet Union began its long-running policy of military intervention in Africa by proxy, be these forces backed by Cuba or Libya, in the mid-1950s, French leaders could begin to portray their own African excursions as responsible acts in response to Soviet imperialism, rather than as the remnants of colonialism. But it seems clear, as Gregory notes, that this elevated role for France was attained, in no small way, through tacit American support and indulgence. If at any moment American Cold War interests had ceased to be served by France's regional activities, then appropriate measures would have been taken and France's autonomy of action curtailed.[8] These missions also seemed to perpetuate the justification for France's global role. At the same time, planners began actively to seek to extend French influence in Africa beyond the old frontiers of empire. Yet, predominantly, French policy towards the 'dark continent' at this time could be described as clinical. To this end, French troops were withdrawn from Chad in 1972 once an accord was reached with Libya, the external aggressor, even though the pro-French Chadian government of President Tombalbaye still faced an internal political conflict. But generally speaking, successive French leaderships, until about the mid-1980s, were not particularly selective with regard to the type of political regime with which they did business, even if it was Marxist as was the case in Benin, Congo and Madagascar. Despite pre-election rhetoric for example, the arrival of Socialist François Mitterrand at the Elysée did not mark the demise of neo-colonial spheres of influence.

One solution to the logistical problem posed by the desire for a global role was to pre-position military forces closer to their probable area of use. As Smouts saw it, '[b]y her presence in strategically important regions (Djibouti, for example), France seeks to play a role of dissuasion and stabilisation'.[9] Hence French forces, and some 950 military advisors, took up residence in Senegal, Côte d'Ivoire, Gabon, Djibouti and the Central African Republic in Africa; Réunion in the Indian Ocean; Tahiti and Nouvel Calédonie in the Pacific and Martinique in the Caribbean. By the mid-1980s, Africa alone was host to some 12,500 French troops. While the system of joint military exercises with local forces implicated these states in the overall French security policy and reinforced the belief that regional security was a collaborative matter and served as a major reason for France's success in maintaining the loyalty of its partners. French military planners placed strong emphasis on this pre-positioning of forces. In each case this implied reassurance for France's friends and a pacifying effect on the unstable. By Mitterrand's time, this policy implied the deferral of any decisions on future strategy, a kind of muddling through, and the contradictory acceptance that France could not continue to meet all its desired commitments.

McNulty was correct in his observation that because of 'France's interpersonal "networks" and treaty-ratified support for the internal status quo in the states of its African sphere, its permanent bases and its peerless power projection capacity on the continent, Franco-African relations are inherently interventionary'.[10] It was evident that 12,000-plus French troops were not stationed permanently in sub-Saharan Africa purely for the possible evacuation of French citizens. The example of Chad probably provides the most graphic illustration of the former imperial power's open volition to intervene with military force in its former colonies. Despite the absence of any actual defence accord, the presence of French troops in the country was to be almost uninterrupted from 1960. In addition, Paris launched successive counter-interventions in the country from 1968 to the end of the Cold War in order to deny success to Libya and its nomadic Arab proxies from the north of the country in their attempts to occupy the Aouzou Strip and, at times, the rest of the country.

Both of the external powers took sides in the ethnically driven civil war. French interests in Chad were almost solely geostrategic, as opposed to fuelling domestic support, or diverting domestic criticism. The country was a potential base from which Libya could dominate the other sub-Saharan states, principally, Niger and Gabon where French economic interests were substantial. At the same time, policy-makers in Paris saw the commitment to Chad's black southerners as crucial to France's credibility with other black African francophone states.[11] To this end, the territorial integrity of Chad itself was for many years not the top priority. Libya was, for example, allowed on several occasions to occupy the Aouzou Strip unopposed. The main objective in Paris was the protection of neighbouring states and the containment of Libyan influence. Incidentally, this potential enemy was continuing to be bestowed with French military aircraft and French training personnel.

Operation Manta, in 1983, comprised several hundred French military instructors and the deployment of some 3000 troops in Chad along the fifteenth parallel (to prevent Libyan-backed forces occupying the capital, N'Djamena). No French troops were sent into action against the Libyans, but troops, equipment and aircraft were lost in accidents. Despite a diplomatic agreement, only French forces subsequently withdrew. In February 1986, in response to an attack by Libyan-backed forces south of the sixteenth parallel, French aircraft bombed the Libyan air base at Ouadi Doum and a new operation, code-named *Epervier*, comprising numerous aircraft and 1200 troops, was launched. Mitterrand sought to guarantee Chad south of the sixteenth parallel, while avoiding direct combat with Libyan troops, leaving forces loyal to Paris' proxy, Habré, to do the fighting in the north. At times, it seemed, Habré's political survival was totally reliant on the French military presence. The Libyans then lost most of their Chadian support, but the fighting continued. *Epervier* was reinforced throughout 1987, helping Habré to push the Libyans back to the border. Paris had avoided any real direct and overt participation in the fighting and its policy objectives were realised. However, this 'temporary' operation was not finally concluded until early 1996!

French troops also undertook reactive deployments in Cameroon, supposedly being threatened by neighbouring anglophone Nigeria (1957-64), Senegal (1962); Gabon (1964), where France had a large economic stake in the manganese and uranium ore deposits; Niger, Mauritania and neighbouring Spanish Sahara (1977-8, 1980), Zaire (1977 and 1978) and Togo (1986). It intervened on behalf of oil-rich Biafra in its attempts to break away from Nigeria. And 18 warships were deployed off Djibouti in 1977 to cover the referendum there and to be prepared to evacuate French nationals if necessary. But troops were not deployed to save the regimes of Presidents Youlou in the Congo, in 1963, Maga in Dahomy (now Benin), in 1965, Diori in Niger and Tsiranana in Madagascar. In September 1979, Giscard authorised *Operation Barracuda*, with the task of deposing 'Emperor' Bokassa in the Central African Republic, following the confirmation of atrocity stories about him, and in order to facilitate the country's transition to a republic. However morally correct the operation may have been, it, like others before it, recalled the gung-ho imperialism of the nineteenth century.

But as France's conventional capability continued to be sacrificed in favour of the nuclear programme, French leaders had to increasingly rely on American logistical support, especially during the 1980s, in order to carry out its numerous military interventions in sub-Saharan Africa. Principally this involved satellite intelligence and air transport. Mitterrand's declaration at the 1985 Franco-African summit in Burundi that he was not going to be the *gendarme* of Africa was perhaps an acknowledgement of France's limited means.

Global Initiatives

Mitterrand's foreign policy towards the wider world would largely mirror that of the Fifth Republic's first President; French armed forces continued to be deployed around the globe. Like de Gaulle, he believed that France had its role to play and its contribution to make. According to Schraeder, decision-makers in Paris strove throughout the Cold War to consolidate and promote the *rayonnement*, or spread, of French culture.[12] One logical outcome of this was to promote the development of *la francophonie*. The Agency for Cultural and Technical Cooperation was established in 1970 and became the Francophone Agency in 1996. Having rested on education and technical cooperation for many years, the Agency was given a higher profile by Mitterrand. This included the putting in place, from 1986, of a system of biennial summits attended by all the relevant Heads of State; 52 states were represented at the 1999 summit held in New Brunswick, Canada. The organisation now has a Permanent Council 15 members representing the Heads of State and Government) and a

Secretariat-General (former UN Secretary General Boutros Boutros-Ghali became its first head in 1997).

Mitterrand was resolute in what he saw as the struggle with the anglo-saxon world. He was determined that this would not simply be a question of language. Only some 160 million people speak French fluently or occasionally out of a *francophonie* population of 450 million and a world population of around six billion. Vietnam, for example, as host of the *francophonie* summit in 1997, could only boast some 0.09 per cent of its population with a working knowledge of French. These summits have been intended to be an instrument with which to challenge the anglo-saxons diplomatically, politically and economically.[13] And the economic motive has become progressively more significant as international trade became the principle battleground for global influence. Moreover, the summits are portrayed as something akin to a family reunion at which already close personal relations between the French President and his francophone counterparts are strengthened. And, no doubt, they are used to boost French international standing. At the UN, for example, a large francophone bloc of states could serve as a further guarantor of French culture.

Meanwhile, Paris sought to multiply its international partners to further extend French influence. To this end, the French took over as the principal Western guarantors of the former-Belgian possessions of Burundi, Rwanda and Zaire and it supplanted Spain in Equatorial Guinea. In addition, France was able to substitute itself for the Soviet Union in Guinea and Congo. Another logical outcome was the decision to resurrect de Gaulle's policy of active engagement in Latin America, often in conflict with the policy of the United States. Hence, there was support in the early 1980s for the left-wing opposition groups in El Salvador and there were simultaneous military sales to the Sandinistas in Nicaragua. The belief in Paris was that the policies pursued by the US were driving these and other nationalist movements into the arms of the Communists.[14] French arms exports to the region were maintained, albeit with increased competition from Britain, Italy, West Germany and, later, Israel.

The sale of French-made arms and military equipment to foreign regimes around the world thus continued unabated throughout Mitterrand's double *septennat*. This included the honouring, in the face of mounting global criticism, of export contracts with Libya and Iraq, both fast becoming international pariahs. Indeed, sales to the former were maintained even in the face of mounting tension between Paris and Tripoli over Chad. The sales were initially justified as fulfilling existing French commitments, then they became the means to protect Arab states against post-revolution Iran.[15] Hence, if the pursuit of *rang* and *grandeur* as strategic objectives could best be served by the sale of military equipment to foreign regimes of questionable moral standing, then so be it.

Elsewhere, French representatives had continued, almost instinctively, to be closely involved, rhetorically at least, in the unfurling events of the Middle East. A major role here, as elsewhere, conformed to the claimed historical mission. De Gaulle's pro-Arab stance during the Arab-Israeli war of 1967 meant that France still retained a certain amount of prestige among the Arab leaders of the region. The nine-year war that broke out in 1980 between Arabic Iraq and Persian Iran thus put the French leadership in a difficult position. French military aircraft would eventually be sold to the former in 1983. But this decision would appear to have been more to do with questions of the regional balance of power (Iran, led by Ayatollah Khomeni, appeared to have gained the upper hand at this time) than with any automatic pro-Arab loyalties. Nevertheless, French citizens would, in the ensuing years after the end of the conflict, become a prime target for hostage-taking by Iranian-sponsored guerrilla groups based in Lebanon.

Experiences in Lebanon during the last years of the Cold War, meanwhile, were to be instrumental in determining the strategy for maintaining France's global role in the security environment of the post-Cold War era. This was to mark the country's first involvement in multilateral peacekeeping. In 1978, President Giscard, at the request of the UNSC, deployed French forces as part of UNIFIL (United Nations Interim Force in Lebanon). Once again the French were attempting to advertise their claim to a place on the highest rung on the global ladder, and to do this they were making increasing use of the UN. The latter was becoming a key instrument for the projection of French *rang* and *grandeur*. This initial action posed some severe problems because France was perceived as an ex-colonial power (Lebanon was a former French protectorate) taking the side of the Christian forces in the conflict. The difficulties were to be a precursor of the much more serious events in the 1980s.[16] French troops then formed part of the international force deployed to Beirut, in August 1982, to assist in the evacuation of the Palestine Liberation Organisation. There were two supplementary motivations behind the intervention; namely the protection of the Christian minority and the determination to demonstrate to Syria that it did not have a 'free hand' in France's former protectorate.[17] In October 1983 the explosion of an Islamic Jihad suicide truck left 58 French soldiers dead. The French force remained in place temporarily but the threshold of unacceptable losses and casualties had been reached and exceeded. The mission was formally ended a month later.

The 1990s: Sub-Saharan Africa – Mission Transformed

Sub-Saharan Africa has long been regarded by French officials as France's own backyard. When discussing French military intervention overseas one is invariably drawn to thoughts of this region. It is here, as discussed above, that French forces appear to have been in almost constant active deployment since the main decolonisation era. Solo French military operations south of the Sahara came to receive minimal media coverage outside of France, so regular had they become. Hence it is interesting to consider whether the re-evaluation of national security policy and the subsequent tactical revisions were extended to the one region where France could, traditionally, legitimately continue to act the Great Power. Here too, there have been clear signs that the French political leadership is reforming its use of military intervention as a policy instrument.

Africa, host to a French military presence for a century and a half, remained a central focus of French security policy throughout the 1990s. In June of the decade's first year, President Mitterrand signalled at La Baule that future assistance for France's African partners south of the Sahara would be conditional on their respective human rights record and the degree of progress in the transition to democracy. With this in mind, Paris did nothing to aid the plight of President Habré in Chad, who was forced to flee the capital N'Djamena in the face of a rebel attack. It had become clear that the man that France had previously backed had become a bloody despot.[18] But, noted Mireille Duteil, this policy of *'prime á la démocratie'*[a] was apparently to be short-lived, giving way to *'prime á la bonne gestion'*[b] and then *'prime au statu quo'*.[c] [19] It was becoming abundantly clear that, in his second *septennat*, Mitterrand was making practical involvement in Africa much less of a priority. As Foreign Minister Dumas put it:

> *[i]l n'est pas question de nous transformer en gendarme de l'Afrique ... Nos engagements s'arrêtent á la sécurité des pays á l'égard desquels nous avons des engagements et á celle des communautés françaises là où elles seraient menacées par des troubles.*[d] [20]

Hence, when France did involve itself, French economic interests and the protection of French nationals still appeared to override everything else. Despite the rhetoric of La Baule, the subsequent years would reveal a French policy for Africa still largely resting on *la permanence*, everything continued to be sacrificed to the dogma of stability. This, rather than development and progress, remained an end in itself. Foreign Legion troops had been sent, for example, only a month prior to that June 1990 speech, to protect Elf's principal oil operation in Gabon (Elf being a major French public company) after the French consulate in Libreville had been set on fire by protesters angry at the suspicious death of an opposition leader. Then, in September 1991, French and Belgian troops were swiftly deployed in the then Zaire after local troops, who had gone unpaid, went on the rampage. French public opinion, by now totally habituated to such overseas operations, appeared indifferent.[21]

It was now uncertain as to whether France's leaders, in the new international security environment, would be prepared to sanction a unilateral intervention at the request of the incumbent regime in a country with which there was a defence agreement. The harder line towards black Africa was further illustrated in January 1994 with the devaluation of the CFA (*Communauté Financière Africaine*) franc by 50 per cent.[22] For Roland Marchal, this represented a challenge to 'one of the privileged instruments of the French hegemony over its backyard (the *pré carré*), the franc zone'.[23] But the military commitment to the African continent, for whatever reasons, remained significant; some 4500 men in Djibouti, 1200 in Senegal, 1000 in the Central African Republic, 600 in Chad, 550 in Gabon and 530 in Côte d'Ivoire.[24] Around 12,000 troops were stationed in the continent as a whole, equal to the size of the force Mitterrand deployed in the Gulf for the liberation of Kuwait. At the same time, policy-

---

[a] 'primacy to democracy'.
[b] 'primacy to good management'.
[c] 'primacy to the status quo'.
[d] 'There is no question of transforming ourselves into the policeman of Africa. ... Our involvement stops at the security of countries to whom we are obliged and at the security of those French communities threatened by unrest'.

makers in Paris moved to make France the privileged partner of certain African states vacated by the Soviet Union with the end of the Cold War. Most notably, one can point to Benin, Congo, Madagascar and Mali.[25] And of course, behind all the rhetoric was the realisation that Africa represented the only region in the world where France could still act like a great power with the deployment of only a few hundred troops. Pretexts would still be found for military interventions if these served French geostrategic interests and boosted France's global prestige. As Mitterrand himself put it in November 1994: *'[l]a France ne serait plus tout-à-fait elle-même aux yeux du monde si elle renonçait à être présente en Afrique'.*[e] [26] In a similar vain, the newly elected President Chirac chose Africa (Côte d'Ivoire, Gabon, Morocco and Senegal) for his first official overseas visit, outside of multinational gatherings. Hence, Africa remained crucial as an almost unique area where French *rang* and *grandeur* could be displayed and remain largely uncontested.

France – Peacekeeper for the International Community

The early 1990s focus on multinational peacekeeping and humanitarian operations 'on behalf' of the international community as legitimisation, as the new *raison d'être*, of French military intervention overseas was introduced in Chapter Four. In this light, participation in the 1992-3 UN-mandated mission in Somalia (UNOSOM) marked a clear signal from the French that they were determined to maintain their global role, and most especially in Africa. UNSC Resolution 794 launched Operation 'Restore Hope' stating 'the magnitude of the human tragedy ... constitutes a threat to international peace and security' and, acting under Chapter VII of the Charter, it went on to authorise the use of 'all necessary means to establish as soon as possible a secure environment for humanitarian relief operations in Somalia'.[27] To this end, the UN empowered an independent group of states to use force, under the operational name UNITAF (Unified Task Force), to establish a secure environment for the provision of humanitarian assistance and to sustain the peace process. The relatively small French contingent of 2400 men (as compared to an American force of 28,000), the BIAS (*Bataillon interarmés de Somalie*), had come from Djibouti and was stationed at Baïdoa, in the south of the country. It was responsible for an area of 95,000 square kilometres in *Opération Oryx*; four French warships stood offshore. The intervention had actually been opposed by French Defence Minister Joxe, citing concern at the nature of the mandate.[28] Moreover, the French were clearly unhappy that the operation had not been under UN control from the outset. There was concern in Paris that the operation could be construed as institutionalising an American military presence in Africa. Certainly, there was deep resentment at having to essentially follow American orders.[29] Nevertheless, it was clearly crucial to French African interests that French troops participate; to have left the operation entirely to the Americans would have been unacceptable to the political elites in Paris. Nevertheless, events in Mogadishu would

---

[e] 'France would no longer be entirely itself in the eyes of the world if it renounced its presence in Africa'.

subsequently mean that this episode did little to boost French claims of *rang* and *grandeur*.

Rwanda

With this in mind, in Africa, as elsewhere, French policy-makers, aware of the relatively diminishing resources at their disposal, began to look to cooperate with allies in order to share the 'burden'. Even here, in sub-Saharan Africa, where France was supposedly a great power, its leaders were struggling to meet all the country's commitments. Their promotion of the idea of an inter-African intervention force, backed by Western logistical support, had not made any real headway before Rwanda, a former Belgian colony and now a close ally of France, slipped into civil war and genocide. Hutus, comprising some 90 per cent of the population, had held power, via one party rule, from independence, when the power of the rival, minority, Tutsis had been smashed. When the latter 'returned', out of Uganda, as a guerrilla army in 1992, Hutu extremists resorted to genocide. At the request of both sides, the UN had deployed a 2500-strong force in November of that year to oversee the peace accord that had been signed the previous August; this principally involved the disarming and demobilisation of combatants. But with the resumption of hostilities, Belgium decided to withdraw its contingent. The UN Secretary General then instructed the commander of UNAMIR (United Nations Assistance Mission to Rwanda) to plan for a total withdrawal, rather than to push for a change to the mandate which would enable the UN force to control the anarchic situation in which the genocide was increasing unabated. In April 1994, some 1000 French troops, in *Opération Amaryllis*, secured the airport outside the capital, Kigali, to ensure the safe evacuation of some 600 French nationals and certain of the Rwandan political elite. The Hutus, in the meantime, continued their systematic slaughter of the Tutsis.[30] In a change of direction, the UNSC then passed Resolution 918, in May 1994, which authorised the reinforcement of UNAMIR, to a total of 5500 soldiers, and the broadening of its mandate. However, the international response was limited. Troops were offered by a number of mostly African states (including Ethiopia, Ghana, Tunisia, Zambia and Zimbabwe) but these lacked the necessary equipment in order to be deployed. In the meantime the slaughter continued apace.

It was in these circumstances that, on June 16 1994, Mitterrand, almost mechanically, decided to act. For Foreign Minister Juppé, *'[l]e sens de l'honneur, la morale la plus élémentaire demandent de prendre des risques calculés'.*[f] [31] Out of 'neutral' and 'humanitarian' concern, 2,500 French special forces troops were deployed (1500 of whom came from bases in Africa). These were supported by Chadian and Senegalese contingents, and in a much smaller way by troops from Congo and Niger (520 African troops in total). The mission of *Opération Turquoise* was to establish a safe haven for refugees, mainly Hutus but also Tutsis, in the south-west of the country. The force was backed by eight Mirage and four Jaguar fighters

---

[f]   'The sense of honour, the most elemental morality, demand the taking of calculated risks'.

and was based in eastern Zaire. UN approval for this largely unilateral action, for want of a better offer and until an adequate UN force could be raised, was quickly extracted; although five Security Council members abstained. And Resolution 929 did not actually refer to France by name, speaking only of a temporary multinational operation 'under national command and control'.

The French actions were controversial to say the least. There was the suspicion, both inside and outside Rwanda, of a secret agenda; namely the defence of France's old friends in the Hutu-dominated former-government. France had begun to arm the Hutu government in 1973, then, from the early 1980s French advisors started to train the Rwandan army to counter rebel Tutsi insurgencies from neighbouring Uganda. Troop numbers jumped from 5000 to 35,000, and attention was particularly paid to strengthening, with assistance from Egypt, Zaïre and South Africa, the Presidential Guard.[32] Then, in *Opération Noroît*, French forces continued to back the government during the 1990-3 civil war, when the latter was already committing atrocities, with military advisors, weapons, armoured cars and helicopters. The 1975 Franco-Rwandan Treaty was revised for this very purpose. Henceforth, not just French nationals would receive French protection, but also the Rwandese armed forces.[33] As far as Eric Fottorin was concerned, with regard to these largely Hutu massacres of Tutsis, '*la France ne voyait rien, n'entendait rien, ne disait rien*'.[g] [34]

This support was largely responsible for keeping the regime of President Habyarimana in power and, more importantly for the Elysée, for halting the advance of the Ugandan-backed RPF (Rwandan Patriotic Front) which, having reached the gates of the capital, had alarmingly looked set to switch Rwanda to the anglophone group of states.[35] This obsession with the containment of 'anglo-saxon' influence in the continent symbolically dates back to 1898, when a British force under Kitchener infamously intercepted and halted at Fashoda the French colonial advance into the Horn of Africa. To this end, much French rhetoric was used up in the 'demonisation' of Uganda. Indeed, Jacques Foccart, Presidential advisor on African affairs for some 35 years, saw the crisis in terms of the struggle with the United States for influence in the African continent, as part of an undeclared battle between Paris and Washington.[36] There was the genuine fear of something akin to that described by domino theory, namely that the overthrow of a French-backed regime, and the failure of Paris to intervene to protect it, would threaten neighbouring pro-French leaders, both by example and by direct conflict overspill. Although the fact that only one Rwandan adult in six spoke French fluently hardly supported the view of the most densely populated country in Africa being truly francophone.[37] For Marc Chavannes:

> [l]e Rwanda n'est pas un pays riche où l'on pouvait s'arracher des marchés intéressants. Mais pour préserver une Afrique francophone et amie, le pays a joué un rôle utile, grâce au régime de Juvénal Habyarimana, resté stable pendant des années. De plus, les Mitterrand et les Habyarimana étaient devenues très amis.[h] [38]

---

g   'France did not see anything, hear anything, say anything'.
h   'Rwanda is not a rich country with interesting markets to fight over. But in the preservation of Francphone Africa, the country has played a useful role, remaining stable for many years under the regime of Juvénal Habyarimana. Moreover, the Mitterrands

Certainly, Mitterrand was not impervious to the widespread international criticism of France's former role in Rwanda; his administration was being accused of having promoted the government which subsequently engineered the genocide. Moreover, is it not plausible that Mitterrand had been looking for France to lead an operation of this type so as to demonstrate to the rest of the world that France, contrary to its subservient role in Desert Storm, was still capable of force projection and of successfully leading an international action? Finally, Rwanda had been one of the few countries in which French influence had actually been growing, Paris was not about to abandon its efforts now.[39] The will of the President to act, backed in particular by his own son Jean-Christophe (a Presidential advisor on African affairs) and by Juppé at the Foreign Ministry, appears to have been decisive in launching the operation. It is clear, for example, that Prime Minister Balladur and Defence Minister Léotard shared the French military's reluctance to mount an action of this kind in which "the enemy" could not easily be determined.[40] Hence, this was very much the President's personal project, often in the face of the counsel of his advisors.[41] As with the Gulf War, the French President became the dominant agent within the domestic political structure. And to this can be added what McNulty describes as the in-built dynamic of French militarism. In his interpretation, '[o]nce alerted to trouble in its African backyard, France always intervened; it had done so more than 30 times since 1960; and in 1990, the outbreak of civil war in Rwanda led to the activation of the same traditional, mechanical interventionary response to a perceived intervention stimulus'.[42]

But if France, or more accurately Mitterrand, truly did have a sense of guilt, why did it move to protect the Hutus? It would not have exactly been good public relations to be seen to be protecting the people associated with perpetrating the genocide.[43] The desire for continued influence cannot be ruled out as a motive. In this way, *Opération Turquoise* could have been a move to get closer to, and to gain leverage over, the new government of the Tutsi-dominated RPF.[44] Certainly, Belgium and Italy, among others, suspected as much.[45] This was, incidentally, the first defeat of a French-armed, trained and sponsored army and administration in sub-Saharan Africa. Observers have also speculated that Mitterrand wanted to demonstrate to France's African partners that, despite all the recent rhetoric, it had not abandoned them completely. In this sense, this was a symbolic action.[46] Alison Desforges of Human Rights Watch, meanwhile, ascribed France's actions to the quest for glory.[47] Whatever the intention, the French troops, whose deployment had been vehemently opposed by the RPF, were welcomed by the Hutus, not as a neutral humanitarian force but as their allies. Certainly, there was the danger that the French would serve as a buffer between retreating former-government troops and the advancing victorious Tutsis. Indeed, clashes with RPF forces were reported.

Prime Minister Balladur denied any ulterior motive behind the operation, stating that France only acted after the international community had failed to respond adequately to an 'unacceptable tragedy'.[48] In addition, while accepting that the Hutus had to respect democratic freedoms, the unrealistic notion of a future Rwanda living in peace when governed by an RPF-led administration, when Tutsis only represented

---

and the Habyarimanas became great friends'.

some 14 per cent of the population, was highlighted.[49] However, Human Rights Watch Africa published a report in May 1995 claiming that France, and Zaire, had flouted the UN arms embargo, established in May 1994, in order to assist the fleeing Hutu government. Furthermore, the organisation claimed that Hutu militias were receiving training at a French military facility in the Central African Republic.[50] Mel McNulty, meanwhile cites French extra-regional support for the Hutus, as one of the belligerents in the conflict, as having served to artificially prolong that conflict, especially once these Hutus came to believe that the support from Paris was open-ended and unconditional.[51]

In *Opération Turquoise*, France applied the lessons learnt from previous post-Cold War international interventions, principally the ill-fated American-led action in Somalia. Firstly, it insisted on a clear mandate from the UN and it applied Chapter VII of the UN Charter, declaring its preparedness to use force, if necessary, in the carrying out of the mandate. The French force cautiously defined the lines within which it could take command without fighting, but which it could defend if necessary. This was, essentially, an area over which it could temporarily rule. Secondly, French policy-makers had become far more prudent towards overseas military undertakings and were now supposedly reluctant, in the new security environment, for France to be seen to be acting alone.[52] Hence, concerted efforts were made to ensure that the intervention force was multinational in make-up. Cooperation was sought from France's west European allies under the auspices of the WEU, but in vain, as the latter were reluctant to get involved.[53] In the end, only a few francophone African states came on board and not to any great extent. A strict short time limit on the operation was imposed. It was made clear from the outset that this was not going to be an open-ended commitment.[54] The French forces withdrew in mid-August, handing over control of the protected zone to new UNAMIR forces.

Many, including representatives of humanitarian agencies had warned that the action would only exacerbate the genocide.[55] And the operation was subsequently criticised for actually making the humanitarian situation worse. The safe-area, created on 5 July, only served to suck-in thousands of refugees from outside, swamping the resources of the aid agencies. Clearly, the operation did not bring about any noticeable improvement in the lot of the local population. But the French would argue that the action was realistic rather than idealistic, being only a stopgap, administering to those in need and protecting them from violence. It was never, so this argument goes, going to be a solution. Thomas Sancton was more dismissive, saying that all this 'humanitarian' operation succeeded in doing was to freeze, temporarily, the situation on the ground.[56] Nevertheless, Mitterrand's France, without doubt, did more than most, whatever its motives, to attempt to bring a halt, if temporary, to the slaughter.[57] In the view of Christian Hoche, '*[a]u milieu de l'indifférence planétaire, elle a été le seul pays a accepter de se salir les mains*'.[i][58]

Andrew Roberts, meanwhile, was not so complimentary. 'Proclaiming their mission's success ..., the French then abandoned the zone, leaving the well-supplied

---

[i]   'In the middle of global indifference, it was the only country to accept getting its hands dirty'.

Hutus with a strong power base and ready to continue the war as soon as they had gone'.[59] And there were claims that Paris had continued to arm the Hutus for some considerable time after they had begun their systematic genocide against the Tutsis.[60] Indeed, Jean-François Bayart speculated that French personnel began to rearm the defeated extremist Hutus concentrated in refugee camps in eastern Zaire.[61] To this end, René Backmann reported a supposed airborne operation, coordinated by French Special Forces, to supply some 100 tons of military equipment to these Hutu camps.[62] And various members of the Hutu political and military elites found refuge in the safe areas established by *Turquoise*. Kirsty Lang reported, for example, that the chief architect of the genocide, Theonestre Bagasora, was 'whisked away' by French troops before he could be captured by the RPF.[63] Philippe Leymarie, meanwhile, described *Turquoise* as late (some ten weeks after the massacres had started), ambiguous, confused and risky.[64] What is clear is that France's standing among other African states and with the Organisation for African Unity took a serious downturn, many being of the opinion that France, given its historical involvement with the Hutu government, should not have got involved. The subsequent non-invitation of the now Tutsi-led Rwanda to the francophone gathering in Biarritz (November 1994) did nothing to quell France's critics.

Post-Rwanda

Meanwhile, with a new President installed at the Elysée, the French, in addition to contributing to the new UN mission, UNAVEM, in Angola, continued to conduct those solo small-scale African military operations that observers had become accustomed to. Chirac would emphasise the high level of continuity with the policy pursued by François Mitterrand.[65] In true gaullist fashion, he considered himself 'African'. To this end, and backed by certain elements within the RPR possessing strong business links with the region, more emphasis was placed on Africa despite strong objections from 'modernists' at the Quai d'Orsay. There had been a recent intervention in Cameroon, *Opération Aramis*, in February 1995, and Chirac authorised *Opération Southern Cross* in Niger, which ran from July to December in his inaugural year.

At this time, the Minister of Cooperation, Jacques Godfrain, announced that France would intervene on behalf of a democratically elected regime if a defence treaty existed with that country. However, this appeared to be a false promise as Niger's democratically elected government was denied French military support in the face of an army coup in February 1996. Paris instead decided to work with the new military regime.[66] Then the French military became particularly active in the Central African Republic, in *Opération Almandin*, in May 1996 (ostensibly to protect French nationals and possibly in the face of local popular opinion)[67] and in the Comoros. In the former, French troops, initially "invited" to intervene by President Patassié, gradually 'handed over' to an inter-African force (MISAB, later replaced by an UN force – MINURCA) comprising troops from six other sub-Saharan states whose mission was to oversee the implementation of the 1997 Bangui peace accords.

The longer-term significance of this all-African initiative has yet to be ascertained, but, certainly, it mirrors ongoing French, and British (supported by the WEU), efforts to create, train and equip an African permanent peacekeeping force reporting to the Organisation for African Unity. Chirac, among others, was now calling for Africans to take responsibility for their own stability and for a clear vision of the security architecture for Africa in which the OAU and sub-regional organisations play a major part.[68] In 1998, to support the Africans, France launched RECAMP (the Reinforcement of African Peacekeeping Capabilities Programme), but continues to stresses that this is not a step towards French disengagement (some 20 per cent of funds allocated for military cooperation in Africa has been redirected to African peacekeeping).[69] It is, rather, a recognition that while African armed forces have the human resources to participate in all types of operations, they often need support in the areas of logistics, transport and specialised training. In January 1998, the material required to equip an African peacekeeping battalion was pre-positioned in Dakar, Senegal, and later that year Zambroko in Côte d'Ivoire became host to training centre for peacekeeping (established with French collaboration). The utility of RECAMP can be seen in the Central African Republic, it also contributed logistics and transport facilities to the ECOMOG operation in Guinea-Bissau.

A mercenary-led coup in the Comoros was foiled in October 1995 by a 900-strong French force, codename *Azalée*, deployed on Chirac's personal directive to 'restore order'.[70] The French took the opportunity to promote the Prime Minister to the Presidency; altogether someone far more favourable and presentable for the French leadership.[71] This was not the first time that France had intervened militarily in the affairs of these tiny islands of high strategic value given their location at the head of the Mozambique Channel.[72] Paris was clearly still prepared to play it tough, and to incur considerable costs in its African policy. Jim Hoagland described these operations as 'thunderbolt diplomacy'.[73] Or as Moïsi put it, 'we intervene, therefore we are'.[74] And clearly, Chirac has been prepared to use the capacity for Presidential initiatives within French security policy-making to stamp his own authority on the process. Here again, we see the Presidency behaving as the principal determining agent within the French political structure. However, it seemed as though France was becoming increasingly less inclined to intervene in the region in order to overthrow a regime. To some extent, it would seem that the Rwanda experience has had the same impact on French policy-makers as Somalia had on the American counterparts.[75] It was certainly striking, through 1995 and 1996, that France was unwilling to act independently and intervene in a turbulent Burundi. Since 1995, French leaders have become increasingly disinclined to authorise unilateral peacekeeping operations, preferring instead to not be involved or to be part of a multinational endeavour.

This appeared to be the message when the Paris decision-makers refused to sanction unilateral military intervention in Zaire towards the end of 1996. The situation was, on the surface at least, largely similar to that which had already prompted French action in Rwanda, another former-Belgian colony absorbed into *la francophonie* under Giscard during the mid-1970s: a perceived 'invasion' of a friendly francophone state by an army of hostile anglophones from a neighbouring state. If, asks McNulty, 1994's *Opération Turquoise*, as France's first milito-humanitarian intervention had been as 'successful' as Paris claimed then why not repeat the exercise elsewhere, not least as a means of boosting French *grandeur* and *rang*?[76] Was this sudden paralysis, asked Philippe Leymarie, a further sign of France's growing *impuissance* in sub-Saharan Africa?[77] And what were the consequences for French influence in the region if political crises in Zaire and the Central African Republic, countries where French military forces had been omnipresent, could not be prevented? The loss of a pro-French regime in Kinshasa (Zaire is the world's second-largest French-speaking country), with President Mobutu being ousted by anglophone Laurent-Désiré Kabila (a long-time opponent of Mobutu), backed by forces from Angola, Rwanda (displaced Tutsis) and Uganda, was in particular a serious blow to Paris' regional standing. Zaire, now the Democratic Republic of Congo, joined Burundi and Rwanda as former-francophone, pro-Paris, states being run by new anglophone rulers. And, seen from Paris, the situation in neighbouring Congo, described by René Backmann as an Elf protectorate (referring to that French company's dominant position in the country), did not look too promising at this time.[78] Whereas Uganda is a strong American ally of long-standing. The worst fears of a central African version of domino theory, as described above, were appearing to be realised. Relations between Paris and Kinshasa quickly deteriorated. Kabila's administration remains deeply suspicious of French motives, and at one point even threatened to withdraw from *la francophonie*.[79] And this distrust can only have been accentuated by repeated claims in early 1998 of French complicity in the arming of the perpetrators of the Rwandan genocide. And this particularly since the Elysée has so far rejected mounting calls for a national enquiry in to the precise nature of France's role in the conflict.[80] Hence, in the short-term at least, France appears somewhat discredited in central Africa and its relative position weakened. French supremacy was no longer unchallenged.

Economic Influence – the New Measure of a Great Power?

Whatever the fate of France's status, it was now clear that the international competition for influence across the African continent was to be fought increasingly in the economic sphere. Paris fears that French business interests could now lose out to their anglophone, principally American, rivals. The subsequent loss of political clout, further accentuated by the diplomatic advances of anglophone Nigeria and South Africa, could have traumatic consequences for a country traditionally used to 'calling the shots' and being the only great power in this region. Traditional power relationships are being turned on their head, with the French, for the sake of national interest, being widely perceived as having sought to preserve the post-colonial status quo. Regional cooperation and collaboration with the US is seemingly being replaced in French African policy by a growing sense of competition. Backmann reported, for example, that Kabila was granting American companies mining concessions in former-Zaire, replacing in the process long-standing agreements with European enterprises.[81] Indeed, the US has noticeably become more economically aggressive in Africa since a President Clinton-led trade initiative in 1993 (American exports to the continent rose by 20 per cent in both 1994 and 1995).[82] For Marchal, here were graphic illustrations of the short-sightedness of French policy which were now placing France in an inferior position in relation to the 'extremely enterprising American diplomacy which was more in tune with the way the continent was changing'.[83]

The reaction in Paris has been, while remaining faithful to France's traditional francophone partners but partly to off-set perceived setbacks in francophone Burundi, Rwanda and Zaire, to engage far more proactively with the continent as a whole, including former British and Portuguese colonies, while simultaneously being more selective. As an illustration of this new approach, the twentieth Africa-France summit, held in Paris during November 1998, welcomed representatives from an unprecedented 49 African states (Libya and Sudan – under UN sanctions – and Somalia – lacking a central government – were not invited), as well as the UN and OAU Secretary-Generals. In the same vein, President Chirac's July 1999 African tour took in three long-standing partners, Cameroon, Guinea and Togo, but Chirac also became the first French Head of State to visit Nigeria (anglophone and the regional superpower). And there is a far greater sense of cooperation with its former Western rivals. In March 1999, for example, Foreign Minister Védrine, undertook a joint diplomatic mission with British Foreign Minister Cook to Côte d'Ivoire and Ghana. On paper at least, there were no longer exclusive or forbidden zones of influence. In September that year, in the wings of the UN General Assembly, the two Foreign Ministers jointly met with their counterparts from Côte d'Ivoire, Gabon, Kenya and Nigeria to discuss various crises. And it was clear that kind of arrangement was not going to be a 'one-off'. And in terms of development policy, France has resolved many of its differences with the International Monetary Fund and the World Bank that had been running since the late 1980s to the extent that it is now fully part of the coordinated international effort.

Domestic Pressures

In addition to reflecting new geopolitical, France's African policy also began to reflect the constraints being imposed by the requirements of the domestic economy and the decision to end conscription and move towards fully professional armed forces (by 2002, the overall size of the French army would have been downsized by 36 per cent).[84] The country's military presence in the region would undergo a radical overhaul. At the beginning of 1997, some 8,200 French troops were stationed across the continent. By July (only four months after the death of France's *Monsieur Afrique*, Jacques Foccart, with whom France's interventionist volition in the continent is most closely associated) it was clear that this presence would be cut by some 40 per cent within three years (to 5,500 by 2000) and consolidated in fewer bases (down from six to five). If anything, Jospin's Socialist-led centre-left coalition government, elected in the May of that year and of a younger generation than the now deceased Mitterrand who had dominated the Party's policy since the 1970s, proved to be even firmer on this than Juppé's and Balladur's centre-right administrations had been, determined as it was to break with the colonialist past. Indeed, Marchal interpreted the new government's stance as indicating that French interventionism in Africa was over.[85] Here was a graphic illustration of the reining back of France's national ambitions, particularly in Africa. Troop numbers in Chad, Djibouti, Gabon and Senegal were thus scaled down (although they were unchanged in Côte d'Ivoire), and there has been a total withdrawal from the Central African Republic and Cameroon. In the past, often almost unnoticed by the international community, French forces had launched more than 30 military operations from that country.[86] A further component of this rationalisation took effect from the start of 1999, namely the transferral of the post of Minister for Cooperation to a more junior rank within the Quai d'Orsay under the authority of the Foreign Minister. Concurrently, the post of Minister for *la francophonie* was abolished and its duties also moved to the Quai. These were also attempts to increase the transparency of France's traditionally opaque African policy.

Did these measures serve to illustrate a reining back of French national ambitions? The official line denied these claims; *désengagement* was not a policy option.

> *Si la France privilégie désormais une approche multilatérale des questions de sécurité sur le continent africain, elle continue d'honorer les accords de défense qui la lient à certains pays et maintient pour l'essentiel le dispositif de ses forces prépositionnées.*[j] [87]

Fitchett saw 'a new policy of benign neglect towards regimes that until recently thought that they could rely on French military might to keep them in power'. He went on to suggest the 'demise of a long-standing view in Paris that the fealty of a bloc of west African nations provided trade advantages and confirmed France's status as a world power'.[88] It was becoming clear that, on paper at least, France would no longer consider Africa as a collective whole, worrying that failure to support one regime would lead to panic among others. And the implementation of this approach can only have been accelerated by the aforementioned events in Zaire. Paris was now looking to adopt a less paternalistic, more selective, approach, focusing on those states that 'show promise', both in terms of political stability and economic viability. And the economic motive is crucial here, at a time when the French were attempting to spread their influence on the continent to non-francophone states, they were no longer in a position to subsidise automatically their traditional partners.

Conclusion

The nature of the international system has changed to the extent that France is no longer in a position to act alone as an agent in pursuit of its fundamental security policy objectives. And, worryingly for some, even France's pre-eminence in much of sub-Saharan Africa is now being seriously challenged. Due not least to a series of significant miscalculations in French policy-making circles, the privileged relationship Paris had enjoyed with many of these countries can no longer be taken for granted. French African policy has suffered because it has failed to keep pace with changing circumstances across the continent, not least the emergence of a new generation of national leaders. Marchal pointed to 'the conservative nature of French politics and its

---

[j]   'If France henceforth promotes a multilateral approach towards security questions on the
        African continent, she continues to honour her defence accords that link her to certain
        countries and to maintain, for the most part, its system of pre-positioned forces'.

understanding of African policy, where personal ties and traditional networks were predominant' as also being to blame.[89] Referring to the Rwandan excursion of 1994, Gregory noted 'France had sleepwalked into a disaster on the assumption that past policy would continue to work'.[90] But equally, there has been a new realisation that even in sub-Saharan Africa France cannot continue to 'try and do it all'. The reasoning is now that if French security policy is to maintain its pursuit of its strategic objectives then even its African policy would have to be rationalised and more multinational solutions, both Western and local, would have to be sought.[91] Observers have noticed since the Rwandan catastrophe an increasing reluctance among hitherto almost 'trigger happy' French leaders to deploy French troops in unilateral peacekeeping operations in sub-Saharan Africa as elsewhere. Thus multinational endeavours have become the *ordre du jour*.[92] And perhaps we are witnessing a gradual but steady process of the normalisation of French relations with the region. It is certainly clear that what we *are* witnessing is a more global approach to the region, an increasingly multilateral approach to African security issues. France's political leadership are attempting to readjust relations with Africa 'by breaking away from the mould of its special influence over the African French-speaking countries and moving towards a policy of aid for all African states regardless of whether they are French-, Portuguese- or English-speaking'.[93] And this has been accompanied by a significant reduction of France's military presence across the continent.

Notes

1 Kolodziej, Edward A. (1974), *French International Policy under De Gaulle and Pompidou*, Cornell University Press, Ithaca, p.447.
2 Gordon, Philip H. (1993), *A Certain Idea of France: French Security Policy and the Gaullist Legacy*, Princeton University Press, Princeton, pp.7-8.
3 France dissolved its two large African colonial federations (French West Africa and French Equatorial Africa) in 1960. Of the 20 francophone African states, 15 had been direct French dependencies: Benin, Burkina Faso, Central African Republic, Chad, the Comores, Congo, Gabon, Djibouti, Guinea, Côte d'Ivoire, Madagascar, Mauritania, Niger, Senegal; two had been French-administered UN trust territories: Cameroon and Togo; and three had been ruled by Belgium: Burundi, Rwanda and Zaïre.
4 McNamara, Francis Terry (1989), *France in Black Africa*, National Defence University Press, Washington DC, 1989, p.235.
5 Roberts, Andrew, 'Zaire, a problem for France alone', *The Sunday Times*, 10 November 1996.
6 McNulty, Mel, 'France's role in Rwanda and external military intervention: a double discrediting', *International Peacekeeping*, vol.4, no.3, Autumn 1997, p.27.
7 Isnard, Jacques, 'La France remanie son dispositif militaire en Afrique', *Le Monde*, 20 July 1997.
8 Gregory, Shaun (2000), *French Defence Policy into the Twenty-First Century*, Macmillan, Basingstoke, p.156.
9 Smouts, Marie-Claude, 'The Fifth Republic and the Third World', in Paul Godt (ed), *Policy-making in France*, Pinter Publishers, London, 1989, p.241.
10 McNulty, Mel, *op cit*, p.31.

11 Betts, Paul, 'France shoulders thankless role of gendarme in Chad', *The Financial Times*, 9 January 1987. See also, McNamara, Francis Terry, *op cit*, p.170.

12 Schraeder, Peter J., 'France and the Great Game in Africa', *Current History*, vol.96, no.610, May 1997, p.206.

13 Védrine, Hubert (1996), *Les Mondes de François Mitterrand: A l'Elysée 1981-1995*, Fayard, Paris, pp.710-11.

14 *Ibid*, p.198.

15 Hoffman, Stanley (1987), 'La politique internationale de Mitterrand ou le gaullisme sous un autre nom', in Stanley Hoffman and Silvia Malzacher (eds), *L'Expérience Mitterrand: Continuité et Changement dans la France Contemporaine*, Presses Univésitaires de France/Basil Blackwell, Cambridge, p.377.

16 Weiss, Thomas G., Forsythe, David P. and Coate, Roger A. (1994), *The United Nations and Changing World Politics*, Westview Press, Boulder, p.53.

17 Gallois (Général [C.R.]), Pierre-Marie (1993), 'Les nouvelles conditions de sécurité de la défense', in Pierre Pascallon (ed), *Quelle Défense pour la France?*, Institut des Relations Internationales et Stratégiques/Dunod, Paris, p.71.

18 Wauthier, Claude, 'La politique Africaine de la France: 1988-1993', *Relations Internationales et Stratégiques*, no.9, Spring 1993, p.200.

19 Duteil, Mireille, 'Les héritiers de l'Afrique', *Le Point*, 12 February 1994, p.41.

20 Dumas, Roland (French Foreign Minister), quoted in Duteil, Mireille, 'La France dans le bourbier', *Le Point*, 6 February 1993, p.19.

21 *The Fourth 'Dossier Noir' de la Politique Africaine de la France*, Coalition pour Ramener a la Raison Démocratique la Politique Africaine de la France, February 1995, p.6.

22 The CFA (the common African Financial Community) had been introduced in 1948 and pegged the currencies of 14 African states to the French franc. By this time, commerce with Africa had fallen to some three per cent of France's overall trade, from around 30 per cent in the 1960s: 'Au revoir to Africa', *Time*, 3 April 1995, p.45.

23 Marchal, Roland, 'France and Africa: the emergence of essential reforms?', *International Affairs*, vol.74, no.2, 1998, p.355.

24 Duteil, Mireille, 'Mitterrand: l'Africain', *Le Point*, 2 July 1994, p.40.

25 Leymarie, Philippe, 'La France et le maintien de l'ordre en Afrique', *Le Monde Diplomatique*, June 1994, p.28.

26 Mitterrand, François, quoted in Subtil, Marie-Pierre, 'François Mitterrand affirme que la France doit "refuser de réduire son ambition africaine"', *Le Monde*, 10 November 1994.

27 *UNSC Resolution 794*.

28 D'Oléon, Michel (Vice-Amiral), then Chargé de Recherche, Western European Union Institute For Security Studies, in an interview with the author, Paris, April 1995.

29 Torrelli, Maurice, *op cit*, p.76.

30 Hertzog, Gilles, 'La peur ou le choléra', *Le Point*, 30 July 1994, p.24.

31 Juppé, Alain, quoted in Duteil, Mireille, 'Rwanda: pourquoi la France intervient', *Le Point*, 25 June 1994, p.14.

32 Schlosser, François, 'Rwanda: la France est-elle coupable?', *Le Nouvel Observateur*, June 30 1994, p.38.

33 McNulty, Mel, 'France's role in Rwanda and external military intervention: a double discrediting', *International Peacekeeping*, vol.4, no.3, Autumn 1997, p.30.

34 Fottorino, Eric, 'Dans le piège rwandais', *Le Monde*, 25 July 1997.

35 Duteil, Mireille, 'Les embarras de Paris', *Le Point*, 18 June 1994, p.14.

36 Lang, Kirsty, 'France plays African power game', *The Sunday Times*, 10 November 1996.
37 Smyth, Frank, 'La France compromise au Rwanda', *Courrier International*, 21 April 1994.
38 Chavannes, Marc, 'Les dessous de l'intervention au Rwanda', *Courrier International*, 7 July 1994, p.8.
39 Bayart, Jean-François and Massiah, Gustave, 'La France au Rwanda', *Les Temps Modernes*, vol.50, no.583, July/August 1995, p.224.
40 McCarthy, Patrick, 'France in the mid-1990s: gloom but not doomed', *Current History*, vol.93, no.586, November 1994, p.364.
41 Bayart, Jean-François and Massiah, Gustave, *op cit*, p.217.
42 McNulty, Mel, *op cit*, p.31.
43 Boniface, Pascal, Directeur, IRIS, in an interview with the author, Paris, April 1995.
44 'Zone of influence', *The Economist*, 9 July 1994, p.58.
45 McCarthy, Patrick, *op cit*, p.368.
46 Duteil, Mireille, 'Mitterrand: l'Africain', *op cit*, p.37.
47 Desforges, Alison, quoted in Elliott, Michael, 'A calculus of incursion', *Newsweek*, 1 August 1994, p.17.
48 Littlejohns, Michael, 'Balladur denies Rwanda agenda', *The Financial Times*, 12 July 1994.
49 Védrine, Hubert, *op cit*, p.703.
50 'Guilty governments', *The Economist*, 3 June 1995, p.65.
51 McNulty, Mel, *op cit*, p.24.
52 D'Oleon, Michel, *op cit*.
53 Italy said that it would 'not exclude' such a commitment but made no promises. Britain, in the meantime, offered 50 trucks, while the Dutch offered a field hospital and air transport. Drozdiak, William, 'Paris finds no backing on Rwanda force', *International Herald Tribune*, 19 June 1994.
54 D'Oleon, Michel, *op cit*.
55 Crawford, Leslie, Buchan, David and Reuters, 'French troops mount first Rwanda patrol', *The Financial Times*, 24 June 1994.
56 Sancton, Thomas, 'Back to central Africa', *Time*, 4 July 1994, p.25.
57 'Zone of influence', *op cit*, p.58.
58 Hoche, Christian, 'La France attend le relève', *L'Express*, 14 July 1994, p.28.
59 Roberts, Andrew, 'Zaire, a problem for France alone', *The Sunday Times*, 10 November 1996, p.5.
60 See for example, Verschave, François-Xavier, 'Connivences françaises au Rwanda', *Le Monde Diplomatique*, March 1995, p.10.
61 Bayart, Jean-François, 'Zaïre: "le fiasco français"', *Le Nouvel Observateur*, 15 May 1997, p.63.
62 Backmann, René, 'Gribouille au Congo', *Le Nouvel Observateur*, 5 December 1996, p.78.
63 Lang, Kirsty, *op cit*, p.19.
64 Leymarie, Philippe, 'Litigieuse intervention française au Rwanda', *Le Monde Diplomatique*, July 1994, p.3.
65 Sotinel, Thomas, 'M. Chirac réaffirme le continuité de la politique africaine de la France', *Le Monde*, 8 December 1996.
66 Schraeder, Peter J., 'France and the Great Game in Africa', *Current History*, vol.96, no.610, May 1997, p.208.

67 French, Howard W., 'West's intervention in Africa: not solving the problems', *International Herald Tribune*, 28 May 1996. France's defence agreement with the Central African Republic only covers external aggression, not internal threats.

68 Chirac, Jacques, at the Twentieth Conference of Heads of State of Africa and France, Paris, 26-8 November 1998.

69 *Idem*.

70 Webster, Paul, 'French troops end coup in Comoros', *The Guardian*, 5 October 1995.

71 Sotinel, Thomas, 'Nouvelle doctrine, vieilles habitudes', *Le Monde*, 6 October 1995.

72 Hélène, Jean, 'La conférence de l'OAU n'a pas résolu la crise des Comores', *Le Monde*, 16 December 1997.

73 Hoagland, Jim, 'France hoists the old "White Man's Burden" in Central Africa', *International Herald Tribune*, 1 June 1996.

74 Moïsi, Dominique, quoted in Hoagland, Jim, *op cit*.

75 'Peacekeeping and Security in Africa' – Conclusions Drawn from the Lisbon Colloquy, Assembly of the Western European Union Document 1648, 19 May 1999, p.23.

76 McNulty, Mel, *op cit*, p.26.

77 Leymarie, Philippe, 'En Afrique, la fin des ultimes "chasses gardées"', *Le Monde Diplomatique*, December 1996, p.4.

78 Backmann, René, 'Afrique: les foyers de crise', *Le Nouvel Observateur*, 19 June 1997, p.64.

79 Fritscher, Frédéric, 'La République démocratique du Congo accuse la France devouloir déstabiliser le pays', *Le Monde*, 2 December 1997.

80 Webster, Paul, 'France "armed killers in Rwanda genocide"', *The Guardian*, 13 January 1998.

81 Backmann, René, *op cit*, p.64.

82 Boulet-Gercourt, Philippe, 'Washington et le gâteau africain', *Le Nouvel Observateur*, 12 December 1996, p.70.

83 Marchal, Roland, *op cit*, p.356.

84 Owen, David, 'France set to lower its guard in Africa', *The Financial Times*, 31 July 1997.

85 Marchal, Roland, *op cit*, p.363.

86 Duval-Smith, Alex, 'France to slash troop numbers in Africa', *The Guardian*, 26 July 1997.

87 French Foreign Ministry Briefing Note *La Politique Africaine de la France*, www.france.diplomatie.fr, 12 November 1999.

88 Fitchett, Joseph, 'New policy for Africa: don't rely on troops from France', *International Herald Tribune*, 11 August 1997.

89 Marchal, Roland, *op cit*, p.368.

90 Gregory, Shaun, *op cit*, p.159.

91 During 1999, and as part of its RECAMP programme (Reinforcement of African Peacekeeping Capabilities [itself part of wider UN-sanctioned Franco-British-American efforts to enable Africans to manage and resolve their own political crises]), France established a training centre for peacekeeping forces in Côte D'Ivoire and in Senegal placed the required equipment for an African peacekeeping battalion. Elsewhere, logistics and transport facilities have been supplied to ECOMOG in Guinea-Bissau.

92 'Peacekeeping and Security in Africa', *op cit*, p.23.

93 *Idem*.

Chapter 8

Conclusion – The Loss of *Spécificité* and the Normalisation of French Security Policy?

The premise of this volume has been that it is an inherent feature of French political culture to claim something of an elevated place within the international community based on the notions of *grandeur* and *rang*. No real alternative to the pursuit of this goal, with its twin, closely inter-related tenets, has been given any serious consideration by the country's leaders since the Second World War. 'France', so the thinking goes, would not be France without its high profile external vocation. Furthermore, the rest of the world supposedly looked to the French to take something of the lead in international affairs. To this end, de Gaulle, writing in 1941, had declared that there was a secular pact between the *grandeur* of France and the freedom of the world.[1] And this eccentric self-promotion was brazenly pushed on all willing to listen despite glaring tensions. In this way, the universal mission described in Chapter One could be claimed in the face of a widely documented aggressive and self-serving colonial past, or the *anglo-saxons* could be held up almost as pariahs while French policy could be virtually identical to that of Britain and the US. In de Montbrial's view meanwhile:

> [i]n very different fields, it is because of this sense of universal mission that the French accept their casualties in Yugoslavia, that Mr. Chirac intends to preserve a deterrent capability for the long-term, and that the French film industry is defended tooth and nail whereas the Italians have let theirs perish. These three examples stem from one and the same idea: France must remain true to itself.[2]

And Tom Lansford wrote of the country having retained its 'idiosyncratic view of its own importance and rank as a world power'.[3] But these pretensions to an elevated global standing have not just rested on empty rhetoric. As Gregory notes, '[g]eography condemns France to engagement; lacking the isolation of the island state or the remoteness of the peripheral state, France has been forced to look outwards to the affairs of its neighbours and beyond'.[4] The characteristic flamboyant gesturing has been backed, for example, by quite a radical overhaul of the armed forces that will enable France to perpetuate its influence around the world through national and multinational military operations. And it has been the French who have consistently led the movement towards the construction of the European Union into a viable international military actor. And these have represented tactical adaptations to changing circumstances through the Fifth Republic in order to ensure that the fixed strategic objective, as crystallised by the actions and legacy of de Gaulle, continues to be attained.

Gaullism in the New Century

Thomas Friedman noted that some specialists referred to gaullism as having been a form of psychotherapy to restore the dignity of a France humiliated by Nazi occupation and subsequent liberation by principally 'anglo-saxon' forces.[5] Many believed that the main elements of gaullism would not outlive their creator.[6] But as described from Chapter Three onwards, the policy choices of de Gaulle and his *certaine idée de la France* were to subsequently develop something of their own momentum. Menon pointed to the increasingly fragmented nature of the French State, to the relative powerlessness of the national leadership to impose its policy preferences.[7] EU founding father Robert Schumann, meanwhile, had always argued that gaullism was much more than the attachment to a single figure.[8] John Gaffney described all of the Fifth Republic's Presidents as gaullist in terms, both through individual choice and the public expectations of the office, of being personally responsible for France's prestige through assertions both of national independence and a leadership role in Europe.[9]

So what does gaullism stand for in terms of French security policy in the twenty-first century? Chirac, as President, described it as pragmatism,[10] and Pompidou referred to it as a way of behaving.[11] It appears, in addition, to represent a conviction of France's special place in the world. And there is the sense of constantly being on the initiative. A lesson from 1940 was that France should not be manipulated by events, rather, it should, as much as possible, be in charge of them. General Michel Cot, former French UNPROFOR commander, described gaullist leadership as both knowing and fearing the French people.[12] Former-Prime Minister Pierre Messmer spoke of the capacity to say 'no'; that is, to be able to produce an alternative to the supposed dictates of the international system.[13] Linked to this has been a clear disposal to display intransigence in international politics in order to ensure that France was heard. Elsewhere, Moïsi wrote:

> [s]ome see it as no more than a style of foreign policy, combining energy, a desire to act and a readiness to engage in confrontation beyond what self-interest might regard as necessary. Others see it as a way of looking at the world that transcends the day-to-day events to capture the real trends in global politics. Harsher critics see Gaullism as a more tragic phenomenon, a desperate, even futile, attempt to establish a role in a world in which France, a defeated country in 1940, is no longer a great power or even a truly significant actor. In this view, Gaullism encourages France to overreach itself by trying to play a role beyond its means with a combination of flamboyant style, rhetoric and political willpower.[14]

Certainly Chipman, writing in 1989, was able to observe: 'no other former great power has been so faithful to its attitudes of the past, no other so successful in transporting seemingly out-dated images of power into the political discourse'.[15]

Klein was correct in his observation that each of the General's successors at the Elysée had the capacity to introduce fundamental changes but that, whether consciously or not, they did not make use of it. *'Il est significatif*, he said, *'que les initiatives prises par la diplomatie française depuis 1990 ne contredisent pas le dessein gaullien des années 1950 et 1960'*.[a] [16] For Dominique David, all of France has become gaullist, in terms of wanting a France *puissante* and believing in its historical universalist mission. He also refers to gaullism as being nothing precise, as being an ongoing *discours politique*, which is consequently open to manipulation.[17] It has, for example, been employed to justify controversial policy decisions such as Chirac's resumption of nuclear testing. De Montbrial was more specific, pointing to the traditional French identification with *le grand homme*, be this Joan of Arc, Louis XIV or Napoleon. De Gaulle thus represents just the latest immortalised incarnation, having saved France from national disaster and restoring its integrity and *grandeur*.[18] However, Joseph Fitchett makes the valid point that admiration for the General's realism and his insight into historical trends ignores the significant degree to which he was driven by unshakeable grudges and skilled opportunism.[19] And as Moïsi acknowledges, realism, unilateralism and a zest for glory comprise key elements of gaullist thinking.[20]

Gaullism was also, at least initially, about reshaping the international system to ensure that no other power was in a position to dictate to France. But can it not now be said that this traditional, gaullist, interpretation of the international system, upon which French foreign policy had rested since the early 1960s, was made obsolete by the end of the Cold War? For example, de Gaulle, in creating the *force de frappe*, insisted that it must remain an unfettered national weapon. French rhetoric, if not actions, has, in recent years, moved away from this rigidity. Is this one sign of the country's gradual substitution of the General's legacy? But it seems equally plausible that gaullism, whatever it finally means, is not being replaced, but that, rather, President Chirac and the other key policy-makers are attempting to adapt it to the new era. After all, contemporary French security policy has lost none of its impassioned pursuit of the *grandes lignes*, continuing as it does to making concerted efforts to influence political developments around the globe.

The very vagueness of gaullism makes it hard to quantify and assess. It has, for example, no doctrine, especially regarding economics, to restrict its appeal. In political terms, it could not be described as being Christian Democrat or Liberal. It can be found across the political spectrum. A 1991 opinion poll found that only 55 per cent of deputies in the RPR, supposed bastion of the General's legacy, actually described themselves as gaullist; however, ten per cent of Socialist deputies and 32 per cent of National Front deputies also described themselves as gaullist.[21] Olivier Duhamel has written of the changing nature of the RPR (the direct descendant of the political grouping built around de Gaulle in the 1960s), claiming that it had been progressively losing much of its gaullist character over the years, certainly losing its links to the General. He added that the inevitable leadership renewal gained momentum from

---

[a] 'It is significant that the initiatives taken by French diplomacy since 1990 do not contradict the Gaullist design of the 1950s and 60s'.

1981, when Chirac, as party leader, used the party's years in opposition to remove older and ineffective individuals from the party hierarchy. In their place he brought in a new generation of leaders loyal to himself as opposed to the grand notion of gaullism.[22] Dabezies even went as far as to denounce the idea of Chirac as gaullist, ascribing him with no ideology at all.[23] He stressed Chirac's wholly pragmatic approach, and yet this is, after all, all that some observers believe gaullism to be.

French Security Policy in the New Century

It has been the contention here that while much has changed within the international security environment during the lifetime of the Fifth Republic, France's security policy-makers have clung resolutely to the twin fundamental objectives of globally recognised greatness and standing. And this stems from a long and turbulent national historical experience that has contributed a mixed legacy of feelings of *grandeur* and insecurity. Mabry and Stanger produced the following analysis of France as a security actor: '[a]n affluent nation. A brilliant culture. A glorious past. France seemed to have it all – and knew it. For a long time it made sure everyone else knew it too'.[24] While Robert A. Levine has referred to what he termed 'the traditional French belief that the facts and logic must be on their side'.[25] Essentially, what has come across has been, on the surface at least, a strong self-reliance. It can never be claimed that 'France' has not been portrayed by its representatives as possessing a strong personality. But it also appears to be the case that despite the outward rhetoric and the plethora of grand gestures, much of French foreign policy during the Fifth Republic has been driven by a pervading sense of insecurity, in place since the defeat of 1870, and by a fear of isolation and of domination by other powers.[26] This anxiety has required constant managing by the political elites. Another interpretation came from Kolodziej, who denied such a methodological approach, describing instead a French global policy which:

> struggled against itself. ... Torn between limited resources and soaring, limitless national aims, French global policy condemned itself to pragmatic tactical adjustments and opportune alignments, waiting for a better day when perhaps the weakness of its rivals rather than its own material strength would return it to the first rank among nations. It was a policy of 'muddling through', obscured by a Gaullist genius for dramatic posturing and arresting turns of phrase that suggested more substance and coherence in French behaviour than close examination could justify.[27]

Jean-Marie Domenach, meanwhile, lambasted his fellow countrymen for erecting a series of conceptual Maginot lines around themselves, and for resting on dreams and self-deception. He went on to cite something of a fortress mentality and bemoaned the country's general reluctance to adopt necessary modernising measures.[28] For a thousand years or so, France has been used to acting largely unimpeded, as it pleased, and to having an influence on the major international issues of the day. And for some 30 years, the political elites have managed to deny to themselves the sentiment of 'relegation' to the 'second division' of world powers. For Doelnitz: '*[l]a nation, confrontée avec cette faiblesse relative, s'est réfugiée dans l'illusion plutôt que de tirer les leçons de la réalité'.*[b][29]

Inevitably, the post-Cold War years have, as elsewhere, seen a considerable amount of self-reflection among France's security policy-makers. There emerged an increasingly deep and unsettling preoccupation in this new global security environment with national and international identity.[30] One explanation for this points to the amount of time that has elapsed since the departure from the political arena of the Fifth Republic's principal architect, General de Gaulle. Certainly, the conjunction of this period of national 'soul-searching' with radical change outside of *l'Hexagone* hinders analysis of contemporary French security policy. According to Lansford, 'France is once again at a point in which it questions both its place and role in both the world and more particularly in the EU'.[31] Doelnitz alluded to the supposed eventual decline of all great powers when he asked the question:

> *[c]ette "difformité" de la France, cette disproportion entre ce qu'elle suggère et ce qu'elle est capable de faire, entre ce qu'elle a été et ce à quoi elle aspire, se réduit-elle à une évolution irréversible, à un principe selon lequel les nations autrefois dominantes seraient vouées à une destinée de second rang?*[c][32]

The French could still play 'the great power' in much of sub-Saharan Africa, an area still associated with misery and turbulence, but they needed partners for threats the size of Bosnia which did not automatically trigger an American intervention.[33] There had to be an acceptance that the global security environment had changed dramatically and that national tactics for the pursuit of *rang* and *grandeur* devised in the 1960s were no longer sufficient.

Nevertheless, the defiant rhetoric continued. Foreign Minister de Charette declared even as recently as August 1995: *'[i]l y a peu de nations comparables à la nôtre. Je crois que l'on peut dire que la France a, par tradition, une politique internationale ambitieuse et de dimension mondiale'.*[d][34] It was clear that there was no question of the French relinquishing their claim to a place among the elite of the international community. One interpretation in Paris of the successive crises in the Persian Gulf, Somalia, former-Yugoslavia and Rwanda, for example, was that the capacity for overseas military action was still a prerequisite for top rank powers in the mid 1990s. Although these mainly multinational operations highlighted France's incapacity to act alone in a foreign crisis of any real size, they did serve to demonstrate that there was still a need for military might. France, as one of Europe's and the world's eldest states, has been one of a handful of countries that has rested on the traditional view that

---

[b] 'confronted with this relative weakness, the nation took refuge in illusion rather than draw the lessons of reality'.

[c] 'With its deformity, this inequality between that which it suggests and that which it is capable of doing, between that which it was and that to which it aspires, is France succumbing to an irreversible evolution, to a principle according to which those previously dominant nations are condemned to a destiny of second rank powers?'

[d] 'There are few nations comparable to ours. I believe that one can say that France has, by its tradition, an ambitious international policy of global dimensions'.

'power' comes with military and diplomatic weight.[35] One of the supposed lessons of the events in former-Yugoslavia, for example, was that (German) economic power could not, by itself, maintain political stability on the European continent.[36]

But equally, wrote Alain Frachon, the measure of power does not solely rest on a nuclear weapons capacity or the number of army divisions that can be mobilised.[37] Thus, how should a country that had relied on the Cold War bipolar system for its distinctive high international profile have maintained its position when that system ruptures and collapses? How can a country endowed with less than one per cent of the world's population and one half of a per cent of its land mass really count for much in the new multipolar international system? Certainly, there were suggestions that France's leaders might be prepared to reassess certain of its gaullist principles that had defined its security policy since the 1960s; namely, national sovereignty, autonomy of decision and freedom of action.[38]

On frequent occasions, when practising security policy, the successive Administrations of the Fifth Republic appeared as though they were making a conscious effort to make France different. They were able to use the country's limited resources to manipulate the global Cold War order and display a certain *singularité*. 'Perhaps', wrote Kramer, 'no European country has been so effective in translating its potential into political influence'.[39] A key characteristic of international diplomacy during the 1960s and, to a lesser extent, the 1970s, was France's ardent defence of autonomy of action. This was the principal mechanism by which national *grandeur* and *rang* were to be promoted and maintained. De Gaulle sought to maximise France's diplomatic margin for manoeuvre within the Western alliance by seeking an independent line on East-West issues, reassured, despite his frequent rhetoric to the contrary, by the knowledge that western Europe was fully protected by the American nuclear umbrella.

This volume has argued that circumstances subsequently combined to make this tactic both impractical and inappropriate. In the new security environment of the 1990s, French policy-makers appeared to lose much of their capacity for *spécificité*. The country's *de facto* 'demotion' to medium power status was confirmed by the Nazi occupation of 1941-5. And yet it was only with the new configuration of the international system in the 1990s that the French, standing alone, have had difficulty getting their diplomacy heard and respected. This has inevitably caused a significant degree of anxiety among national policy-makers. And the unease has not solely been attributable to the demise of bipolarity. At the dawn of the twenty-first century, states are bound by a whole range of interdependencies and constraints that strongly impinge on their ability to act autonomously. In this environment, gaullist-style national isolation no longer serves French national interests. In the words of Maurice Couve de Murville, '*[l]a France a perdu sur le plan international la considération et l'influence dont elle bénéficiait historiquement, et sa voix est du moins en moins écoutée dans le concert des nations*'.[e] [40] Flora Lewis has offered a less sympathetic interpretation. All that the French are losing, she argues, is the illusion of French *grandeur*.[41]

---

[e]   'France has lost at the international level the respect and influence from which it historically benefited, and its voice is listened to less and less in the concert of nations'.

French security policy characteristically continues to conduct the occasional display of independent muscle-flexing, having retained a need for grand gestures to ease the trauma of relative national decline. On the diplomatic front, this has been demonstrated in the Middle East with attempts to counter almost exclusive American influence in the region. One can equally point to policy towards Iraq. There has been, specifically in 1996, a reluctance to continue following the American-driven policy with regard to the maintenance of the no-fly zone in the south of the country and concerning the airborne surveillance operation in the Kurdish north, as well as with the maintenance of economic sanctions. And more recent events concerning Iraq have confirmed this. On the military front meanwhile, the 1990s were sprinkled by small-scale unilateral French military operations in sub-Saharan Africa. Although this volition for solo interventions was brought into serious question by the mid-decade negative experiences in central Africa's Great Lakes region. In addition, the inherent flamboyance with which French international representatives 'perform' only serves to accentuate the notion of France being a country apart, a country that mattered more than most.

Nevertheless, over the last decade or so, the architects of French security policy have lost several degrees of freedom of action and a significant amount of leverage on the global course of events. Several of the props for maintaining what was largely an illusion have been swept away. At the same time, claims to national exceptionalism through France's role as the natural defender of human rights have, according to some, appeared increasingly tenuous, given the policy towards the likes of China, Iran, Iraq and Saudi Arabia. At the same time, the promotion of democracy and of human rights have only spasmodically gained prominence in France's African policy. Moreover, assertions that France is the privileged partner of the Third World have progressively lost credence. The scope for gaullist-style dramatic political gestures has been drastically reduced, both by the post-Cold War security environment and by economic constraints. French excursions into international relations are becoming more ad hoc as opposed to automatic. There is no longer the capacity, nor perhaps even the volition, for the latter. The approach has become progressively circumspect.

The French economy has traditionally been among the most 'statist' in Europe. Its public sector was still spending some 55 per cent of France's GDP in 1995. This further symbol of *spécificité* has steadily been eroded with the growth of economic globalisation and international interdependence. As with other developed countries, market forces have gradually gained increased prominence. France inevitably lost much of its *singularité* as these forces permeated through policy-making structures. Perhaps the time is at an end when its leaders can enjoy the best of both the capitalist and collectivist worlds. At the same time, these leaders have followed, if somewhat fitfully, since Mitterrand's *volte-face* of 1983, the path of economic liberalisation and of opening-up to the outside world. By embracing economic integration in western Europe, they were implicitly committing themselves to the eventual abandonment of protectionism and the embracing of open markets and free competition. This move shattered any remaining pretensions, which had always been based more on rhetoric than reality, that France was blazing a 'third way' between the industrialised and Third worlds, between the Western and Communist models for social and economic life.

Then, France's ratification of the (Maastricht) Treaty of European Union marked the reluctant admission that either it had already lost, or would in the future have to lose, much of its sovereignty in the areas of commercial, economic and monetary policy. The final stage in this process has been the adoption of the single European currency. All the mainstream domestic political parties in France have now been converted, with a few factional exceptions, to the apparent logic of economic integration and the open market. Even within the gaullist RPR, there is a sizeable 'modernist' wing, led by former Prime Minister Edouard Balladur, which envisages a rational, free-enterprise, conservative party like any other.[42]

Europe and the Transferral of Ambitions

It is now some four decades since de Gaulle restored France's honour and a certain degree of abrasive nationalism.[43] According to Paul Webster, the nuclear testing programme concluded in early 1996 looked like 'the last big bang of a government that may seem arrogant from the outside, but has proved too small for its boots'. While Daniel Vernet saw the move '*aussi bien ... comme un dernier coup de chapeau à de Gaulle, avant les grandes remises en question, que comme une manifestation de fidelité*'.[f] [44] And Webster continued, '[e]conomic policy is made in Germany and intervention politics in the United States. Paris can make as much noise as it likes, but it has to sit back and wait for ad hoc alliances before any serious action is taken on the world stage'.[45] And, to a large extent, the reunified Germany has assumed the French mantle of principle conduit for east-west relations across the European continent. And it had become abundantly clear that even if some form of European 'superpower' was eventually to emerge, it was now unlikely that it would be centred on French leadership. However, Bozo, for one, does not necessarily foresee a period of inevitable decline for French global influence. After all, he notes, the French managed to come up with a considerable role for themselves, on paper at least, in the apparent adverse conditions of the bipolar Cold War.[46] Jacques Cordy was less optimistic:

> *[l]a France suit davantage les Nations unies et ne prend pas de grande décision de grand pays comme auparavant. Elle a globalement abandonné sa politique de prestige extérieur de manière assez évidente, même s'il reste un dernier pré carré en Afrique. Pour la France, l'Europe et l'alliance non dite avec les Etats-Unis compte de plus en plus.*[g] [47]

Is France slipping into 'normality' as an international actor, behaving just as its Western partners do?

---

[f]   'as much as a last tip of the cap to de Gaulle before some of his main legacies are called into question, as a sign of loyalty'.

[g]   'France is increasingly following the United Nations and no longer takes the major decisions of a great power. It has quite clearly abandoned its foreign policy of global prestige, even if it retains its African backwater. For France, Europe and the unspoken alliance with the United Nations count for more and more'.

Successive French leaderships throughout the life of the Fifth Republic have repeatedly failed to reconcile France's fundamental European dilemma: the contradictory objectives of promoting, initially west, European integration as a check on probable German political and economic regional hegemony and the construction of a unified Europe that provided considerable scope for national autonomy and allowed France to maintain its cherished level of global influence. Yves Boyer declared, in 1992:

> *[l]es responsables politiques agissent comme s'ils voulaient poursuivre toutes les politiques possibles en même temps, c'est à dire renforcer la coopération ouest-européenne sans mettre en danger ni la constitution d'un système pan-européen, ni la connection transatlantique entre l'Europe et les Etats-Unis, ou l'indépendance de la France en matière de dissuasion nucléaire.*[h] [48]

But ever since the Second World War, France's leaders have been searching for ways to build some meaningful form of European-only security identity, each of which to date has ended in relative disappointment. In this sense, the mid-1990s moves towards NATO did not represent a significant break in policy. Paris is still working for a European 'solution'. Europe has to achieve the goals that France can no longer attain by itself. To this end, the recent British-led moves to bestow the European Union with an autonomous and effective military capacity have been received in Paris with surprised enthusiasm.

The pursuit of rank and *grandeur* remains the principal security policy quest for the French. But whereas before, during the Cold War, this was done by constant demonstrations of French exceptionalism (namely, acting differently to their partners) and national independence, the emphasis is now on actively working and cooperating within organisations like NATO and the EU to boost European cohesion. National ambitions in terms of French *spécificité* have had to be cut back. This is what is meant by the normalisation of France as a security actor. Commentators like Edwy Plenel are now even referring to what he calls France's *petitesse*, or modestness, when it is evaluated by itself.[49] This is not to say that a policy resting on the French exception will not be restored in the future, it is just that as a tactic in the current security environment French planners have deemed it inappropriate. With this in mind, French leaders aimed to preserve France's international *rang* by raising the collective stock of Europe, and this has implied the toning down of the impulse to act alone. Europe is required to function as a multiplier for French power. This represents a significant tactical shift. As Bavarez noted, France was able, while the international system was rigid and governed by the bipolar nuclear stand-off, to conduct high profile, proactive, diplomacy which strove to circumvent the East-West cleavages, as well as those between North and South. But with the sudden disappearance of this system and its

---

[h]   'The politicians are acting as if they would like to pursue all the possible policies at the same time, namely to reinforce west European cooperation without putting in danger neither the construction of a pan-European system, nor the transatlantic connection between Europe and the United States, nor French independence with regard to nuclear dissuasion'.

replacement by one which is multipolar and fluid, French representatives have seen their margins for manoeuvre dramatically reduced. Bavarez believes France to be a major loser' of the end of the Cold War.[50]

Hence, the argument now goes that the special role in the international system that France carved out for itself under de Gaulle was not an end in itself but a specific answer to a certain geopolitical situation. But the political elites in Paris still strive to give the impression, by rhetoric and gestures, that France remains on the top rung of world powers. Nevertheless, the country is going through an enormous struggle with itself in letting go of its glorious past and facing up to the realities of its present position. Bavarez writes of a France with a free hand as a result of the systemic changes of 1989-91, but also of a France with an empty hand.[51] Nevertheless, French leaders retain their remarkable capacity to forge a myth that transforms national self-belief into a form of universal greatness.

The *rapprochement* with NATO and the ongoing reform of the armed forces are two major indications of the continued determination in Paris to protect and promote national rank among the global community of states, even if this necessitates symbolic losses of national sovereignty and the discarding of much of the apparently cherished national *singularité*. But this is not to deny that France has renounced the desire to be first among European equals. For the Economist, '[f]ar from signalling retreat from the world, this revolution, military and industrial, is meant to enable France to play the global role to which it has always aspired – even though it will now cooperate more often with others'.[52] Gone is the sentiment that the French should distance themselves from all international initiatives that they cannot control. This marks the normalisation of France as a security actor, but only in terms of the tactics it adopts. The quest for continued *rang* and *grandeur* remains as instinctive and fervent as ever.

This has clearly been the message put across by President Chirac, in office since May 1995. Indeed, Alain Duhamel actually saw in Chirac a reassertion of gaullist diplomacy: '*l'instinct du volontarisme et le goût de la différenciation s'affirment de nouveau*'.[i][53] The first months of his *septennat* were characterised by high profile and forthright foreign policy initiatives (particularly regarding Bosnia and nuclear testing) that temporarily served to put France back on the map and set it apart from other international actors. But after this initial flurry, partly to herald Chirac's arrival at the Elysée, French exceptionalism was not much in evidence on the world stage. Perhaps, Chirac's tenure will have marked, either by design or by the weight of circumstances, France's transition from living according to vague gaullist legacies to a country willing to come to terms with the security environment of the twenty-first century.

This requires a careful juggling act, keeping dreams and the reality of structural pressures in the air together. French policy-makers have concluded that the changing nature of the international system has greatly diminished the efficacy of the policy of non-dependence and the promotion of the French exception. As an agent, France is no longer in a position to operate relatively freely within the global structure, setting itself apart as something special. If this capacity has lost much of its value, then the tactic

---

[i]   'the instinct of voluntarism and the taste for differentiation are asserting themselves once
        more'.

should be abandoned. French planners, having in the Cold War been initially responsive to structural pressures, were able to adapt policy and ultimately make it proactive in its support of the status quo. French security policy is once again reactive. If the structural pressures are to be manipulated, then France can only do this with the cooperation of other state-agents. At a lower level of analysis, the French domestic political system, the present period of *cohabitation*, the Fifth Republic's third, has significantly impacted on the President's ability to dictate French security policy. The experience at these times has been of the President being a major agent, but not the dominant agent. President Chirac, for example, backed, from 1995 to 1997, by a government from his own centre-right political family, was able to instigate major tactical changes in French security policy, from relations with NATO to the professionalisation of the armed forces to the privatisation of defence industries. All these were called into question the moment Juppé's Administration was replaced by Jospin's left-wing coalition. What has emerged has been a security policy directed by two primary agents. Chirac was able, for example, to introduce a radical overhaul of the armed forces, but he has largely lost control over its implementation.[54] In addition, this volume has highlighted the increasingly determinant role played in security policy by the Finance Ministry. And there have been instances such as Charles Pasqua, as Interior Minister under Edouard Balladur, expanding his domain into key areas of security policy. William Drozdiak pointed in particular to Pasqua's initiatives concerning, Iran, Iraq, Saudi Arabia and Morocco.[55]

The Cultural Struggle

Any future serious attempts to promote French exceptionalism in a largely American-dominated global society look set to be increasingly focused on the cultural domain. The latter, in the view of former Foreign Minister de Charette, represents:

> *l'une des dimensions les plus originales de l'action extérieure de la France, celle qui correspond à une demande forte de la plupart de nos partenaires qui voient en la France autre chose qu'une puissance, autre chose qu'un pays au sens classique du terme, mais un pays qui porte des valeurs, qui exprime une culture.*[j] [56]

The French retain, according to de Montbrial, 'a lofty conception of their history, and of the wealth of their literary, philosophical, artistic or scientific culture'.[57] And their leaders will continue to push France's claim to having fostered the values of the eighteenth century enlightenment. An especially high priority has always been given to projecting its culture abroad. In the nineteenth century, France was the cultural centre of the Western universe and French was the language of diplomacy. Since then the pretence of French cultural pre-eminence has become increasingly difficult to maintain.[58] However, French leaderships are still prepared to spend billions upon

---

[j] 'one of the most original elements of France's overseas activity, one which corresponds to the strong demands from most of our partners who see in France something more than a power, more than a country in the classical sense of the word; they see a country which has values, which expresses a culture'.

billions of francs, despite the budgetary constraints, on extending France's cultural reach around the globe.[59] The principal vehicle for this has become the increasingly institutionalised *francophonie*. Nevertheless, Paul-Marie De La Gorce remarked that the post-Cold War preponderance of the Americans in the international arena has not been seriously challenged in Paris.[60] For one French official, '[t]his is the hour of the worldwide media village and it speaks American'.[61]

National Soul-Searching

One less disturbing conclusion for the French would be that their country no longer has anything to prove, either to itself or to the outside world. In the words of Didier Grange:

> *[r]éconcilié avec le monde, notre pays l'est également avec son passé puisqu'il ne souffre plus de ce besoin d'affirmation qui traverse toute sa politique étrangère depuis 1945 et lui a souvent conféré une agressivité qui était autant une volonté de retrouver un rang de grande puissance après le désastre de juin 1940 que la manifestation d'un sentiment d'insécurité.*[k] [62]

After years of internal torment, the French political elites are becoming reconciled with their country's real position and standing in the world. The sense of insecurity, as demonstrated by an almost aggressive international assertiveness, is steadily diminishing. As each successive generation grows-up in the Hexagon so the national memory of 1940 and of previous humiliations fades. Concurrently, the sense of national accommodation with France's medium power status increases.[63] Conversely, the rest of the world has become accustomed to the French behaving as they do on the world stage, so that their exceptionalism is less evident. France is expected to sometimes behave in a unique manner and to be less sensitive than most countries to international criticism; although it should be stated that this is perhaps increasingly more a question of style rather than substance.

Final Remarks

It has been the endeavour of this volume to bring a degree of coherence to the conduct of French security policy. It has argued that there has been a high degree of logic behind the various policy decisions. For a multiplicity of reasons, the pursuit of global standing and the promotion of national *grandeur* have been the instinctive twin and interlinked strategic goals of French security policy during the Fifth Republic. Gilles Martinet, former *ambassadeur de France*, commented that *rang* has become an obsession. For him, whereas before the Second World War it was not talked about because France had it, this disappeared with the occupation of 1940 and the collective

---

[k]   'Reconciled with the world, our country is similarly with its past since it no longer suffers the need for self-affirmation which spans across all its foreign policy since 1945 and which gave France a certain aggression, which was as much a desire to regain the country's rank of great power after the June 1940 disaster as a display of insecurity'.

acquiescence of many in making France a satellite of Germany.[64] Hence, the obsession lay with seeking to reclaim something that had been lost. It has been demonstrated here that what has changed over the years have been the tactics adopted in order to attain these unwavering strategic objectives. Reacting to a particular set of circumstances, de Gaulle, a key architect of the Fifth Republic, devised a distinctive set of policies resting on national non-dependence and the promotion of French *spécificité*, as epitomised by the development of the autonomous *force de frappe* and the withdrawal from NATO's integrated military command structure. Subsequently, gaullism was held up as *the* model for French policy-makers. But this was only the most vaguest of notions, able to be manipulated to any political advantage. If anything, gaullism could represent the crystallisation of the very purpose of French security policy into the pursuit of *rang* and *grandeur*. In addition, gaullism could been the resolute determination to use all available means to achieve these goals.

To this end, as circumstances evolved, it became apparent that French leaders would have to enlist the rest of western Europe to attain what France could no longer achieve by itself. Economic imperatives, for example, demanded a review of policy tactics. Rather than being cut-back or scaled down, French security ambitions were simply transferred from the national to west European level. Only really in sub-Saharan Africa did French claims to great power status hold any credibility. The end of the Cold War transformed the nature of the international system in which France operated. For one, there was, for the first time in centuries, no definable enemy threatening the Hexagon's territorial integrity. For another, the West German neighbour had reunified with its eastern half, unbalancing in the process the long-standing Franco-German equal partnership. Not only did the French lose much of their political and military leverage, but also Germany's population was now some 31 per cent greater than France's and its economy some 40 per cent larger. Clearly, major tactical adjustments had to be made.

The claim to an elevated global standing would, for instance, henceforth be justified on the grounds of France's disproportionate contributions to multinational peacekeeping and humanitarian operations on behalf of the international community. For Cole, in an effort to attain its strategic objectives, recent French leaders have played up those areas in which they perceive their country preserves an advantage, 'notably in terms of diplomatic prestige, international peacekeeping missions and troop deployments'.[65] Through the 1990s, French forces were repeatedly deployed to meet what could be termed low-level threats. In this way notes Gregory, French influence was enhanced at relatively little cost.[66] To this end, one can additionally point to the ongoing, and often augmented, logistical support to the Dom-Toms; notably Guyane, Nouvelle-Calédonie and Réunion. Experiences in the Gulf War and Bosnia, meanwhile, prompted a serious reappraisal of tactics with regard to the forging of a European security and defence identity that was deemed so crucial to the furtherance of French interests. At the time, prospects for ESDI appeared to focus on creating some form of European pillar within the Atlantic Alliance structure. More recently, and largely not of French doing, there has been some not inconsiderable momentum for ESDI within the EU, but this is still fraught with obstacles. What is clear is that the statements emanating from France on this issue now only talk of some intergovernmental structure. At the same time, France's armed forces are undergoing a major process of professionalisation. The reasoning here is that a conventional capability resting on conscription and on the force of numbers (a large standing army) no longer serves the requirement of the *grandes lignes*. Elsewhere, the military presence in sub-Saharan Africa is being reduced, perhaps epitomising France's loss of influence, particularly in central Africa. All these tactical adjustments, which will be replaced by others in the future when deemed necessary, have served, for the time being at least, to 'normalise' French security policy. This is in terms of, for example, the *rapprochement* with NATO, the loss of leverage over Germany, the dissolution of the traditionally symbolic 'nation in arms', multinational approaches to the development of future military equipment and to military formations and the possible demise of the role as *gendarme* in large parts of Africa. The *grandes lignes* of *rang* and *grandeur* remain sacrosanct, they are inherent in the political culture. But the tactics adopted to achieve them have been transformed during the life of the Fifth Republic. This has been the shift away from exceptionalism towards normalisation.

Notes

1 De Gaulle, Charles, quoted in Plenel, Edwy, 'L'illusion française', *Le Monde*, 31 August 1994.
2 De Montbrial, Thierry, 'French "exception" yes, and it isn't likely to fade away soon', *International Herald Tribune*, 14 September 1995.
3 Lansford, Tom, 'The question of France: French security choices at century's end', *European Security*, vol.5, no.1. Spring 1996, p.47.
4 Gregory, Shaun (2000), *French Defence Policy into the Twenty-First Century*, Macmillan, Basingstoke, p.7.
5 Friedman, Thomas L., 'J'appuie sur le bouton, donc j'existe', *Courrier International*, 14 September 1995, p.7.
6 Buchan, David, 'A general theory of Gaullism', *The Financial Times*, 3 February 1997.
7 Menon, Anand, 'Continuing politics by other means: defence policy under the Fifth Republic', *West European Politics*, vol.17, no.4, October 1994, p.86.
8 Johnson, Douglas, 'A true child of France', *The Guardian*, 11 February 1998.
9 Gaffney, John, 'What difference will Chirac make?', *European Brief*, June 1995.
10 Chirac, Jacques, quoted in Sancton, Thomas, 'France seeks a mission for the next century', *Time*, 4 December 1995, p.49.
11 Hoagland, Jim, 'Chirac has hit a comfortable stride', *International Herald Tribune*, 20 April 1996.
12 Cot, Michel (Général d'Armée), Président de Groupe de Réflexion, Fondation pour les Etudes De Défense, in an interview with the author, Paris, July 1996.
13 Messmer, Pierre, Secrétaire perpétuel de l'Académie des Sciences Morales et Politiques and former French Prime Minister, in an interview with the author, Paris, July 1996.
14 Moïsi, Dominique, 'The allure of Gaullism', *The Financial Times*, 19 April 1996.
15 Chipman, John (1989), *French Power in Africa*, Blackwell Press, Oxford, p.9.
16 Klein, Jean, 'La France, la réorganisation du système de sécurité occidental et la sécurité européenne', paper presented at the Pan-European International Relations Conference – ECPR, Standing Group on International Relations, Paris, 13-16 September 1995, p.1.

17 David, Dominique, Chargé de Recherche, Institut Français des Relations Internationales (IFRI), in an interview with the author, IFRI, Paris, 1996.
18 In an interview with the author, IFRI, Paris, August 1997.
19 Fitchett, Joseph, 'France in the 1990s: has the time arrived to shatter the Gaullist icon?', *International Herald Tribune*, 7 May 1990.
20 Moïsi, Dominique, 'The urge to be different', *The Financial Times*, 25 July 1995.
21 Buchan, David, 'A general theory of Gaullism', *op cit*.
22 Duhamel, Olivier (1989), 'President and Prime Minister', in Paul Godt (ed), *Policy-making in France*, Pinter Publishers, London, p.58.
23 Dabezies, Pierre, Professeur, Université de Paris I and former advisor to Jacques Chirac, in an interview with the author, Paris, June 1996.
24 Stanger, Theodore and Mabry, Marcus, 'The glory that was France', *Newsweek*, 9 May 1994, p.17.
25 Levine, Robert A. (1995), *France and the World: A Snapshot at Mid-decade*, RAND, Santa Monica, p.12.
26 Kramer, Steven Philip, 'The French question', *The Washington Quarterly*, vol.14, no.4, Autumn 1991, p.83.
27 Kolodziej, Edward A. (1974), *French International Policy Under De Gaulle and Pompidou: The Politics of Grandeur*, Cornell University Press, Ithaca, p.569.
28 Domenach, Jean-Marie, quoted in Walden, George, 'France says no', *The Observer* (Prospect Section), 19 October 1997.
29 Doelnitz, Tristan (1993), *La France Hantée par sa Puissance*, Belfond, Paris, p.14.
30 Moïsi, Dominique, 'The place for France is in NATO', *International Herald Tribune*, 7 November 1991.
31 Lansford, Tom, *op cit*, p.60.
32 Doelnitz, Tristan, *op cit*, p.207.
33 Fitchett, Joseph, 'France drops Gaullist boycott of NATO's military', *International Herald Tribune*, 6 December 1995.
34 De Charette, Hervé, speech to France's ambassadors, Paris, 31 August 1995.
35 A belief expressed by among others, Pierre Jacquet and Dominique Moïsi, both Directeurs-adjoint, Institut Français des Relations Internationales, in interviews with the author, Paris, July 1996.
36 Kramer, Steven Philip (1994), *Does France Still Count?: The French Role in the New Europe*, Praeger/The Center for Strategic and International Studies, Washington DC, p.12.
37 Frachon, Alain, 'La construction européenne est restée au coeur de la politique étrangère', *Le Monde*, 2 April 1995.
38 Yost, David S., 'France and west European defence identity', *Survival*, vol.33, no.4, July/August 1991, p.336.
39 Kramer, Steven Philip, *Does France Still Count?: The French Role in the New Europe*, *op cit*, p.99.
40 Couve de Murville, Maurice, 'Y a-t-il encore une politique étrangère?', *Le Figaro*, 14 October 1991.
41 Lewis, Flora, 'Today's French are faring well, most of them, and feeling bad', *International Herald Tribune*, 1 December 1995.
42 Davidson, Ian, 'Gulf shakes Gaullist taboos', *The Financial Times*, 27 September 1990.
43 Ogden, Christopher, 'Mending fences between prickly allies', *Time*, 25 November 1996, p.68.
44 Vernet, Daniel, 'Chirac, le gaullisme et la défense', *Le Monde*, 1 March 1996.

45 Webster, Paul, 'Chirac proving too small for his boots', *The Guardian*, 16 November 1996.
46 Bozo, Frédéric (1995), 'France and security in the new Europe: between the Gaullist legacy and the search for a new model', in Gregory Flynn (ed), *Remaking the Hexagone*, Westview Press, Boulder, p.230.
47 Cordy, Jacques, 'L'époque de la grandeur est finie', *Libération*, 2 September 1994.
48 Boyer, Yves, 'La France et la sécurité dans la nouvelle Europe', in Yves Boyer (ed), *Les Européens Face aux Défis d'une Politique de Sécurité Commune*, Les Cahiers de CREST, 7 June 1992, p.16.
49 Plenel, Edwy, 'L'illusion française', *op cit.*
50 Bavarez, Nicolas, 'Pavane pour une politique étrangère défunte', *Commentaire*, vol.15, no.57, Spring 1992, p.130.
51 *Ibid*, p.131.
52 'A French projection', *The Economist*, 2 March 1996, p.26.
53 Duhamel, Alain, 'La revanche de la diplomatie gaulliste', *Libération*, 12 April 1996.
54 Gregory, Shaun, *op cit*, p.102.
55 Drozdiak, William, 'French foreign policy: tied up in politics at home', *International Herald Tribune*, 24 January 1994.
56 De Charette, Hervé, New Year message to the media in his capacity as Foreign Minister, Paris, 4 January 1996.
57 De Montbrial, Thierry, *op cit.*
58 Hayward, Jack (1973), *The One and Indivisible French Republic*, Weidenfeld and Nicolson, London, p.232.
59 The cultural budget for 1996 was set to rise by 8.7 per cent on 1995 to \$3.2 billion. Russell Chaddock, Gail, 'France strives to rejuvenate its past glory', *Christian Science Monitor*, 6 October 1995, p.10.
60 De La Gorce, Paul-Marie, 'Les occasions manqueés de la politique étrangère française', *Le Monde Diplomatique*, November 1994, p.9.
61 Grange, Didier (pseudonym), 'Pour une nouvelle politique étrangère', *Esprit*, no.186, November 1992, p.15.
62 *Ibid*, p.20.
63 *Idem.*
64 Martinet, Gilles, 'La politique de l'apparence', *Le Monde*, 13 March 1991.
65 Cole, Alistair (1998), *French Politics and Society*, Prentice Hall, Hemel Hempstead, p.236.
66 Gregory, Shaun, *op cit*, p.181.

Bibliography

'A French projection', *The Economist*, 2 March 1996.

'A Gaullist defiance', *Newsweek*, 31 July 1995.

'A new NATO', *The Economist*, 9 December 1995.

'A prime minister for France', *The Economist*, 20 May 1995.

Allison, Graham T. (1971), *Essence of Decision: Explaining the Cuban Missile Crisis*, Little Brown and Co., Boston.

Arnaud, Jean-Louis, 'L'interprétation Mitterrandienne du "domaine réservé"', *Le Matin*, 18 December 1984.

Aron, Raymond (1965), *The Great Debate*, Doubleday, New York.

'Au revoir to Africa', *Time*, 3 April 1995.

Backmann, René, 'Gribouille au Congo', *Le Nouvel Observateur*, 5 December 1996.

Backmann, René, 'Afrique: les foyers de crise', *Le Nouvel Observateur*, 19 June 1997.

Balaj, Barbara S., 'France and the Gulf War', *Mediterranean Quarterly*, vol.4, no.3, Summer 1993.

Baumel, Jacques, 'La France et l'OTAN', *Relations Internationales et Stratégiques*, no.7, Autumn 1992.

Bavarez, Nicolas, 'Pavane pour une politique étrangère défunte', *Commentaire*, vol.15, no.57, Spring 1992.

Bayart, Jean-François, 'Zaïre: "le fiasco français"', *Le Nouvel Observateur*, 15 May 1997.

Bayart, Jean-François and Massiah, Gustave, 'La France au Rwanda', *Les Temps Modernes*, vol.50, no.583, July/August 1995.

Berstein, Serge (1989), *The Republic of De Gaulle: 1958-1969*, Cambridge University Press/Editions de la Maison des Sciences de l'Homme, Paris.

Betts, Paul, 'France shoulders thankless role of gendarme in Chad', *The Financial Times*, 9 January 1987.

Beylau, Pierre, 'Bosnie: veillée d'armes', *Le Point*, 7 May 1993.

Beylau, Pierre, 'La France revient', *Le Point*, 24 September 1994.

Block, Robert, 'Fighting talk may mask subtle campaign of bluff', *The Independent*, 7 June 1995.

Blondel, Jean (1974), *The Government of France*, Methuen, London.

Blunden, Margaret, 'France after the Cold War: inching closer to the Alliance', *Defense Analysis*, vol.9, no.3, 1993.

Borger, Julian and Duval Smith, Alex, 'French threaten Bosnia pullout', *The Guardian*, 17 April 1995.

Boulet-Gercourt, Philippe, 'Washington et le gâteau africain', *Le Nouvel Observateur*, 12 December 1996.

Boulmer, Michel, 'Les errements de la politique française', *Le Monde*, 27 March 1993.

Bourgeois, Bernard, 'L'apport de la pensée française à une organisation collective du monde', in André Lewin (ed), *La France et l'ONU (1945-1995)*, Collection Panoramiques, Condé-sur-Noireau.

Boyer, Yves, 'La France et la sécurité dans la nouvelle Europe', in Yves Boyer (ed), *Les Européens Face aux Défis d'une Politique de Sécurité Commune*, Les Cahiers de CREST, 7 June 1992.

Bozo, Frédéric (1991), *La France et l'OTAN: De la Guerre Froide au Nouvel Ordre Européen*, Masson, Paris

Bozo, Frédéric (1993), 'La France, l'Europe et l'OTAN', in Pierre Pascallon (ed), *Quelle Défense pour la France?*, Institut des Relations Internationales et Stratégiques/Dunod, Paris.

Bozo, Frédéric (1995), 'France and security in the new Europe: between the Gaullist legacy and the search for a new model', in Gregory Flynn (ed), *Remaking the Hexagone: The New France in the New Europe*, Westview Press, Boulder.

Bozo, Frédéric, 'La France et l'Alliance: les limites du rapprochement', *Politique Etrangère*, vol.60, no.4, Winter 1995.

Briseul, Jean-Paul, 'Structures territoriales françaises et construction de l'Europe', *Défense Nationale*, vol.49, January 1993.

Brouillet, Alain, 'Le Parlement français et la politique étrangère', *Le Monde Diplomatique*, May 1979.

Brown, Kevin and Clark, Bruce, 'UK and France in nuclear pact', *The Financial Times*, 31 October 1995.

Buchan, David, 'France unveils first N-carrier', *The Financial Times*, 9 May 1994.

Buchan, David, 'A general theory of Gaullism', *The Financial Times*, 3 February 1997.

Burghardt, A.F., 'The bases of geographical review', *Geographical Review*, vol.63, 1973.

Buzan, Barry (1983), *People, States and Fear*, The University of North Carolina Press, Chapel Hill.

Canivez, Patrice (1994), *Questions de Responsabilité: La France et l'Idée d'Europe Face a la Guerre dans l'Ex-Yougoslavie*, Colibri, Paris.

Cerny, P.G. (1980), *The Politics of Grandeur*, Cambridge University Press, Cambridge.

Chamard, Michel, 'Les fissures du "domaine réservé"', *Le Figaro*, 27 August 1991.

Chartouni-Dubarry, May, *France and the Gulf War*, IFRI Report, Paris, February 1992.

Chavannes, Marc, 'Les dessous de l'intervention au Rwanda', *Courrier International*, 7 July 1994.

Chevènement, Jean-Pierre (1985), *Le Pari sur l'Intelligence; Entretiens avec Hervé Hamon Et Patrick Rotman*, Flammarion, Paris.

Chevènement, Jean-Pierre, 'La France et la sécurité de l'Europe', *Politique Etrangère*, no.3, 1990.

Chevènement, Jean-Pierre, 'Chevènement: on abaisse la France', *Le Nouvel Observateur*, 15 February 1996.

Chipman, John (1989), *French Power in Africa*, Blackwell Press, Oxford.

Cohen, Roger, 'Form and substance: France's dual model', *International Herald Tribune*, 25 August 1997.

Cohen, Samy (1986), *La Monarchie Nucléaire: Les Coulisses de la Politique Etrangère sous la Cinquième République*, Hachette, Paris.

Cohen, Samy, 'Le Président chef des armées', *Pouvoirs*, no.58, 1991.

Cole, Alistair (1998), *French Politics and Society*, Prentice Hall, Hemel Hempstead.

Colombani, 'Le rang de la France', *Le Monde*, 5 March 1991.

Colomès, Michel, ' L'OTAN: le révélateur yougoslave', *Le Point*, 8 January 1994.

Colomès, Michel, 'Bosnie: la première épreuve de Chirac', *Le Point*, 3 June 1995.

Cordy, Jacques, 'L'époque de la grandeur est finie', *Libération*, 2 September 1994.

Couve de Murville, Maurice (1971), *Une Politique Etrangère 1958-1969*, Plon, Paris.

Couve de Murville, Maurice, 'Y a-t-il encore une politique étrangère?', *Le Figaro*, 14 October 1991.

Craig, Gordon. A. and George, Alexander L. (1990), *Force and Statecraft: Diplomatic Problems of our Time*, Oxford University Press, Oxford.

Cranston, Maurice (1988), 'The sovereignty of the nation', in Colin Lucas (ed), *The Political Culture of the French Revolution*, Pergamon Press, Oxford.

Crawford, Leslie, Buchan, David and Reuters, 'French troops mount first Rwanda patrol', *The Financial Times*, 24 June 1994.

David, Dominique (1994), 'France: l'illusion de la puissance', in *Les Fractures de l'Occident: Eliments de Géopolitique*, La Découverte, Paris, 1994.

David, Dominique (1996), 'The search for a new security strategy in a shifting international arena', in Tony Chafer and Brian Jenkins (eds), *France: From the Cold War to the New World Order*, Macmillan, Basingstoke.

Davidson, Ian, 'Gulf shakes Gaullist taboos', *The Financial Times*, 27 October 1990.

Davidson, Ian, 'Platform for historic ambitions', *The Financial Times*, 22 June 1992.

Debré, Michel, 'La France n'existe plus', *Le Figaro*, 7 October 1998.

De Charette, Hervé, 'A new dialogue between equals', *Time*, 27 January 1997.

De Gaulle, Charles (1954), *Mémoires de Guerre*, Plon/Livres De Poche, Paris.

Dejevsky, Mary, 'Chirac spells out role of French force', *The Independent*, 2 June 1995.

De La Gorce, Paul-Marie, 'Les occasions manqueés de la politique étrangère française', *Le Monde Diplomatique*, November 1994.

De La Rose, François (1989), *Défendre la Défense*, Commentaire Julliard, Paris.

De Montbrial, Thierry, 'French "exception", yes, and it isn't likely to fade away soon', *International Herald Tribune*, 14 September 1995.

De Sarajevo á Kigali: Deux Années d'Interventions Extérieures de l'Armée Française Fin 92-Fin 94, Ministère de la Défense, Paris.

Deniau, Jean-François, 'Le rang de la France', *Le Monde*, 7 September 1994.

'Des intellectuels dénoncent le "manque de détermination" de la France en ex-Yougoslavie', *Le Monde*, 20 December 1997.

Desaubliaux, Patrice-Henry, 'Le test de la défense', *Le Figaro*, 10 July 1997.

Desforges, Alison, quoted in Elliott, Michael, 'A calculus of incursion', *Newsweek*, 1 August 1994.

Doelnitz, Tristan (1993), *La France Hantée par sa Puissance*, Belfond, Paris.

Domenach, Jean-Marie, quoted in Walden, George, 'France says no', *The Observer* (Prospect section), 19 October 1997.

D'Orcival, François, 'Chirac au pont de Vrbanja', *Valeurs Actuelles*, 3 June 1995.

Drozdiak, William, 'French foreign policy: tied up in politics at home', *International Herald Tribune*, 24 January 1994.

Drozdiak, William, 'Paris finds no backing on Rwanda force', *International Herald Tribune*, 19 June 1994.

Duhamel, Alain, 'Le monarque républicain', *Le Point*, 22 April 1995.

Duhamel, Alain, 'La revanche de la diplomatie gaulliste', *Libération*, 12 April 1996.

Duhamel, Olivier (1989), 'President and Prime Minister', in Paul Godt (ed), *Policy-Making in France*, Pinter Publishers, London.

Duteil, Mireille, 'La France dans le bourbier', *Le Point*, 6 February 1993.

Duteil, Mireille, 'Les héritiers de l'Afrique', *Le Point*, 12 February 1994.

Duteil, Mireille, 'Les embarras de Paris', *Le Point*, 18 June 1994.

Duteil, Mireille, 'Rwanda: pourquoi la France intervient', *Le Point*, 25 June 1994

Duteil, Mireille, 'Mitterrand: l'Africain', *Le Point*, 2 July 1994.

Duval-Smith, Alex, 'France to slash troop numbers in Africa', *The Guardian*, 26 July 1997.

Eagar, Charlotte, 'Stench of war shrouds city as sniper takes its toll', *The Observer*, 11 June 1995.

Eyal, Jonathan, 'France freezes as Europe melts', *The Independent*, 3 December 1994.

Faringdon, Hugh (1986), *Confrontation: The Strategic Geography of NATO and the Warsaw Pact*, Routledge, and Kegan Paul, London.

Favier, Pierre and Martin-Roland, Michel (1991), *La Décennie Mitterrand: Les Epreuves* Seuil, Paris.

Fitchett, Joseph, 'France in the 1990s: has the time arrived to shatter the Gaullist icon?', *International Herald Tribune*, 7 May 1990.

Fitchett, Joseph, 'France drops Gaullist boycott of NATO's military', *International Herald Tribune*, 6 December 1995.

Fitchett, Joseph, 'French-German military vision clouds again', *International Herald Tribune*, 30 May 1996.

Fitchett, Joseph, 'New policy for Africa: don't rely on troops from France', *International Herald Tribune*, 11 August 1997.

Flynn, Gregory, *French NATO Policy: The Next Five Years*, RAND, Santa Monica, June 1990.

Foley, James B. (1985), 'Pacifism and anti-nuclearism in France: perceptions of the crisis of deterrence and détente', in James E. Dougherty and Robert L. Pfaltzgraff (eds), *Shattering Europe's Defence Consensus: The Antinuclear Movement and the Future of NATO*, Pergamon/Brasseys, Oxford.

Fontaine, André, 'Diplomatie française: Jacques Chirac et l'ombre du Général', *Politique Internationale*, no.70, Winter 1995-96.

Fortier, Jacques, 'Lionel Jospin confirme la mise à contribution de budget de la défense', *Le Monde*, 30 July 1997.

Fottorino, Eric, 'Dans le piège rwandais', *Le Monde*, 25 July 1997.

Fowler, Michael Ross and Bunck, Julie Marie, 'What constitutes the sovereign state?', *Review of International Studies*, vol.22, no.4, October 1996.

Frachon, Alain, 'La construction européenne est restée au coeur de la politique étrangère', *Le Monde*, 2 April 1995.

Frachon, Alain, 'M. Chirac revendique un "partenariat plus égal" entre l'Europe et les Etats-Unis au sein de l'OTAN', *Le Monde*, 2 February 1996.

Frachon, Alain, 'La France peine à imposer sa conception de la sécurité en Europe', *Le Monde*, 4 December 1996.

'France increases its participation in the transformation of the Alliance', *NATO Review*, vol. 44, no.1, 1996.

'France's changing view of the world', *The Economist*, 10 February 1996.

Franco-British Joint Declaration on European Defence, St-Malo, 3-4 December 1998.

Frears J.B. (1981), *France in the Giscard Presidency*, Allen and Unwin, London.

Freedman, Lawrence (1989), *The Evolution of Nuclear Strategy*, Macmillan/IISS, Basingstoke.

French, Howard W., 'West's intervention in Africa: not solving the problems', *International Herald Tribune*, 28 May 1996.

Friedman, Thomas L., 'J'appuie sur le bouton, donc j'existe', *Courrier International*, 14 September 1995.

Friend, Julius W. (1989), *Seven Years in France: François Mitterrand and the Unintended Revolution 1981-1988*, Westview Press, Boulder.

Fritscher, Frédéric, 'La République démocratique du Congo accuse la France de vouloir déstabiliser le pays', *Le Monde*, 2 December 1997.

Gaffney, John (1991), 'Language and politics: the case of neo-Gaullism', in John Gaffney and Eva Kolinsky (eds), *Political Culture in France and Germany*, Routledge, London.

Gaffney, John, 'What difference will Chirac make?', *European Brief*, June 1995.

Gallois (Général [C.R.]), Pierre-Marie (1993), 'Les nouvelles conditions de sécurité de la défense', in Pierre Pascallon (ed), *Quelle Défense pour la France?*, Institut des Relations Internationales et Stratégiques/Dunod, Paris.

Gnesotto, Nicole, *The Lessons of Yugoslavia*, Chaillot Paper 14, WEU Institute for Security Studies, Paris, March 1994.

Gnesotto, Nicole, 'La défense européenne au carrefour de la Bosnie et de la CIG', *Politique Etrangère*, vol.61, no.1, Spring 1996.

Gnesotto, Nicole, 'CFSP and defence: how does it work?', Western European Union Institute for Security Studies Newsletter, no.30, July 2000.

Goldstein, Avery, 'Discounting the free-ride: alliances and security in the postwar world', *International Organization*, vol.49, no.1, Winter 1995.

Gonin, Jean-Marc and Pierre-Brossolette, Sylvie, 'Armée: 10 questions en suspens', *L'Express*, 29 February 1996.

Gordon, Philip H., 'The Franco-German security partnership', in France-Germany, 1983-1993: *The Struggle to Cooperate*, St. Martin's Press, New York.

Gordon, Philip H. (1993), *A Certain Idea of France: French Security Policy and the Gaullist Legacy*, Princeton University Press, Princeton.

Gordon, Philip. H., 'Charles de Gaulle and the nuclear revolution', *Security Studies*, vol.5, no.1, Autumn 1995.

Goubert, Pierre (1991), *The Course of French History*, Routledge, London.

Graham, Robert, 'Defence: pledge on European capability', *The Financial Times*, 31 May 1999.

Graham, Robert, 'Defence: Government faces a financial squeeze', *The Financial Times* (country survey), June 2000.

Grange, Didier (pseudonym), 'Pour une nouvelle politique étrangère', *Esprit*, no.186, November 1992.

Gregory, Shaun (2000), French Defence Policy into the Twenty-First Century, Macmillan, Basingstoke.

Grimond, John, 'First nation singular', *The Economist*, 25 November 1995.

Grosser, Alfred, 'General de Gaulle and the foreign policy of the Fifth Republic', *International Affairs*, vol.41, no.2, April 1963.

Grosser, Alfred (1984), *Affaires Extérieures: La Politique de la France 1944-1984*, Flammarion, Paris.

Grosser, Alfred (1985), 'Un "Giscardisme" en politique extérieure?', in Samy Cohen and Marie-Claude Smouts (eds), *La Politique Extérieure de Valéry Giscard d'Estaing*, Presses de la Fondation Nationale des Sciences, Paris.

Grosser, Alfred (1995), 'Le rôle et le rang', in André Lewin (ed), *La France et l'ONU (1945-1995)*, Collection Panoramiques, Condé-sur-Noireau.

'Guilty governments', *The Economist*, 3 June 1995.

Guisnel, Jean, '"L'exception militaire" française', in *L'Etat de la France 1994-5*, Editions De La Découverte, Paris, 1994.

Hague, Rod, Harrop, Martin and Breslin, Shaun (1992), *Comparative Government and Politics: An Introduction*, Macmillan, London.

Hampson, Norman, 'La Patrie', in Colin Lucas (ed), *The Political Culture of the French Revolution*, Pergamon Press, Oxford.

Hayward, Jack (1973), *The One and Indivisible French Republic*, Weidenfeld and Nicolson, London.

Hazareesingh, Sudhir (1994), *Political Traditions in Modern France*, Oxford University Press, Oxford, 1994.

Heisbourg, François (1991), 'La France et la crise du Golfe', in *L'Europe Occidentale et la Golfe*, in Nicole Gnesotto and John Roper (eds), WEU Institute for Security Studies, Paris.

Hélène, Jean, 'La conférence de l'OAU n'a pas résolu la crise des Comores', *Le Monde*, 16 December 1997.

'Helmet blues', *The Economist*, 22 April 1995.

Hertzog, Gilles, 'La peur ou le choléra', *Le Point*, 30 July 1994.

Hoagland, Jim, 'Chirac has hit a comfortable stride', *International Herald Tribune*, 20 April 1996.

Hoagland, Jim, 'France hoists the old "White Man's Burden" in Central Africa', *International Herald Tribune*, 1 June 1996.

Hoche, Christian, 'La France attend le relève', *L'Express*, 14 July 1994.

Hoffman, Stanley (1987), 'La politique internationale de Mitterrand, ou le gaullisme sous un autre nom', in Stanley Hoffman and Sylvia Malzacher (eds), *L'Expérience Mitterrand: Continuité et Changement dans la France Contemporaine*, Presses Universitaires de France.

Hollis, Martin and Smith, Steve, 'Two stories about structure and agency', *Review of International Studies*, vol.20, no.3, July 1994.

Howorth, Jolyon (1987), 'Budgets et choix stratégiques: la politique de défense sous François Mitterrand', in Stanley Hoffman and Sylvia Malzacher (eds), *L'Expérience Mitterrand: Continuité et Changement dans la France Contemporaine*, Universitaires de France/Basil Blackwell, Cambridge.

Howorth, Jolyon (1990), 'Foreign and defence policy: from independence to interdependence', in Jack Hayward, Peter A. Hall and Howard Machin (eds), *Developments in French Politics*, Macmillan, London.

Howorth, Jolyon (1993), 'The President's special role in foreign and defence policy', in Jack Hayward (ed), *De Gaulle to Mitterrand: Presidential Power in France*, Hurst and Co., London.

Howorth, Jolyon (1994), 'The debate in France over military intervention in Europe', in Lawrence Freedman (ed), *Military Intervention in European Conflicts*, Blackwell, Oxford.

Howorth, Jolyon (1996), 'France and European security 1944-94: re-reading the Gaullist "consensus"', in Tony Chafer and Brian Jenkins (eds), *France: From the Cold War to the New World Order*, Macmillan, London.

Howorth, Jolyon, 'Britain, France and the European Defence Initiative', *Survival*, vol.42, no.2, Summer 2000.

Isnard, Jacques, 'L'Allemagne et la France cherchent à harmoniser leurs besoins en matière d'armement', *Le Monde*, 10 December 1996.

Isnard, Jacques, 'La France remanie son dispositif militaire en Afrique', *Le Monde*, 20 July 1997.

Isnard, Jacques, 'Solitaire mais solidaire', *Le Monde*, 4 December 1997.

Jenkins, Brian (1987), 'Nation, nationalism and national identity in France since 1789: some theoretical reflections', in Jeff Bridgford (ed), *France: Image and Identity*, Newcastle Upon Tyne Polytechnic Products, Newcastle.

Johnson, Douglas, 'A true child of France', *The Guardian*, 11 February 1998.

Kennedy, Paul (1988), *The Rise and Fall of the Great Powers*, Fontana Press, London.

Kohl, Wilfred (1971), *French Nuclear Diplomacy*, Princeton University Press, Princeton.

Kolodziej, Edward A. (1974), *French International Policy under de Gaulle and Pompidou: The Politics of Grandeur*, Cornell University Press, Ithaca.

Kramer, Steven Philip, 'The French question', *The Washington Quarterly*, vol.14, no.4, Autumn 1991.

Kramer, Steven Philip (1994), *Does France Still Count?: The French Role in the New Europe*, Center for Strategic and International Studies/Praegar, Washington DC.

Lacouture, Jean (1993), *De Gaulle - The Ruler 1945-1970*, Harper Collins, London.

'La France souhaite que le problème soit reglé au sein de la communauté arabe', *Le Monde*, 11 August 1990.

Lagarde, Dominique, 'Le retour de la France', *L'Express*, 5 December 1996.

Lagarde, Dominique, 'OTAN: la bataille d'Europe', *L'Express*, 5 December 1996.

Laird, Robbin (1992), 'The renovation of French defence policy', in Stuart Croft and Phil Williams (eds), *European Security without the Soviet Union*, Frank Cass.

Lang, Kirsty, 'France plays African power game', *The Sunday Times*, 10 November 1996.

Lansford, Tom, 'The question of France: French security choices at century's end', *European Security*, vol.5, no.1, Spring 1996.

Lanxade, Jacques, 'French defence policy after the White Paper', *RUSI Journal*, vol.139, no.2, April 1994.

Lasserre, Isabelle, Laporte, Benoît and Roche, Marc, 'Sarajevo: les Français pour la manière forte', *Le Point*, 12 February 1994.

Latter, Richard, European Security and Defence: Forging an EU Role, Wilton Park, December 2000.

Laulan, Yves-Marie, 'La défense de la France á l'heure des choix: puissance mondiale où puissance régionale?', in Pierre Pascallon (ed), *Quelle Défense pour la France?*, Institut Français des Relations Internationales/Dunod, Paris, 1993.

'Le mariage manqué du blindé et du sac de riz', *Le Nouvel Observateur*, 18 November 1993.

Lellouche, Pierre (1988), 'Guidelines for a European defence concept', in Jonathan Alford and Kenneth Hunt (eds), *Europe in the Western Alliance*, Macmillan/IISS, London.

Lellouche, Pierre, 'Mitterrand ou l'art du zigzag', *Le Figaro*, 9 February 1991.

Lellouche, Pierre, 'La France et l'OTAN', *Relations Internationales et Stratégiques*, no.7, Autumn 1992.

Lellouche, Pierre, 'France in search of security', *Foreign Affairs*, vol.72, no.2, Spring 1993.

Lellouche, Pierre, 'L'utilité militaire du service est dépassé', *Libération*, 13 May 1996.

Léotard, François, 'Défense européenne: le temps de la volonté', *Le Figaro*, 3 January 1995.

'L'épreuve cruelle de vérité aura lieu. Il faut que les Français y préparent leur esprit', *Le Monde*, 9 February 1991.

Les débats, *Défense Nationale*, Décembre 1982.

'Les positions de la France depuis le début de la crise', *Libération*, 10 January 1991.

Levine, Robert A. (1995), *France and the World: A Snapshot at Mid-Decade*, RAND, Santa Monica.

Lewin, André (1995), 'La France et la coopération multilatérale', in André Lewin (ed), *La France Et L'ONU (1945-1995)*, Collection Panoramiques, Condé-sur-Noireau.

Lewis, Flora, 'Today's French are faring well, most of them, and feeling bad', *International Herald Tribune*, 1 December 1995.

Lewis, J.A.C., 'Fitter, leaner forces for multi-polar world', *Jane's Defence Weekly*, 11 June 1997.

Leymarie, Philippe, 'La France et le maintien de l'ordre en Afrique', *Le Monde Diplomatique*, June 1994.

Leymarie, Philippe, 'Litigieuse intervention française au Rwanda', *Le Monde Diplomatique*, July 1994.

Leymarie, Philippe, 'En Afrique, la fin des ultimes "chasses gardées"', *Le Monde Diplomatique*, December 1996.

Lintner, Bertil, 'Not neighbourly', *Far Eastern Economic Review*, 30 November 1995.

Littlejohns, Michael, 'Balladur denies Rwanda agenda', *The Financial Times*, 12 July 1994.

Livre Blanc Sur La Défense 1994, Union Générale d'Editions, Paris, 1994.

'L'opposition s'inquiète du risque de "repli" de l'industrie de défense', *Le Monde*, 15 July 1997.

Marchal, Roland, 'France and Africa: the emergence of essential reforms?', *International Affairs*, vol.74, no.2, 1998.

Marnham, Patrick, 'Not quite as American as pomme tarte', *The Independent*, 26 February 1991.

Marr, Andrew, 'Vive la république! Et vive le roi!', *The Independent*, 8 August 1995.

Marshall, Andrew, 'Old rivals unite in a military embrace', *The Independent*, 5 June 1995.

Martinet, Gilles, 'La politique de l'apparence', *Le Monde*, 13 March 1991.

Mason, John G. (1989), 'Mitterrand, the Socialists and French nuclear policy', in *French Security Policy in a Disarming World: Domestic Challenges and International Constraints*, Lynne Reinner, London.

Massie, Allan, 'Arrogance meets its match at the barricades', *The Observer*, 10 December 1995.

McCarthy, Patrick (1993), 'Condemned to partnership: the Franco-German relationship, 1944-1983', in *France-Germany, 1983-1993: The Struggle to Cooperate*, St. Martin's Press, New York.

McCarthy, Patrick, 'France in the mid-1990s: gloom but not doomed', *Current History*, vol.93, no.586, November 1994.

McLynn, Frank, 'Napoleon', as reviewed in *The Times*, 20 November 1997.

McMillan, James F. (1992), *Twentieth Century France: Politics and Society 1898-1991*, Edward Arnold, London.

McNamara, Francis Terry (1989), *France in Black Africa*, National Defence University Press, Washington DC, 1989.

McNulty, Mel, 'France's role in Rwanda and external military intervention: a double discrediting', *International Peacekeeping*, vol.4, no.3, Autumn 1997.

Mendl, Wolf (1970), *Deterrence and Persuasion: French Nuclear Armament in the Context Of National Policy 1945-69*, Faber and Faber, London.

Menon, Anand, 'Continuing politics by other means: defence policy under the French Fifth Republic', *West European Politics*, vol.17, no.4, October 1994.

Menon, Anand, 'From independence to cooperation: France, NATO and European security', *International Affairs*, vol.71, no.1, 1995.

Menon, Anand (1996), 'The "consensus" on defence policy and the end of the Cold War: political parties and the limits of adaptation', in Tony Chafer and Brian Jenkins (eds), *France: From the Cold War to the New World Order*, Macmillan, London.

Menon, Anand (2000), *France, NATO and the Limits of Independence 1981-97*, Macmillan, Basingstoke.

Mény, Yves (1989), 'Interest groups and politics in the Fifth Republic", in Paul Godt (ed), *Policy-Making in France*, Pinter Publishers.

Merchet, Jean-Dominique and Schneider, Vanessa, 'Millon subit l'assaut des députés', *Libération*, 6 June 1996.

Merchet, Jean-Dominique, 'La défense dépense tous azimuts', *Libération*, 5 June 1996.

Mitterrand, François (1986), *Réflexions sur la Politique Extérieure*, Fayard, Paris.

'Mitterrand vows to pursue peace plan until last dawn', *International Herald Tribune*, 19 January 1991.

Moïsi, Dominique, 'Mitterrand's foreign policy: the limits of continuity', *Foreign Affairs*, Winter 1981/2.

Moïsi, Dominique (1989), 'Franco-Soviet relations and French foreign policy: between adjustment and ambition', in Paul Godt (ed), *Policy-Making in France*, Pinter Publishers.

Moïsi, Dominique, 'De Mitterrand à Chirac', *Politique Étrangère*, vol. 60, no. 4, Winter 1995.

Moïsi, Dominique, 'The urge to be different', *The Financial Times*, 25 July 1995.

Moïsi, Dominique, 'The allure of Gaullism', *The Financial Times*, 19 April 1996.

Moreau Defarges, Philippe, 'La France et l'ONU: le ralliement', *Relations Internationales et Stratégiques*, no.9, Spring 1993.

Morse, Edward L. (1973), *Foreign Policy and Interdependence In Gaullist France*, Princeton University Press, Princeton.

Nayeri, Farah, 'Chirac takes his cue from de Gaulle', *Wall Street Journal Europe*, 11 August 1995.

Ogden, Christopher, 'Mending fences between prickly allies', *Time*, 25 November 1996.

O'Neill, Michael, 'The pursuit of a grand illusion', *European Brief*, vol.3, no.1, October 1995.

Owen, David, 'France set to lower its guard in Africa', *The Financial Times*, 31 July 1997.

'Paris takes a European line on defence', *The Financial Times*, 28 June 1985.

Parker, George, 'Europe: Minister to urge less reliance on US forces', *The Financial Times*, 13 May 1999.

Pascallon, Pierre (ed), *Quelle Défense pour la France?*, Institut des Relations Internationales et Stratégiques/Dunod, Paris.

Patry, Jean-Jacques, 'L'OTAN dans l'oeil du cyclone', *Défense*, no.67, March 1995.

'Peacekeeping and Security in Africa' – Conclusions Drawn from the Lisbon Colloquy, Assembly of the Western European Union Document 1648, 19 May 1999.

Pfaff, William, 'The ill-grasped logic behind France's "return" to NATO', *International Herald Tribune*, 31 January 1996.

Plenel, Edwy, 'L'illusion française', *Le Monde*, 31 August 1994.

Pointon, Clare, 'The French identity crisis', *European Trends*, no.2, 1992.

Price, Roger (1993), *A Concise History of France*, Cambridge University Press, Cambridge.

Quilès, Paul, 'Défense européenne et l'OTAN: la dérive', *Le Monde*, 11 June 1996.

Randal, Jonathan C, 'Outlook for France in Chad: at best, a standoff', *International Herald Tribune*, 14 March 1986.

Rhodes, Tom, 'Chirac pushes for more balanced Atlantic alliance', *The Times*, 1 February 1996.

Riding, Alan, 'Paris moves to end isolation in NATO', *International Herald Tribune*, 30 September 1992.

Roberts, Andrew, 'Zaire, a problem for France alone', *The Sunday Times*, 10 November 1996.

Rosenzweig, Luc, 'Les ministres de la défense de l'OTAN approuvent la réforme des commandements alliés', *Le Monde*, 4 December 1997.

Ross, George, 'Chirac and France: prisoners of the past?', *Current History*, vol.96, no.608, March 1997.

Routier, Airy, 'Armement: la campagne du Général Chirac', *Le Nouvel Observateur*, 25 January 1996.

Ruiz-Palmer, Diego A., *French Strategic Options in the 1990s*, Adelphi Paper 260, Brasseys/IISS, Summer 1991.

Russell Chaddock, Gail, 'France strives to rejuvenate its past glory', *Christian Science Monitor*, 6 October 1995.

Sancton, Thomas, 'Back to central Africa', *Time*, 4 July 1994.

Sancton, Thomas, 'France seeks a mission for the next century', *Time*, 4 December 1995.

Sancton, Thomas, 'Farewell to some arms', *Time*, 4 March 1996.

Schlosser, François, 'Rwanda: la France est-elle coupable?', *Le Nouvel Observateur*, June 30 1994.

Schmitt, Jean, *'Polémique sur le nucléaire'*, *Le Point*, 17 July 1993.

Schraeder, Peter J., 'France and the Great Game in Africa', *Current History*, vol.96, no.610, May 1997.

Schubert, Klaus (1991), 'France', in Regina Cowen Karp (ed), *Security with Nuclear Weapons?: Different Perspectives on National Security*, Oxford University Press, Oxford.

Sewell (jr), William H., 'Activity, passivity, and the revolutionary concept of citizenship', in Colin Lucas (ed), *The Political Culture of the French Revolution*, Pergamon Press, Oxford.

Smith, Tony, 'In defense of intervention', *Foreign Affairs*, vol.73, no.6, Nov/Dec 1994.

Smouts, Marie-Claude, 'The external policy of François Mitterrand', *International Affairs*, vol.59, no.2, Spring 1983.

Smouts, Marie-Claude (1989), 'The Fifth Republic and the Third World' in Paul Godt (ed), *Policy-Making in France*, Pinter Publishers, London.

Smyth, Frank, 'La France compromise au Rwanda', *Courrier International*, 21 April 1994.

Sotinel, Thomas, 'Nouvelle doctrine, vieilles habitudes', *Le Monde*, 6 October 1995.

Sotinel, Thomas, 'M. Chirac réaffirme le continuité de la politique africaine de la France', *Le Monde*, 8 December 1996.

Stanger, Theodore and Mabry, Marcus, 'The glory that was France', *Newsweek*, 9 May 1994.

'Still in step, mostly', *The Economist*, 27 October 1990.

Subtil, Marie-Pierre, 'François Mitterrand affirme que la France doit "refuser de réduire son ambition africaine"', *Le Monde*, 10 November 1994.

Tardy, Thierry, 'French policy towards peace support operations',

Taylor, Paul, 'Chirac hits at left's U-turn', *The Guardian*, 15 July 1997.

Taylor, Trevor (1988), 'European institutions and defence', in Jonathan Alford and Kenneth Hunt (eds), *Europe in the Western Alliance*, Macmillan/IISS, London.

'The defence of Europe: it can't be done alone', *The Economist*, 25 February 1995.

The Fourth 'Dossier Noir' De La Politique Africaine De La France, Coalition Pour Ramener a la Raison Démocratique La Politique Africaine De La France, February 1995.

The Military Balance 1994-95, IISS/Oxford University Press, 1994.

Timmerman, Kenneth R., 'Defense policy shifts from isolationism toward Europe', *International Herald Tribune*, 1 June 1987.

Torrelli, Maurice, 'Les missions humanitaires de l'armée française', *Défense Nationale*, vol.49, March 1993.

Touraine, Marisol, *'La France doit revoir son organisation de défense'*, *Le Point*, 17 July, 1993.

Touraine, Marisol, 'La représentation de l'adversaire dans la politique extérieure française depuis 1981', *Revue Française de Science Politique*, vol.43, no.5, October 1993.

Tréan, Claire, 'La relation de la France à l'OTAN n'est pas modifiée, affirme M. Roland Dumas', *Le Monde*, 23 March 1991.

Tréan, Claire, 'Sursaut français en Bosnie', *Le Monde*, 9 June 1995.

Urquhart, Brian (1995), 'Un regard extérieur sur 50 ans de présence française', in André Lewin (ed), *La France et l'ONU 1945-1995*, Collection Panoramiques, Condé-sur-Noireau.

Utley, R.E. (2000), *The French Defence Debate: Consensus and Continuity in the Mitterrand Era*, Macmillan, Basingstoke.

Valance, Georges (1990), *France-Allemagne: Le Retour de Bismark*, Flammarion, Paris.

Védrine, Hubert (1996), *Les Mondes de François Mitterrand: A l'Elysée 1981-1995*, Fayard, Paris.

Vernet, Daniel, 'The dilemma of French foreign policy', *International Affairs*, vol.68, no.4, Winter 1992.

Vernet, Daniel, 'Chirac, le gaullisme et la défense', *Le Monde*, 1 March 1996.

Vernet, Daniel, 'L'OTAN fait une place à l'Europe en son sein', *Le Monde*, 4 June 1996.

Vernet, Daniel, 'La France toujours à la recherche d'un arrangement avec L'OTAN', *Le Monde*, 2 December 1997.

Verschave, François-Xavier, 'Connivences françaises au Rwanda', *Le Monde Diplomatique*, March 1995.

Walden, George, 'France says no', *The Observer* (Prospect Section), 19 October 1997.

Wallerstein, Immanuel (1992), *Geopolitics and Geoculture*, Cambridge University Press, Cambridge.

Wauthier, Claude, 'La politique Africaine de la France: 1988-1993', *Relations Internationales et Stratégiques*, no.9, Spring 1993.

Webster, Paul, 'French troops end coup in Comoros', *The Guardian*, 5 October 1995.

Webster, Paul, 'Chirac proving too small for his boots', *The Guardian*, 16 November 1996.

Webster, Paul, 'France "armed killers in Rwanda genocide"', *The Guardian*, 13 January 1998.

Weiss, Thomas G., Forsythe, David P. and Coate, Roger A. (1994), *The United Nations and Changing World Politics*, Westview Press, Boulder.

Wells Jr, Samuel F., 'Les politiques étrangères de Mitterrand: bilan d'un premier septennat', *Commentaire*, no.43, Autumn 1988.

Wendt, Alexander, 'Levels of analysis vs. agents and structures: part III', *Review of International Studies*, vol.18, no.2, April 1992.

Wetterqvist, Fredrik (1990), *French Security and Defence Policy: Current Developments and Future Prospects*, National Defence Research Institute, Stockholm.

Whitney, Craig. R., 'France sells a third of Aerospatiale to Groupe Lagardère', *The New York Times*, 16 February 1999.

Whitney, Craig R., 'Military posture of Europe to turn more independent', *The New York Times*, 13 December 1999.

Winand, Pascaline (1997), *Eisenhower, Kennedy and the United States of Europe*, Macmillan, Basingstoke.

Winock, Michel, quoted in Jeambar, Denis, 'La France et les Frances', *Le Point*, 28 January 1995.

Wood, Pia Christina., 'France and the post-Cold War era: the case of Yugoslavia', *European Security*, vol.3, no.1, Spring 1994.

Woollacott, Martin, 'The great Atlantic drift away', *The Guardian*, 10 February 1995.

Yost, David S., 'France and west European defence identity', *Survival*, vol.33, no.4, July/August 1991.

'Zone of influence', *The Economist*, 9 July 1994.

Index